Camus's *The Plague*

OXFORD STUDIES IN PHILOSOPHY AND LITERATURE

Richard Eldridge, Philosophy, Swarthmore College

EDITORIAL BOARD

Anthony J. Cascardi, Comparative Literature, Romance, Languages, and Rhetoric, University of California, Berkeley
David Damrosch, Comparative Literature, Harvard University
Moira Gatens, Philosophy, University of Sydney
Garry Hagberg, Philosophy, Bard College
Philip Kitcher, Philosophy, Columbia University
Joshua Landy, French and Comparative Literature, Stanford University
Toril Moi, Literature, Romance Studies, Philosophy, and Theater Studies, Duke University
Martha C. Nussbaum, Philosophy and Law School, University of Chicago
Bernard Rhie, English, Williams College
David Wellbery, Germanic Studies, Comparative Literature, and Committee on Social Thought, University of Chicago
Paul Woodruff, Philosophy and Classics, University of Texas at Austin

PUBLISHED IN THE SERIES

Jane Austen's *Emma*: Philosophical Perspectives
Edited by E. M. Dadlez

Murasaki Shikibu's *The Tale of Genji*: Philosophical Perspectives
Edited by James McMullen

Dostoevsky's *Crime and Punishment*: Philosophical Perspectives
Edited by Robert E. Guay

Joyce's *Ulysses*: Philosophical Perspectives
Edited by Philip Kitcher

The Poetry of Emily Dickinson: Philosophical Perspectives
Edited by Elisabeth Camp

Proust's *In Search of Lost Time*: Philosophical Perspectives
Edited by Katherine Elkins

Camus's *The Plague*: Philosophical Perspectives
Edited by Peg Brand Weiser

Camus's *The Plague*

Philosophical Perspectives

EDITED BY PEG BRAND WEISER

OXFORD
UNIVERSITY PRESS

Oxford University Press is a department of the University of Oxford. It furthers
the University's objective of excellence in research, scholarship, and education
by publishing worldwide. Oxford is a registered trade mark of Oxford University
Press in the UK and certain other countries.

Published in the United States of America by Oxford University Press
198 Madison Avenue, New York, NY 10016, United States of America.

© Oxford University Press 2023

All rights reserved. No part of this publication may be reproduced, stored in
a retrieval system, or transmitted, in any form or by any means, without the
prior permission in writing of Oxford University Press, or as expressly permitted
by law, by license, or under terms agreed with the appropriate reproduction
rights organization. Inquiries concerning reproduction outside the scope of the
above should be sent to the Rights Department, Oxford University Press, at the
address above.

You must not circulate this work in any other form
and you must impose this same condition on any acquirer.

Library of Congress Cataloging-in-Publication Data
Names: Weiser, Peg Brand, author.
Title: Camus's The plague : philosophical perspectives / edited by Peg Brand Weiser.
Description: New York, NY : Oxford University Press, [2023] |
Series: Oxford studies in philosophy and literature | Includes index.
Identifiers: LCCN 2022038837 (print) | LCCN 2022038838 (ebook) |
ISBN 9780197599334 (paperback) | ISBN 9780197599327 (hardback) |
ISBN 9780197599358 (epub)
Subjects: LCSH: Camus, Albert, 1913-1960. Peste. | Philosophy in literature. |
Epidemics in literature. | LCGFT: Literary criticism. | Essays.
Classification: LCC PQ2605 .A3734 P4394 2023 (print) | LCC PQ2605 .A3734 (ebook) |
DDC 843/.914—dc23/eng/20220916
LC record available at https://lccn.loc.gov/2022038837
LC ebook record available at https://lccn.loc.gov/2022038838

DOI: 10.1093/oso/9780197599327.001.0001

Triumph of Death.
From: Francesco Petrarca, "I Trionfi" (The Triumphs). Miniature. Neapolitan School, 1449–1460
Tempera and gold on parchment.
Ms. It. 103 alfa W 925, Folio 30v
Alfredo Dagli Orti / Art Resource, NY

*This volume is dedicated to the millions of lives lost from Covid-19,
to those who tried to save them,
and to the loved ones left behind.*

Because I could not stop for Death—
He kindly stopped for me—
The Carriage held but just Ourselves—
And Immortality.

We slowly drove—He knew no haste
And I had put away
My labor and my leisure too,
For His Civility—

We passed the School where Children strove
At Recess—in the Ring—
We passed the Fields of Gazing Grain—
We passed the Setting Sun—

Or rather—He passed us—
The Dews drew quivering and Chill—
For only Gossamer, my Gown—
My Tippet—only Tulle—

We paused before a House that seemed
A Swelling of the Ground—
The Roof was scarcely visible —
The Cornice—in the Ground—

Since then—'tis Centuries—and yet
Feels shorter than the Day
I first surmised the Horses' Heads
Were toward Eternity—

—Emily Dickinson (1830–1886)

Contents

Series Editor's Foreword	ix
Acknowledgments	xiii
Contributors	xv

Introduction: The Relevance of Camus's *The Plague* 1
  Peg Brand Weiser

1. *The Plague* and the Present Moment 31
  Steven G. Kellman

2. Present in Effacement: The Place of Women in
  Camus's Plague and Ours 53
  Jane E. Schultz

3. The Meaning of a Pandemic 77
  Andrew Edgar

4. Grief and Human Connection in *The Plague* 103
  Kathleen Higgins

5. Examining the Narrative Devolution of the Physician
  in Camus's *The Plague* 127
  Edward B. Weiser

6. Horror and Natural Evil in *The Plague* 147
  Cynthia A. Freeland

7. "I Can't Breathe": Covid-19 and *The Plague*'s Tragedy
  of Political and Corporeal Suffocation 175
  Margaret E. Gray

8. Modern Death, Decent Death, and Heroic Solidarity
  in *The Plague* 199
  Peg Brand Weiser

Index 225

Series Editor's Foreword

At least since Plato had Socrates criticize the poets and attempt to displace Homer as the authoritative articulator and transmitter of human experience and values, philosophy and literature have developed as partly competing, partly complementary enterprises. Both literary writers and philosophers have frequently studied and commented on each other's texts and ideas, sometimes with approval, sometimes with disapproval, in their efforts to become clearer about human life and about valuable commitments—moral, artistic, political, epistemic, metaphysical, and religious, as may be. Plato's texts themselves register the complexity and importance of these interactions in being dialogues in which both deductive argumentation and dramatic narration do central work in furthering a complex body of views.

While these relations have been widely recognized, they have also frequently been ignored or misunderstood, as academic disciplines have gone their separate ways within their modern institutional settings. Philosophy has often turned to science or mathematics as providing models of knowledge; in doing so, it has often explicitly set itself against cultural entanglements and literary devices, rejecting, at least officially, the importance of plot, figuration, and imagery in favor of supposedly plain speech about the truth. Literary study has moved variously through formalism, structuralism, poststructuralism, and cultural studies, among other movements, as modes of approach to a literary text. In doing so, it has understood literary texts as sample instances of images, structures, personal styles, or failures of consciousness, or it has seen the literary text as a largely fungible product, fundamentally shaped by wider pressures and patterns of consumption and expectation that affect and figure in

X SERIES EDITOR'S FOREWORD

nonliterary textual production as well. It has thus set itself against the idea that major literary texts productively and originally address philosophical problems of value and commitment precisely through their form, diction, imagery, and development, even while these works also resist claiming conclusively to solve the problems that occupy them.

These distinct academic traditions have yielded important perspectives and insights. But in the end none of them has been kind to the idea of major literary works as achievements in thinking about values and human life, often in distinctive, open, self-revising, self-critical ways. At the same time readers outside institutional settings, and often enough philosophers and literary scholars, too, have turned to major literary texts precisely in order to engage with their productive, materially and medially specific patterns and processes of thinking. These turns to literature have, however, not so far been systematically encouraged within disciplines, and they have generally occurred independently of each other.

The aim of this series is to make manifest the multiple, complex engagements with philosophical ideas and problems that lie at the hearts of major literary texts. In doing so, its volumes aim not only to help philosophers and literary scholars of various kinds to find rich affinities and provocations to further thought and work; they also aim to bridge various gaps between academic disciplines and between those disciplines and the experiences of extrainstitutional readers.

Each volume focuses on a single, undisputedly major literary text. Both philosophers with training and experience in literary study and literary scholars with training and experience in philosophy are invited to engage with themes, details, images, and incidents in the focal text, through which philosophical problems are held in view, worried at, and reformulated. Decidedly not a project simply to formulate A's philosophy of X as a finished product, merely illustrated in the text, and decidedly not a project to explain the literary work entirely by reference to external social configurations and forces, the effort is instead to track the work of open thinking in literary forms, as they lie both neighbor to and aslant from philosophy. As Walter Benjamin once wrote, "new centers of reflection are continually forming," as problems of commitment and value of all kinds take on new shapes for human agents in relation to changing historical circumstances, where reflective address remains possible. By considering how such centers of reflection are formed and expressed in and through literary works, as they engage with philosophical problems of agency, knowledge, commitment, and value, these volumes undertake to present both literature and philosophy as, at times, productive forms of reflective, medial work in relation both to each other and to social circumstances and to show how this work is specifically undertaken and developed in distinctive and original ways in exemplary works of literary art.

Richard Eldridge
Swarthmore College

Acknowledgments

The idea first came to me during spring break in March 2020 when in-person teaching on campus was delayed one week, then two, then for the rest of the semester. No one had any idea how long the "temporary" situation would last. We hardly thought it would be two years with still no end in sight to the interruption of normal activities in our lives. Too many deaths have occurred. Too much pain and suffering and political posturing. To write about Camus's *The Plague* during a pandemic seemed both logical and urgent.

My sincere thanks to Richard Eldridge, Series Editor of the Oxford University Press Philosophy and Literature series—good friend and colleague in the American Society for Aesthetics—for his support and insightful suggestions. Thanks also to Lucy Randall, Commissioning Editor at Oxford University Press, New York, and her Production Team.

I am indebted to the students of my two classes in Philosophy in Literature at the University of Arizona who learned about plagues in history and deftly analyzed fictional Oran. Their strength in studying subject matter that could easily have eroded one's confidence in human nature as the pandemic wore on and on attested to their hope in solidarity: Camus's message to us all.

Finally, my husband, Ed Weiser—one of the authors in this volume—has been steadfast throughout. As a retired gynecologic oncologist and surgeon, he has seen illness and death up close. His understanding of the uncontrollable force of nature known as Covid-19 has sustained and inspired me. I thank him for navigating a worldwide catastrophe . . . at my side.

Contributors

Andrew Edgar is Reader Emeritus at Cardiff University, where he was a member of the School of English, Communication and Philosophy. He is an honorary staff member of Swansea University's School of Sport Science. His research interests include critical theory, the philosophy of art, and the philosophy of sport. He is the author of two books on Jürgen Habermas's philosophy and social theory, *The Philosophy of Habermas* (2005) and *Habermas: Key Concepts* (2006). He is currently editor of the journal *Sport, Ethics and Philosophy*, and he published a monograph of the aesthetics of sport entitled *Sport and Art: An Essay in the Hermeneutics of Sport* (2014). Most recently, he edited *Somaesthetics and Sport* (2022).

Cynthia A. Freeland is Professor Emerita of Philosophy at the University of Houston. She has published on topics in ancient philosophy, feminist philosophy, film theory, and aesthetics. Her books include *Philosophy and Film*, coedited with Thomas Wartenberg (Routledge, 1995), *Feminist Interpretations of Aristotle* (Penn State Press, 1998), *The Naked and the Undead: Evil and the Appeal of Horror* (Westview Press, 1999), *But Is It Art?* (Oxford University Press, 2001), and *Portraits and Persons* (Oxford University Press, 2010). From 2014 to 2016, she served as president of the American Society for Aesthetics.

Margaret E. Gray is an Associate Professor in the French and Italian Department at Indiana University, Bloomington. She has published on Proust (*Postmodern Proust*, 1992) and such authors as George Sand, Colette, Camus, Simone de Beauvoir, Beckett, Jean-Philippe Toussaint, Calixthe Beyala, and Noémi LeFebvre. Most recently, she published *Stolen Limelight: Gender, Display, and Displacement in Modern Fiction in French* (University of Wales Press, 2022).

Kathleen Higgins is Professor of Philosophy at the University of Texas at Austin, where she specializes in aesthetics, continental philosophy, and philosophy of emotion. Her primary research interests in aesthetics include philosophy of music, emotion and the arts, beauty, popular culture,

xvi CONTRIBUTORS

kitsch, and non-Western aesthetics. She is author of many articles related to these topics as well as a several books, including *The Music of Our Lives* (1991; rev. ed. 2011) and *The Music between Us: Is Music the Universal Language?* (2012). She is also coeditor of *A Companion to Aesthetics* (2nd ed., 2009) and *Artistic Visions and the Promise of Beauty: Cross-Cultural Perspectives* (2017). She is a former delegate-at-large in the International Aesthetics Association and a former president of the American Society for Aesthetics.

Steven G. Kellman is Professor of Comparative Literature at the University of Texas at San Antonio. His books include *Rambling Prose: Essays* (Trinity University Press, 2020); *Nimble Tongues: Studies in Literary Translingualism* (Purdue University Press, 2020); *The Restless Ilan Stavans: Outsider on the Inside* (University of Pittsburgh Press, 2019); *Redemption: The Life of Henry Roth* (Norton, 2005); *The Translingual Imagination* (University of Nebraska Press, 2000); *The Plague: Fiction and Resistance* (Twayne, 1993); *Loving Reading: Erotics of the Text* (Archon, 1985); and *The Self-Begetting Novel* (Columbia University Press, 1980). Kellman served four terms on the board of the National Book Critics Circle and received its Balakian Citation for Excellence in Reviewing.

Jane E. Schultz is Professor of English, History, and Medical Humanities at Indiana University in Indianapolis and coeditor of Manchester University's Nursing History and Humanities book series. *Women at the Front: Hospital Workers in Civil War America* (University of North Carolina Press, 2004)—a finalist for the Lincoln Prize—and *This Birth Place of Souls* (Oxford University Press, 2011) concern nursing and relief work in wartime military hospitals. Schultz published a new edition of Sarah Edmonds's *Nurse and Spy in the Union Army* (Lakeside Press, 2019) and was historical consultant for the PBS drama *Mercy Street* from 2014 to 2017. She continues to chip away at *Lead, Blood, and Ink*—a study of the relationship between wartime surgical language and practice. In addition to her work as board president of the Indiana Medical History Museum, which houses one of the last remaining nineteenth-century surgical amphitheaters in the United States, she has written widely on cancer memoirs and other kinds of illness narratives.

Edward B. Weiser is a board-certified obstetrician-gynecologist and gynecologic oncologist who has held medical school appointments at Uniformed Services University, Upstate Medical University of New York,

Emory University, Mercer University, and Indiana University. After retiring from over thirty years of clinical practice, he is now Professor of Practice teaching medical ethics, a career-long parallel pursuit at the University of Arizona in the Philosophy Department and the W.A. Franke Honors College.

Peg Brand Weiser is Laureate Professor and Research Professor of Philosophy at the University of Arizona who teaches in the W.A. Franke Honors College. She is affiliated with the Gender and Women's Studies Department and the Applied Intercultural Arts Research graduate program (AIAR). She is also Emerita Associate Professor of Philosophy and Women's Studies at Indiana University. Editor of *Beauty Unlimited* (Indiana University Press, 2013) and *Beauty Matters* (Indiana University Press, 2000), she recently guest coedited a Special Issue of the *Journal of Intercollegiate Sport* (2021) and published an essay in *Somaesthetics and Sport* (Brill Press, 2022). She is coauthor with Carolyn Korsmeyer of "Feminist Aesthetics" in the *Stanford Encyclopedia of Philosophy* (2021).

1. Argelino Con Turbante [Algerian with Turban] En El Patio De La Mezquita, Oran, Algeria. Album/Art Resource, NY.

Introduction

The Relevance of Camus's *The Plague*

Peg Brand Weiser

[T]here's no substitute for finally sitting down and reading the 1947 novel "The Plague," by Albert Camus. Its relevance lashes you across the face."[1]

Camus's classic narrative *La Peste* (*The Plague*)[2] is a timely philosophical read in an era when a deadly pandemic rages worldwide. An allegory rich with suggestion, it rewards an imaginative reader with innumerable meanings as our own lived experiences mirror the novel. We witness protesters who argue for individual freedom and the autonomy to defy government-imposed regulations. They openly clash with followers of science who recommend shared actions of self-sacrifice to mitigate the spread of infection. Choosing either to act in one's own interest or to sacrifice for the good of all has become a haunting theme of American life in which the "richest nation on earth" experienced the highest number of cases and deaths in the world while under the leadership of former president Donald Trump as well as through the first

[1] Metcalf, "Albert Camus' 'The Plague' and Our Own Great Reset," March 23, 2020.
[2] Camus's *La Peste* was published in French in 1947, and as *The Plague*, in English, in 1948.

Camus's The Plague. Peg Brand Weiser, Oxford University Press. © Oxford University Press 2023.
DOI: 10.1093/oso/9780197599327.003.0001

2 CAMUS'S *THE PLAGUE*

year, 2021, of the administration of President Joe Biden.[3] Political divisions over wearing masks, social distancing, police killings, Black Lives Matter, the January 6, 2021, assault on the United States Capitol, and recommended or mandated vaccines sow discord at a time when solidarity could have united the United States to lead the world against the pandemic. Instead, misinformation campaigns have stoked opposition among the populace and away from the virus. "We're all in this together," was repeatedly uttered by Dr. Bernard Rieux, Camus's narrator. How seldom did we hear that call for unity from the podiums of power, for example, the leaders of America, Brazil, and India (the three countries with the highest death counts in the world)? After two years into the coronavirus pandemic with over 1 million deaths in the United States and over 6 million worldwide, we might ask ourselves, do we measure up to Camus's optimistic assessment of human behavior under duress? Do we collectively meet the minimum threshold of ethical behavior posed by Camus who wrote, "What's true of all the evils in the world is true of plague as well. It helps men to rise above themselves"?[4]

His Life and Work

Albert Camus was born on November 7, 1913, in Mondovi, Algeria. As a *pied noir* (black foot), he was the second-generation offspring of European colonists who settled in North Africa from 1830 until the 1960s, when indigenous independence was regained after the Algerian War of 1954–1962. Unlike Arab and Berber inhabitants, he was born a French citizen: a unique status. He was described by one scholar, Stephen G. Kellman, as both "a stranger in his native land" and "a ragged interloper among the literary sophisticates of Paris."[5]

---

[3] Bassett and Linos, "Trump Gave Up on Fighting the Virus," July 14, 2020. See also World Health Organization (WHO) Coronavirus (COVID-19) Dashboard, July 4, 2022.

[4] Camus, *The Plague*, 125.

[5] Kellman, "On Albert Camus," 4.

INTRODUCTION 3

His father, killed in World War I in 1914, prompted his Spanish mother (born deaf) to relocate him and his older brother (born deaf-mute) to an apartment in Algiers where they lived with three other persons without electricity or running water. Diagnosed with tuberculosis at age seventeen, a transmitted disease for which there was then no cure nor satisfactory treatment, he was forced to leave home and live in self-imposed quarantine with an uncle. A lycée professor influenced him to study philosophy, particularly the ancient Greeks and Nietzsche. Forced to abandon his love of swimming and aspirations of becoming a professional football player, he relinquished the position of goalkeeper for a local team, later remarking, "What little I know on morality, I learned it on football pitches and theater stages. Those were my true universities."[6]

Beginning in 1933, he studied philosophy at the University of Algiers and completed his studies (equivalent to a master's degree) in 1936 with a thesis on Plotinus. First married in 1934 and divorced in 1936, he wrote theatrical works and traveled Algeria as an actor. He visited Paris for the first time in 1937, where he wrote for several socialist newspapers, and in 1940 moved to Paris to become editor-in-chief of *Paris-Soir*. As the buildup to World War II intensified, he attempted to join the army but was rejected due to his illness. As Germany invaded Paris, he fled to Lyon, married again in 1940, and by 1942 had published *The Stranger*, *The Myth of Sisyphus*, and *Caligula*. He and his wife moved to Oran where he taught in primary schools, but due to a recurrence of tuberculosis, he moved again in 1942 to a mountain village in the French Alps where he began writing *La Peste*. Stranded in France, he was separated from both his wife and mother who were back in Algeria. In 1943, he returned to Paris to edit the underground newspaper *Combat* as part of the French Resistance. In 1944, he met Jean-Paul

---

[6] Mezahi, "Goalkeeper, Philosopher, Outsider," November 7, 2013. Speculation is that Camus might have become a professional football player.

4 CAMUS'S *THE PLAGUE*

Sartre, André Gide, Simone de Beauvoir, André Breton, and, since he was already well-known, easily assimilated into the group of French intellectuals living in Paris. In Paris after the war in 1945, his wife gave birth to twins, and in 1946, as a celebrated writer, he visited the United States and Canada, delivering a speech at Columbia University and publishing a series of essays from *Combat* entitled "Neither Victims nor Executioners."

La Peste was published in 1947 and translated into English the following year. He continued to write, to travel to other countries—including Algeria where he expressed disapproval of oppressive French colonialist policies—and to see performances of his dramatic works on stage. In 1951, he published *The Rebel* to negative reviews, broke off his friendship with Jean-Paul Sartre, and rejected the label "existentialist."[7] He repeatedly took political stands against oppressive governments, including France in the 1950s, when he tried to find a way to negotiate Algerian freedom amid anticolonialist uprisings.[8] Conflicted by a complicated social dynamic of sympathy for the Algerian cause but also identification with his French lineage, he failed to satisfy both the Left—particularly those sympathetic to communism—and the Right. Yet the complexity of his views continues to provide opportunities for present-day readers to study his words and actions more carefully: to credit him for meeting his literary and humanitarian goals while withholding praise for what we judge, in retrospect, as failures and omissions. A pensive short story published in 1957, "The Artist at Work," captured the "good luck" and rise in popularity of a painter who, like Camus, vacillated between solidarity and solitude as he came to lose prestige and influence.[9] That same

---

[7] See also Aronson, *Camus and Sartre: The Story of a Friendship and the Quarrel That Ended It.*

[8] Kabel and Phillipson, "Structural Violence and Hope in Catastrophic Times," 5.

[9] For a detailed chronicle of critics of Camus's *The Plague*, see Krapp, "Time and Ethics in Albert Camus's *The Plague*."

INTRODUCTION 5

year, Camus accepted the Nobel Prize in Literature whereupon he wrote in his journal, "Strange feeling of overwhelming pressure and melancholy."[10] He died in a car crash at age forty-six on January 4, 1960. An unfinished manuscript found with him at the scene of his death was later published in 1994 as *Le Premier Homme (The First Man)*.[11]

Then and Now

As winter turns into spring of an unspecified year in the 1940s, Camus's narrator, Dr. Bernard Rieux (whose identity is revealed only at the end of the novel), leads us through dire events in Oran as it is voluntarily shut off from the outside world. Oran is cast as a "treeless, glamourless, soulless" town of 200,000.[12] Beginning with the first dead rat on April 16 and ending the following February with the ceremonial opening of the town gates, Rieux tracks time, the promise of a curative serum, and corpses. Death rates climb through the hot summer and into the fall. At first counted by the week—at 16, 24, 28, 32, 40, 100, 302, then nearly 700 per week—administrators switch to counting them by the day to report "lower" numbers (reaching 92, 107, then 130 deaths per day) in order to forestall panic. The narrative chronicles the progression of deadly bubonic plague through the town as its inhabitants deny the obvious, struggle to comply with orders of quarantine, and cope with denial, fear, isolation, and loss of loved ones. The invasion of the plague bacillus is unexpected, unwanted, and uncontrollable: exemplifying for Camus the inevitable human condition of "the absurd" and man's helplessness in the face of it. The

---

[10] Kellman, "On Albert Camus," 6. From Camus, *Notebooks 1951–1959*.
[11] Camus, *Le Premier Homme*, was first published in French in 1994 and in English in 1995.
[12] Camus, *The Plague*, 6.

6   CAMUS'S *THE PLAGUE*

response of Rieux is not to succumb, however, but to fight, thereby finding meaning in resistance. He cites his duty, urges others to decency, and invokes their shared concern for humanity. The novel raises issues of truth, honesty, ethics, the problem of evil, faith, the pathology of illness, death, the absurd, freedom, love, heroism, and time.

One might trace the relevance of the novel along at least three notable lines: (1) the narrative's depiction of a range of human reactions to the absurd, (2) its historical weight within the context of plague literature and pandemic fiction, and (3) its fictional triumph over the facts—the numbers, the data, and the daily developments—in chronicling a story of diverse individuals thrown together by fate who succeed in pulling together, acting in solidarity, and surviving the worst conditions of the plague. This story of plague could have easily resulted in a shallow, documentary-style work of nonfiction or a dry, didactic philosophical tome that, either way, ended on a less optimistic note. An alternative informed reading, on the other hand, casts the relevance of the novel in terms of three additional features conceptualized as what the novel lacks, namely (4) any significant description of women as fully functioning human beings—female caregivers, doctors, workers, wives, partners; (5) depictions of Algerian and Arab characters who represent the majority indigenous population; and (6) an awareness and analysis of class differences, only minimally represented in the text by starving, rioting, destructive mobs. On this competing interpretation, Camus's novel is relevant for revealing the long-standing hierarchical power structures of the privileged that maintained systemic inequalities and oppression of the less powerful, non-male, non-white, non-European, poor, and vulnerable populations. As a result, some readers of *The Plague* find Camus's advocacy of solidarity, cooperation, and hope a form of "naïve idealism" that ignores pervasive structural differences and ideologies that continually harm those who are truly suffering and dying, particularly during a pandemic. On this reading, according to critics Kabel and Phillipson, Camus's book fails to inspire social change.[13]

The unraveling of our own story parallels that of Oran. Some say we began to mark "Covid time" as early as December 2019, with March 11, 2020, as the official pronouncement of pandemic by the World Health Organization (WHO) due to a novel coronavirus that emerged from Wuhan, China, to blanket world populations in sickness and death.[14] For over two years, government agencies and concerned citizens have tracked daily statistics of contracted cases, hospitalizations, and deaths. "The United States continues to have the highest cumulative number of cases and deaths globally . . . despite the widespread availability of vaccines in the country" and now lags behind in vaccines in comparison to much of the rest of the developed world.[15] Reporters chronicled the experiences of front line medical workers in overcrowded hospitals. Families awaited a plan, a cure, and finally, a vaccine, while politicians and pundits posited an "existential crisis" to describe our world in peril.[16] Under the new administration of President Biden—which began on January 20, 2021—vaccines-in-arms came to exceed 3 million per day while simultaneously more transmissible variants of the virus began to spread. Citizens cautiously sought a return to "normal" but medical epidemiologists doubted that even if at least 60–70 percent of the country's population received at least one vaccine, it could escape the reach of the virus when other countries were unable to attain sufficient vaccines or control recurring outbreaks. What the vaccine has done, however, is severely limit

---

[13] Kabel and Phillipson, "Structural Violence and Hope in Catastrophic Times," 4.

[14] "WHO Director-General's Opening Remarks," March 11, 2020.

[15] The United States had recorded more than 52 million of the world's 281 million cases and 820,000 deaths of the world's 5.4 million. WHO Coronavirus (COVID-19) Dashboard, December 31, 2021. According to *The Washington Post* coronavirus data on December 31, 2021, 62 percent of Americans were fully vaccinated (73.4 percent partially vaccinated) in spite of vaccine availability since April 2021, lagging far behind dozens of other European and Asian countries, including Britain.

[16] Mark Leibovich, "For A.O.C., 'Existential Crises' as Her District Becomes the Coronavirus Epicenter," May 4, 2020.

8 CAMUS'S *THE PLAGUE*

the death toll, particularly in America.[17] Not so in other parts of the world. On May 19, 2021, India reported the highest number of deaths in one day worldwide—4,500, surpassing the highest number of 4,400 in the United States on January 20, 2021.[18] Photos revealed dozens of Covid-infected bodies floating down the Ganges River due to shallow graves unable to hold them.[19] After a long respite from conflict in the Middle East, fighting between Hamas and Israel posed the dual threat of war injuries and spread of the virus in Gaza.[20] With severe shortages and unequal distribution of vaccines—"only 0.3% were in low-income countries, while richer countries administered around 85%"—some countries are not expected to obtain vaccines until 2024.[21]

It should be noted that the numbers of both cases and deaths are assumed to be severely underreported in the United States as well as elsewhere, due to lack of testing and transparency of reporting. In May 2021, one study estimated an actual number of 912,345 deaths—compared to a then reported 578,555—in the United States alone.[22] The uneven distribution of medical treatment, ventilators, vaccines, and proper burials worldwide has been criticized as evidence of the "catastrophe" of Covid that "makes indigenous peoples acutely vulnerable to the ravages of the virus, further deepening their material, physical and spiritual plight and collective loss."[23]

---

[17] On May 18, 2021, the seven-day average dropped to 589 from a high of 4,000 per day in January. But as of October 2021, it once again reached heights of over 2,000 per day; see *The Washington Post* Coronavirus data, November 14, 2021. By December 31, 2021, the highly transmissible Omicron variant rose to an average of 344,543 cases per day, but deaths stabilized at 1,551 per day; see *The Washington Post* Coronavirus data, December 31, 2021.

[18] Slater, "In India, the Deadliest Day," May 19, 2021, and "India Sets Pandemic Record with More Than 400,000 New Cases," May 1, 2021.

[19] Pandy, "India's Holiest River Is Swollen with Covid Victims," May 18, 2021.

[20] Hendrix and Balousha, "Gaza Struggles with Twin Crises," May 22, 2021.

[21] Petrequin, "EU Leaders Agree to Donate 100 Million Doses of Vaccines," May 25, 2021.

[22] "Estimation of Total Mortality," Institute for Health Metrics (IHME), May 13, 2021.

[23] Kabul and Phillipson, "Structural Violence and Hope," 13.

INTRODUCTION 9

Camus Sets the Stage

Consider the speech delivered by Camus at Columbia University on March 28, 1946, during his only trip to America, entitled, "La Crise de L'homme" ("A Human Crisis")—judged by one scholar as providing us with a "blueprint" to a number of Camus's works, including *The Plague, The Fall, The Rebel,* and *First Man.*[24] Fresh from postwar France, the thirty-two-year-old Camus represented "his generation" of young French citizens as he addressed American academics sitting comfortably in a packed auditorium in New York City.[25] Few listeners had undergone the unspeakable horrors of World War II, survived the occupied rule of Hitler, been stripped of freedoms that resulted in being held prisoner in one's own country—trapped in one's home, separated from loved ones—as if attacked by a veritable plague. After the novel was published in 1947, Camus acknowledged its allegorical nature as a chronicle of Nazi invasions of Europe, but, as many authors in this volume have argued, it was so much more: it offers us relevance beyond its original place in time. It opens a lens that probes deep and wide; it portrays any person in any town at any unspecified time anywhere that becomes "victim" to the brutality of "the executioner" (referred to by Camus in his speech as "the brutes taking charge in the four corners of Europe"). Recall that in 1946, Camus also published a collection of essays from *Combat* entitled, "Neither Victims nor Executioners."

As Camus came to write in *The Plague,* through the words of Dr. Rieux's friend, Tarrou, who was adamantly opposed to capital punishment and violence: "on this earth there are pestilences and

[24] Kaplan, *Looking for the Stranger: Camus and the Life of a Literary Classic.* Kaplan was a panelist following the May 9, 2016, reading of Camus's 1946 speech by actor Viggo Mortensen in the same Columbia University auditorium of Camus's appearance seventy years prior. See https://www.youtube.com/watch?v=aaFZJ_ymueA. All quotes are taken from this video.

[25] Renewed attention to the speech is the focus of Robert Emmet Meagher's 2021 publication, *Albert Camus and the Human Crisis.*

10 CAMUS'S *THE PLAGUE*

there are victims, and it's up to us, so far as possible, not to join forces with the pestilences."[26] Foreshadowing the main themes of resistance against an oppressor, disease, or injustice by inspiring solidarity among men and women who come together in a common fight, Camus added, "I grant we should add a third category: that of the true healers."[27] Surely this explains why Camus chose a physician, Dr. Rieux, as the main character and narrator:

> Nonetheless, he knew that the tale he had to tell could not be one of a final victory. It could be only the record of what had had to be done, and what assuredly would have to be done again in the never ending fight against terror and its relentless onslaughts, despite their personal afflictions, by all who, while unable to be saints but refusing to bow down to pestilences, strive their utmost to be healers.[28]

In his 1946 speech, Camus outlined four symptoms of "the human crisis" resulting from human indifference and passivity within a world of violence, "mistrust, resentment, greed, and the race for power": (1) the rise of terror consisting in an uncertain future that begets fear and anxiety, solitude and unhappiness; (2) the impossibility of persuasion, that is, the failure of reason and passion to trump irrationality and indifference; his example is a concentration camp victim "who cannot hope to explain to the SS men who are beating him that they ought not to"; (3) the growth of bureaucracy where paperwork replaces persons; and (4) a "cult of efficiency" where "real men" are replaced by "political men" who engage in destructive abstractions (like Nazism) in which harmful instincts are "elevated to the status of an idea or theory."[29]

---

[26] Camus, *The Plague*, 254.
[27] Camus, *The Plague*, 254.
[28] Camus, *The Plague*, 308.
[29] All quotes taken from the video at https://www.youtube.com/watch?v=aaFZJ_ymueA.

INTRODUCTION 11

The remedy for "the human crisis"—Camus's suggested "lesson of those years . . . of blood spilled"—is an end to "the cult of silence" in the face of "the reign of abstraction" and a rediscovery of "the freedom of thought" needed "to resolve any of the problems facing the modern conscience." This consists of freely seeking "the common good" in "communion among men" and in forming a "brotherhood of men struggling against fate." For the sake of justice, Camus argues, we must eliminate lying, violence, slavery, and terror.

It is too easy in this matter to simply accuse Hitler and to say, "Since the beast is dead, its venom is gone." We know perfectly well that the venom is not gone, that each of us carries it in our own hearts.

Consider that at the end of *The Plague*, Dr. Rieux ominously "remembered" to himself:

He knew what those jubilant crowds did not know but could have learned from books: that the plague bacillus never dies or disappears for good; that it can lie dormant for years and years in furniture and linen-chests; that it bides its time in bedrooms, cellars, trunks, and bookshelves; and that perhaps the day would come when, for the bane and the enlightening of men, it would rouse up its rats again and send them forth to die in a happy city.[30]

On a positive note, Camus shares Dr. Rieux's reasoning for chronicling the story of the plague in fictional Oran with another direct link to his speech that serves to explain why he himself was motivated to write his own fictional account, *La Peste*:

---

[30] Camus, *The Plague*, 308.

12   CAMUS'S *THE PLAGUE*

> Dr Rieux resolved to compile this chronicle, so that he should not be one of those who hold their peace but should bear witness in favor of those plague-stricken people: so that some memorial of the injustice and outrage done them might endure; and to state quite simply what we learn in time of pestilence: that there are more things to admire in men than to despise.[31]

This conclusion, in the face of the incomprehensible and insurmountable absurd—man's suffering, evil, and death—reflects a change in Camus's writings when he moved beyond advocating that one merely face the absurd, alone, like Sisyphus, to instead combat it by forming "a brotherhood of men":

> [I]f there is one fact that these last five years have brought out, it is the extreme solidarity of men with one another. Solidarity in crime for some, solidarity in the upsurge of resistance in other. Solidarity even between victims and executioners.[32]

We, too, witness a monumental human crisis enacted in real time. Our full story is yet to be written but one might conclude that ultimately nearly 81 million Americans (51.3 percent of the votes cast) denied Donald Trump a second term in favor of Joseph Biden and Kamala Harris, and that the state of Georgia elected two Democrats to the U.S. Senate to split the numbers 50-50 with Vice President Harris becoming the deciding majority vote. In keeping with campaign promises, Biden met and surpassed his goal of 100 million vaccines within his first one hundred days in office and signed economic relief into law for economically disadvantaged citizens. No such political accounting surfaces in Camus's story while it is integral to understanding ours. The highest number of American

---

[31] Camus, *The Plague*, 308. Interestingly, there is a second chronicle within the narrative as well: that recorded by Tarrou.

[32] Camus's *Notebooks 1951–1959*, cited in Birdsall, "Albert Camus' *Jonas, or the Artist at Work*," 8. See also Camus, "The Artist at Work," 1957.

INTRODUCTION 13

citizens voted in a safe election that insured the country's turn toward fighting the pandemic rather than ignoring it or calling it a "hoax." President Biden acknowledged both the dead and grieving as he held the first communal memorial for the nation on the eve of his inauguration. Camus would have called this a form of resistance and a form of solidarity. He would have empathized with victims lost to the virus while valorizing the healers, particularly health care personnel and other essential workers, for whose ordinary, everyday deeds of decency and healing he reserved the term "heroic."

Range of Human Reactions to the Absurd

Camus's characters adopt a variety of stances from the extremes of exploitation (Cottard) and religious fervor (the Jesuit priest, Father Paneloux) with a host of options in-between: the narrator, Dr. Rieux, who seeks to cure but cannot; Rieux's new friend and confidant, Jean Tarrou, who organizes squads of workers to fight the disease; the visiting journalist, Raymond Rambert, who longs to escape and return to his lover in Paris; the heroic yet nondescript office clerk, Joseph Grand, who diligently tallies the dead; other doctors, citizens, and the family of Monsieur Othan, particularly his young, innocent son—recipient of a long-awaited serum—who dies a painful death nonetheless. Rieux's inability to cure the sick moves him to lead others to volunteer, work, organize: to do something—anything—against an invading, unwieldy, arbitrary killing force. Doing nothing constitutes complicity with the enemy.

It is not until the New Year that hope begins to return to the inhabitants of Oran, although Dr. Rieux remarks, "it is doubtful if this could be called a victory."[33] The story takes on new relevance

---

[33] Camus, *The Plague*, 271.

14   CAMUS'S *THE PLAGUE*

and meaning as we, too, lived sequestered-in-place in our respective homes and communities—waiting: for adequate testing, for the death toll to drop, for social distancing requirements to ease, for a possible "next wave," for businesses and schools to remain open, for ample doses of a vaccine, and for the normalcy we once knew. *The Plague* teaches us to neither covet nor expect what we so casually took for granted. As we progress through long, drawn-out stages of our own twenty-first-century "plague," the passing of time reveals new problems such as loss of employment, hunger, eviction, lack of internet access for children to attend school remotely, and the disproportionate susceptibility to contracting the disease if one is a person of color, an "essential" worker forced to continue laboring in an unsafe environment, an "undocumented/unauthorized noncitizen,"[34] poor, or someone lacking health insurance. As with the growing spread of the disease in Oran, crises we experience multiply over time. Covid "variants"—such as the deadly Delta and highly contagious Omicron variants of 2021—pose new threats to health and welfare, just as the extension of vaccines to young children and a third "booster" shot offer a glimmer of hope to the weary. Millions of anti-vaxxers, however, complicate recovery for all.

The Narrative's Historical Weight

Consider how Camus crafted the novel in its historical and literary contexts. Numerous commentaries have been written during our current pandemic to motivate readers to appreciate the novel's plot and details. For example, Clay Jenkinson gleans commonalities with other plagues from a study of pandemic literature dating back to the Justinian Plague of 541 CE, the Black Death (1348–1352), the Great Plague of London (1665–1666), the Third Plague Pandemic beginning in 1894 (China, Australia, India), and the Spanish Flu

---

[34] Aguilera, "Another Word for 'Illegal Alien,'" July 22, 2016.

INTRODUCTION 15

(1918). These documents record a pattern of human reactions of denial, flight (for the wealthy), suffering of the poor who are often essential workers unable to flee, legitimate strategies to mitigate the spread of the disease (government laws, quarantine, social distancing, masks), confidence men and conspiracy theories, economic fallout, and a rush to normalcy that often causes prolonged infection and death.[35] Kim Willsher notes that the novel is loosely based on a cholera epidemic in Algeria which reportedly killed a large proportion of the population in 1849, almost twenty years after French colonization began.[36] Sean Illing suggests, "The beauty of *The Plague* is that it asks the reader to map the lessons of the pandemic onto everyday life. The principles that drive the hero, Rieux, are the same principles that make every society worthwhile—empathy, love, and solidarity."[37]

Alain de Botton credits Camus with both exposing the absurdity of one's life which can end at any moment, for any reason, as well as encouraging an internalization of human vulnerability that necessitates loving our fellow man.[38] Robert Zaretsky suggests that the lessons learned from Camus are complex wherein "ordinary" characters can function as role models who exemplify "resistance against the inhuman force of the plague," but it is the ignorance of the politicians and powerful that are the real threat (although, in the end, not a reason for despair, given Camus's faith in man).[39] Simon Critchley argues that basic anxiety about vulnerability and death—experienced acutely during a pandemic—can actually function as a "vehicle of liberation."[40] Ronald Aronson offers the observation that "there is nothing political about his plague, while our situation is profoundly so. . . . our plague takes place through

---

[35] Jenkinson, "Why We Should Be Reading Albert Camus during the Pandemic," May 26, 2020.
[36] Willsher, "Albert Camus Novel *The Plague*," March 28, 2020.
[37] Illing, "This Is a Time for Solidarity," March 15, 2020.
[38] Botton, "Camus on the Coronavirus," March 19, 2020.
[39] Zaretsky, "The Unwilling Guide: Camus's *The Plague*," Summer 2020.
[40] Critchley, "Our Fear, Our Trembling," April 11, 2020.

16   CAMUS'S *THE PLAGUE*

the social and political madness of Trumpism. . . . its viciousness, its sense of grievance, its cult of personality, its proud rejection of science and reason."[41] No comparable critique of Oran's leadership appears in *The Plague*.

Orhan Pamuk cites Daniel Defoe's chronicle of seventeenth-century London, *A Journal of the Plague Year*, as "the single most illuminating work of literature ever written on contagion and human behavior."[42] That work influenced Camus, but it is worth noting that while Dafoe's narrator ends his chronicle bemoaning "all manner of wickedness among us,"[43] Camus cautiously celebrates the cooperation that sustained the doctors, workers, and the general populace. Moreover, Defoe notes the contributions of women as nurses, their tribulations as mothers, the many burdens of caregiving relegated to women: all of which are absent from *The Plague*. Other epidemic literature that preceded *La Peste* includes *History of the Wars* by Procopius (542 CE, The Justinian Plague), *The History of the Peloponnesian War* by Thucydides (431 BCE, The Plague of Athens), Giovanni Boccaccio's 1353 *Decameron* (fourteenth-century Black Death in Italy), and *The Diary of Samuel Pepys* (seventeenth-century bubonic plague in London). The closest factual description of plague in Algeria to that fictionalized by Camus is that referenced by the Centers for Disease Control and Prevention that occurred in 1946, just when Camus is writing *The Plague* (in France).[44] Clearly he was able to pick and choose how to craft his version, resulting in an uplifting testament to men's strength united against an enemy, fighting a foe.

---

[41] Aronson, "Camus' Plague Is Not Ours," April 14, 2020. For a philosophical overview of Camus's oeuvre, see Aronson, "Albert Camus," *Stanford Encyclopedia of Philosophy* as well as the previously mentioned *Camus and Sartre: The Story of a Friendship*.

[42] Pamuk, "What the Great Pandemic Novels Teach Us," April 23, 2020. Pamuk is the winner of the 2006 Nobel Prize in Literature and is currently writing a novel set in 1901 based on the Third Plague Pandemic.

[43] Defoe, *A Journal of the Plague Year*, 143.

[44] Bertherat et al., "Plague Reappearance in Algeria after 50 Years, 2003," October 2007.

INTRODUCTION   17

Not everyone responded positively. Even early criticisms by Jean-Paul Sartre and Roland Barthes found fault with Camus's moral message overwhelming his aesthetic concerns.[45] More recent readings further problematize Camus's intentions, style, and overall effect on generations of readers and critics. Scholars influenced by the writings of Frantz Fanon, Edward Said, and other race theorists fault Camus for ignoring the indigenous population of Algeria, its struggle for autonomy, and the pervasive inequalities a colonized country bears: all of which were apparent to the author. As he engaged in various political pronouncements and publications in real life, he omitted them from his fictional account of Oran. He is criticized for deliberately evading the topic of French colonial oppression and violence, "erasing" the Algerian uprising and resultant 1945 massacre of at least 20,000 Algerians, and "masking" the indigenous peoples' fight for freedom.[46] For some critics, Camus silences the voice of the North African "subaltern" who fails to see herself reflected in the text; that is, "Individual travails overshadow the decimation of Arabs by the plague."[47] More pointedly, as argued by Robert Solomon in a 2008 essay, "In *The Stranger* the Arabs who make up most of the population don't have names, but in *The Plague* they don't seem to have deaths either."[48] Camus is accused of choosing to write a "classic imperialist discourse that, directly, overtly, and with complicity, accepts the racist hierarchy that all European countries imposed on other parts of the world.[49] Solomon added, "Camus describes Algeria here as in *The Stranger* as if it is nothing but a European colony."[50]

---

[45] Krapp, "Time and Ethics," 655.
[46] Kabel and Phillipson, "Structural Violence and Hope in Catastrophic Times," 4.
[47] Kabel and Phillipson, "Structural Violence and Hope in Catastrophic Times," 5.
[48] Solomon, "Facing Death Together," 174.
[49] Kabel and Phillipson, "Structural Violence and Hope in Catastrophic Times," 6.
[50] Solomon, "Facing Death Together," 174.

18   CAMUS'S *THE PLAGUE*

Fictional Triumph over Fact

The shift toward critical readings of the novel lies in the difference in time periods—ours and that of Camus—as well as what is considered to be Camus's outdated response to "the executioner," oppressor, or purveyor of injustice. Scholars Kabel and Phillipson write, "The anti-fascism that was important for Camus in occupied France is largely immaterial to Algerian politics. His advocacy of assimilation in Algeria predated and continued after the 'demise' of fascism."[51] In effect, he grew out of step with the times—his own—with an exhortation to "universal humanism" that was said to exclude the indigenous population and conceal "his parochial colonialist politics," thereby rendering his "hope" for the future "romanticized."[52] More awareness of what is missing, eliminated, and structurally barred from the novel results in reading the novel's advocacy of solidarity as incomplete, hollow, and empty.

LeBlanc and Jones, however, offer a 2002 reading of *The Plague* in which they see Camus offering an alternative narrative model that moves beyond "conflict models of discourse" to one in which "the binary logic of the conflict between France and Algeria" is rejected and "far from embodying and promulgating a colonial mentality, his second published novel actually anticipates post-colonial critiques of French control of Africa."[53] They argue, "The intersections of religion, art, and politics in his work problematize models of political discourse and open a way to think about the place of narrative and story-telling and their meaning for being at home with 'others' and the self, in community, in a place."[54]

Specifically with regard to the inequities seemingly perpetuated by Camus's neglect of the Arab population, David Carroll tracks

---

[51] Kabel and Phillipson, 5, refers to Tony Judt, *The Burden of Responsibility: Blum, Camus, Aron, and the French Twentieth Century* (University of Chicago Press, 1998), 87–135.

[52] Kabel and Phillipson, "Structural Violence and Hope in Catastrophic Times," 6, 14.

[53] Kellman, "About This Volume," ix.

[54] LeBlanc and Jones, "Space/Place and Home," 209.

INTRODUCTION 19

the origins of the earliest and most intensely negative claims against the novel to a 1970 book by Conor Cruise O'Brien to which Camus never had a chance to respond.[55] Carroll defends what he insists is Camus's clear and consistent anticolonialist stance with ample documentation from both his fictional and political writings. In explaining the complexity of Camus's strategic choice of Oran—"his least favorite Algerian city," Carroll offers evidence of contrasting procolonialist writings of Camus's literary predecessors, particularly from 1938.[56] Carroll's incisive historical and textual analysis provides evidence that cannot be denied: "The charge that 'Camus and his friends' did not find colonial racism and oppression repugnant and that he did not denounce them and see a link between colonial and Nazi racism and violence simply does not hold up to scrutiny."[57] Carroll's analysis also considers the literary fact stressed by Camus himself, namely, that the novel was fictional and allegorical and thus necessarily resistant to historical-political accuracy. Carroll emphatically argues that Camus was not only anticolonialist but also an Algerian who did not ignore his fellow Algerians. Moreover, Camus had always advocated multireferentiality, that is, multiple readings of "the plague"—for instance, Stalinism in addition to Nazism as a form of unacceptable political oppression (much debated by fellow French intellectuals of the day). Previously, O'Brien had questioned Camus's intentions on this matter, claiming that the author only intended "the plague" to refer to Nazism. Perhaps this entire controversy surrounding Camus's portrayal of Oran's citizens as colonialists would be moot if characters had just been given non-French names.

---

[55] Carroll, *Albert Camus the Algerian*, 49 and ff.
[56] Carroll, *Albert Camus the Algerian*, 45 and ff. For instance, René Lespès, in his *Oran: etude de géographie et d'histoire urbaine* (Paris: Librairie Félix Alcan, 1938), considered Oran a model city in Algeria *only because of* one hundred years of French occupation.
[57] Carroll, *Albert Camus the Algerian*, 53.

20   CAMUS'S *THE PLAGUE*

Thus, at this unique time in the wake of the work, when readers accumulate lived experiences of their own during an unprecedented pandemic and are acutely aware of systemic injustices, new commentators and critics should be given wide berth to find additional "layers of meaning" in the words on the page as well as names and phrases that do not appear.[58] As informed readers and critics, we continue to question the author's literary and philosophical intentions, choices, and omissions in order to judge for ourselves. The essays in this volume begin that discussion in the twenty-first century, mid-pandemic.

Strategically, Camus chose fiction to convey facts. *The Plague* is *not just fiction*, since it is based on haunting facts from the historical past; nor is it *merely literary journalism*, as it attends to newsworthy details of everyday life in a storytelling setting.[59] It may function as *escape fiction*, but our escape is illusory as we ourselves—living in a pandemic reproducing the restrictive conditions like those of bubonic plague in 1940s Oran—identify with the actions of fictional characters like those we witness in real life: in the media, on the streets, in hospitals, on Zoom, within our own families. Our lived experiences—the starting point for phenomenologists seeking to chart the theoretical—map onto Camus's narrative, confirming Simone de Beauvoir's similar intuition to choose to write fiction over philosophy. Her mode of existentialist writing, with an "emphasis on the particular and the concrete, from which philosophical propositions may be drawn, invites the use of fiction as a medium for philosophical discovery, especially at the ontological level."[60] A similar observation might be offered of Camus, namely, "there is no question but that Camus's philosophical concerns were best captured in literary form."[61] Even in English translation, Camus's

---

[58] See Gray, "Layers of Meaning in *La Peste*."
[59] Hartsock, *Literary Journalism and the Aesthetics of Experience*.
[60] Fullbrook and Simons, "Simone de Beauvoir," March 25, 2020.
[61] Sherman, *Camus*, 3.

INTRODUCTION 21

prose is vivid, powerful, and arresting; it is often so pleasing that one risks becoming too absorbed in his words, similes, and metaphors, thereby forgetting the horrors of plague. Simple and direct, Camus elevates the words of everyday sights and sounds to an aesthetically high level of creative endeavor. Perhaps the frustrated writer, the clerk named Grand, said it best when he insisted, "It's only artists who know how to use their eyes."[62] Borrowing from Defoe—in an epigraph intended to appear at the beginning of *The Plague*—Camus also chose fiction to convey what he imagined might have happened in a town called Oran: "It is as reasonable to represent one kind of imprisonment by another as it is to represent anything which really exists by that which exists not."[63]

New Perspectives

This collection of essays invites contemporary thinkers to reflect—in light of Camus's original fictional narrative—upon the progression of the coronavirus as it spread worldwide, felled millions of victims, and posed moral challenges to us as individuals, governments, and global societies. Conversely, readers are encouraged to reread and reconsider Camus's fiction in light of contemporary life. Authors range from fields as diverse as philosophy, French and comparative literature, English, history, gender and women's studies, medicine, medical ethics, feminist bioethics,[64] and medical humanities. Informative and provocative essays were penned at different times over the duration of one year, 2021, within an atmosphere that posed a dangerous and lethal level of political discourse: one of falsehoods, denials, and "alternative facts." This anthology seeks to explain what constitutes

[62] Camus, *The Plague*, 136.
[63] The quote is from Daniel Defoe's *Robinson Crusoe* (1719): the epigraph is missing from the 1948 and 1975 Stuart Gilbert translations of the paperback Vintage publication.
[64] See also *The American Philosophical Association Feminism and Philosophy Newsletter*, "Special Issue: Feminist Responses to COVID-19 and Pandemics.".

22 CAMUS'S *THE PLAGUE*

the timeliness and timelessness of Camus's fictional plague by drawing on contemporary commentary, prevailing scholarship, and personal observations, interpretation, and (aesthetic) judgments.

First, Steven G. Kellman interrogates the social context of our time in "*The Plague* and the Present Moment" when American protesters resisted both oppressive government tactics against their civil liberties and expressed demands for racial justice. These actions—during the 2020 presidential election—parallel the Algerian population's war for independence in the 1950s and 1960s. The dissimilarity to Oran's naturally occurring plague—for which no one was held morally responsible—highlighted the autocratic and punitive practices of former president Trump, who exacerbated an already urgent medical situation by denying its importance and calling it a hoax. Both the novel and the 2020 pandemic raise questions about human behavior that ranges from the heroic to the unethical, conspiratorial, and criminal.

The absence of women on the front lines of fighting the plague in Camus's Oran raises the specter of medicine as a masculinized and exclusionary profession at odds with our own contemporary situation. In "Present in Effacement: The Place of Women in Camus's Plague and Ours," Jane E. Schultz notes that the mid-twentieth-century context of Algerian society is dominated by Camus's choice of nearly all male characters in the novel: leaders like Dr. Rieux, doctors, workers, and even patients. Women are relegated to marginal roles: maternal, spousal, or desired and distant lover. In contrast, the history of nursing illuminates the role of women who function as risk takers and caregivers in a profession in which they labor as active agents of change and comfort.

Camus's treatment of the arbitrariness and contingency of life—the absurd—leaves us, like many characters in Camus's novel, searching for order and purpose. Andrew Edgar examines the underlying foundations of this loss of control in an essay entitled, "The Meaning of a Pandemic." Invoking Camus's *Myth of Sisyphus* from

1955, Edgar contrasts various coping strategies in human behaviors that either acquiesce to the absurdity of existence or find meaning in the challenge the absurd inevitably presents. The influence of phenomenology, particularly the work of Heidegger, informs a reading of *The Plague* that elucidates the current pandemic. According to Kathleen Higgins, those impacted by plague or pandemic are naturally afflicted with common psychological symptoms of grief following loss, but also with a sense of anticipatory grief that might be diminished or overcome by means of collective action. In "Grief and Human Connection in *The Plague*," Higgins casts this sense of expected dread as contributing to one's sense of isolation, exhaustion, and apathy. We, however, like Camus's more heroic characters, can extract ourselves from loss and progress toward healing by working together toward common goals that benefit all.

The erosion of the physician's role as healer when faced with a fast-spreading disease in the absence of any prevention or cure is analyzed by Edward Weiser through a comparison between Dr. Rieux and contemporary medical practice in "Examining the Narrative Devolution of the Physician in Camus's *The Plague*." Much like the situation in Oran, the current pandemic thwarts medical successes which physicians routinely seek and expect. Comparisons between Dr. Rieux and today's physicians serve to highlight the achievements of medical practice in spite of its limitations.

Cynthia A. Freeland presents Camus's exploration of the multi-faceted problem of evil—evidenced as great human suffering—in her essay, "Horror and Natural Evil in *The Plague*." She probes "zoonotic villains" such as rats and bats which function like monsters (reminiscent of Dracula) as well as Camus's use of natural phenomena like the incessant winds that rattle Oran. These non-humanmade causes inspire dread, placing the novel in the category of "natural horror" to which Dr. Rieux must respond.

Particular words uttered by both patients on ventilators as well as Black Lives Matter protesters in the streets open a path to interpreting the tragedies of Covid-19 and Camus's plague. An essay

24 CAMUS'S *THE PLAGUE*

by Margaret E. Gray, "'I Can't Breathe': Covid-19 and *The Plague*'s Tragedy of Political and Corporeal Suffocation," recalls the last words spoken by George Floyd on May 25, 2020, that inspired mask-wearing protestors to take to the streets by the thousands in the name of justice. The act of breathing, particularly when thwarted, prevented, or denied, functions as a trope for freedom and life—in opposition to oppression, death, and sociopolitical tyranny.

Not everyone faces "modern" death equally, whether in Oran or today's world.[65] In the essay, "Modern Death, Decent Death, and Heroic Solidarity in *The Plague*," Peg Brand Weiser argues that the "difficulty" in Oran of "modern death" as described by Camus is still with us today in that Americans neither faced death *together* in any form of solidarity under the Trump administration nor faced death individually in any traditional "decent" manner (as proposed by the character Tarrou), that is, comforted by family or friends. One reason is overwhelming fear of death—what neuroscientists call "existential anxiety"—that can motivate human behavior toward either selfishness or an ethics of care. As a result of lived experiences of the pandemic, a sense of "heroic solidarity" has perhaps finally been achieved that moves us from despair to hope, confirming Camus's faith in humanity.

Conclusion

Within a year of its publication, *The Plague* had been translated into nine languages; current translations number at least twenty-eight. It is currently a worldwide bestseller with its British publisher, Pelican/Penguin Classics (now part of Viking Penguin, Penguin Random House, publisher of the original 1948 translation by Stuart Gilbert), struggling to meet demand. A second English translation by Robin Russ appeared in November 2001, with a commentary

---

[65] See Warraich, *Modern Death: How Medicine Changed the End of Life.*

INTRODUCTION   25

by Tony Judt noting the relevancy of reading the novel just after the September 11th attack on New York and the Pentagon.[66] A new translation for the original English publisher (Alfred A. Knopf, Inc.) by Laura Marris was begun before the current pandemic and arrived in print in November 2021; she argues that "while Camus was writing for the moment, he was also writing for the future. He knew that his book would be needed again, long after his death, in a context he couldn't predict or imagine."[67] Indeed, an entirely new field of pandemic bioethics has begun.[68]

Readers are invited to engage with Camus's text in new and innovative ways, allowing the fictional flow of events and imaginary human actions to triumph over the facts of the matter, the undeniable truths of our current state of affairs. The plague never really ends; it lies dormant while time passes and while we choose—or not—to address the persistent inequalities and sufferings of a world under siege. Remedies require solidarity and sacrifice, but we can imagine a future when the elimination of exterminators and the safety and health of *all* victims are realized. "Perhaps with the lockdown we will have some time to reflect about what is real, what is important, and become more human," observed Catherine Camus, seventy-four-year-old daughter of Albert Camus, early in the Covid-19 pandemic (March 2020).[69] Camus may not have provided the most complete account of how to achieve "a brotherhood of man," but he starts us down a path of self-awareness toward inclusivity and justice when he warns us early on, "no one will ever be free so long as there are pestilences."[70]

---

[66] Judt, "On 'The Plague,'" November 29, 2001.

[67] Marris, "Camus's Innoculation against Hate," April 16, 2020. Marris and Alice Kaplan have coauthored a book of essays, *States of Plague: Reading Albert Camus in a Pandemic* (2022).

[68] See Pence, *Pandemic Bioethics* (2021) and Schwartz, *The Ethics of Pandemics* (2020).

[69] Willsher, "Albert Camus Novel *The Plague*," March 28, 2020. Catherine Camus first read the novel when she was fourteen, two months before the death of her father at age forty-six by car accident in 1960. Catherine Camus is editor of *Albert Camus: Solitude and Solidarity* (2012).

[70] Camus, *The Plague*, 37.

26 CAMUS'S *THE PLAGUE*

Works Cited

Aguilera, Jasmine. "Another Word for 'Illegal Alien' at the Library of Congress: Contentious." *The New York Times*, July 22, 2016. https://www.nytimes.com/2016/07/23/us/another-word-for-illegal-alien-at-the-library-of-congress-contentious.html.

American Philosophical Association Feminism and Philosophy Newsletter 20, no. 1 (2020). "Special Issue: Feminist Responses to COVID-19 and Pandemics." https://cdn.ymaws.com/www.apaonline.org/resource/collection/D03EBDAB-82D7-4B28-B897-C050FDC1ACB4/FeminismCovidSpecialIssueV20n1.pdf.

Aronson, Ronald. "Albert Camus." *Stanford Encyclopedia of Philosophy* (April 10, 2017). https://plato.stanford.edu/entries/camus/.

Aronson, Ronald. *Camus and Sartre: The Story of a Friendship and the Quarrel That Ended It.* Chicago: University of Chicago Press, 2004.

Aronson, Ronald. "Camus' Plague Is Not Ours." *Tikkun*, April 14, 2020. https://www.tikkun.org/camus-plague-is-not-ours/.

Bassett, Mary T., and Natalia Linos. "Trump Gave Up on Fighting the Virus: Now We're Paying for His Laziness." *The Washington Post*, July 14, 2020. https://www.washingtonpost.com/outlook/2020/07/14/trump-gave-up-coronavirus/.

Bertherat, Eric, Souad Bekhoucha, Saada Chougrani, Fathia Razik, Jean B. Duchemin, Leila Houti, Larbi Deharib, Corinne Fayolle, Banaouda Makrerougrass, Radia Dali-Yahia, Ramdan Bella, Leila Belhabri, Amina Chaieb, Evgueni Tikhomirov, and Elisabeth Carniel. "Plague Reappearance in Algeria after 50 Years, 2003." *Emerging Infectious Diseases* 13, no. 10 (October 2007), 1459–1462. https://wwwnc.cdc.gov/eid/article/13/10/07-0284_article.

Birdsall, William F. "Albert Camus' *Jonas, or the Artist at Work*: Deciphering a Painting, Solving a Contradiction." *Albert Camus Society Downloads* (February 3, 2015). https://www.academia.edu/12293455/Albert_Camus_Jonas_or_the_Artist_at_Work_Deciphering_a_Painting_Solving_a_Contradiction.

Botton, Alain de. "Camus on the Coronavirus." *The New York Times Magazine*, March 19, 2020. https://www.nytimes.com/2020/03/19/opinion/sunday/coronavirus-camus-plague.html.

Camus, Albert. *Neither Victims nor Executioners: An Ethic Superior to Murder.* Translated by Dwight Macdonald. Second edition. Eugene, OR: Wipf and Stock, 2008. Reprint of "Ni Victimes Ni Bourreaux," in *Actuelles: Écrits Politiques; Tome I: Chroniques 1944–1948.* Paris: Editions Gallimard, 1950.

Camus, Albert. *La Peste.* Paris: Editions Gallimard, 1947.

Camus, Albert. *The Plague.* Translated by Stuart Gilbert. London: Hamish Hamilton, 1948.

Camus, Albert. *The Plague.* Translated by Stuart Gilbert. New York: Vintage Books, 1991.

INTRODUCTION 27

Camus, Albert. *Le Premier Homme* (*The First Man*). Translated by David Hapgood. New York: Alfred A. Knopf, 1995. [Originally published 1994 by Editions Gallimard, Paris.]

Camus, Albert. *Notebooks 1951–1959*. Translated by Ryan Bloom. Chicago: Ivan R. Dee, 2008.

Camus, Albert. *The Plague*. Translated by Laura Marris. New York: Alfred A. Knopf, 2021.

Camus, Albert. "The Artist at Work." In *Exile and the Kingdom*, edited by Albert Camus. Translated by Justin O'Brien, 36–49. New York: Vintage Books, 1957.

Camus, Catherine, ed. *Albert Camus: Solitude and Solidarity*. Zurich: Edition Olms, 2012.

Carroll, David. *Albert Camus the Algerian: Colonialism, Terrorism, Justice*. New York: Columbia University Press, 2008.

Critchley, Simon. "Our Fear, Our Trembling, Our Strength." *The New York Times*, April 11, 2020. https://www.nytimes.com/2020/04/11/opinion/covid-philosophy-anxiety-death.html.

Defoe, Daniel. *A Journal of the Plague Year, Written by a Citizen Who Continued All the While in London*. London: Penguin, 2003.

Fullbrook, Edward, and Margaret Simons. "Simone de Beauvoir." *Oxford Bibliographies* (March 25, 2020). https://www.oxfordbibliographies.com/view/document/obo-9780195396577/obo-9780195396577-0277.xml.

Gray, Margaret E. "Layers of Meaning in *La Peste*." In *The Cambridge Companion to Camus*, edited by Edward J. Hughes, 165–177. Cambridge: Cambridge University Press, 2007.

Hartsock, John C. *Literary Journalism and the Aesthetics of Experience*. Amherst: University of Massachusetts Press, 2016.

Hendrix, Steve, and Hazem Balousha, "Gaza Struggles with Twin Crises of War Injuries and Feared Coronavirus Surge." *The Washington Post*, May 22, 2021. https://www.washingtonpost.com/world/middle_east/gaza-isr ael-hospitals-coronavirus/2021/05/22/8b64d080-ba67-11eb-bc4a-62849cf 6cca9_story.html.

Illing, Sean. "This Is a Time for Solidarity; What Albert Camus's 'The Plague' Can Teach Us about Life in a Pandemic." *Vox*, March 15, 2020. https://www.vox.com/2020/3/13/21172237/coronavirus-covid-19-albert-camus-the-plague.

Institute for Health Metrics and Evaluation. "Estimation of Total Mortality Due to COVID-19, May 13, 2021. https://www.healthdata.org/sites/default/files/files/Projects/COVID/2021/Estimation-of-excess-mortality-due-to-COVID.pdf.

Jenkinson, Clay S. "Why We Should Be Reading Albert Camus during the Pandemic." *Governing*, May 26, 2020. https://www.governing.com/context/Why-We-Should-Be-Reading-Albert-Camus-During-the-Pandemic.html.

28   CAMUS'S THE PLAGUE

Judt, Tony. "On 'The Plague.'" *The New York Review of Books*, November 29, 2001. https://www.nybooks.com/articles/2001/11/29/on-the-plague/.

Kabel, Ahmed, and Robert Phillipson. "Structural Violence and Hope in Catastrophic Times: From Camus' *The Plague* to Covid-19." *Race & Class* 62, no. 4 (December 2, 2020): 3–18. https://journals.sagepub.com/doi/full/10.1177/0306396820974180.

Kaplan, Alice. *Looking for the Stranger: Camus and the Life of a Literary Classic*. Chicago: University of Chicago Press, 2016.

Kellman, Stephen G. "About This Volume." In *Critical Insights: Albert Camus*, edited by Stephen G. Kellman, vii–xii. Pasadena, CA: Salem Press, 2011.

Kellman, Stephen G. "On Albert Camus." In *Critical Insights: Albert Camus*, edited by Stephen G. Kellman, 3–17. Pasadena, CA: Salem Press, 2011.

Krapp. John. "Time and Ethics in Albert Camus's *The Plague*." *University of Toronto Quarterly* 68, no. 2 (Spring 1999): 655–676. https://utpjournals.press/doi/abs/10.3138/utq.68.2.655.

LeBlanc, John Randolph, and Carolyn M. Jones. "Space/Place and Home: Prefiguring Contemporary Political and Religious Discourse in Albert Camus's *The Plague*." In *Critical Insights: Albert Camus*, edited by Stephen G. Kellman, 201–230. Pasadena, CA: Salem Press, 2011. [Originally published in *Contemporary Political Theory* 2 (2002): 209–230.]

Leibovich, Mark. "For A.O.C., 'Existential Crises' as Her District Becomes the Coronavirus Epicenter." *Washington Post*, May 4, 2020. https://www.nytimes.com/2020/05/04/us/politics/coronavirus-alexandria-ocasio-cortez.html.

Marris, Laura. "Camus's Innoculation against Hate." *The New York Times*, April 16, 2020. https://www.nytimes.com/2020/04/16/books/review/the-plague-albert-camus-coronavirus.html.

Marris, Laura, and Alice Kaplan. *States of Plague: Reading Albert Camus in a Pandemic*. Chicago: University of Chicago Press, 2022.

Meagher, Robert Emmet. *Albert Camus and the Human Crisis*. New York: Pegasus Books, 2021.

Metcalf, Stephen. "Albert Camus' 'The Plague' and Our Own Great Reset." *The Los Angeles Times*, March 23, 2020. https://www.latimes.com/entertainment-arts/books/story/2020-03-23/reading-camu-the-plague-amid-coronavirus.

Mezahi, Maher. "Goalkeeper, Philosopher, Outsider: Albert Camus." *French Football Weekly*, November 7, 2013. http://frenchfootballweekly.com/2013/11/07/goalkeeper-philosopher-outsider-albert-camus/.

Mortensen, Viggo. "La Crise de L'homme" ("A Human Crisis"): A Reading of Albert Camus's March 28, 1946 speech at Columbia University. May 9, 2016. https://www.youtube.com/watch?v=aaFZJ_ymueA. Accessed August 2, 2022.

O'Brien, Conor Cruise. *Albert Camus of Europe and Africa*. New York: Viking Press, 1970.

Pamuk, Orhan. "What the Great Pandemic Novels Teach Us." *The New York Times*, April 23, 2020. https://www.nytimes.com/2020/04/23/opinion/sunday/coronavirus-orhan-pamuk.html.

Pandy, Geeta. "India's Holiest River Is Swollen with Covid Victims." *BBC News*, Delhi, May 18, 2021. https://www.bbc.com/news/world-asia-india-57154564.

Pence, Gregory E. *Pandemic Bioethics*. Peterborough, Ontario: Broadview Press, 2021.

Petrequin, Samuel. "EU Leaders Agree to Donate 100 Million Doses of Vaccines." *The Washington Post*, May 25, 2021. https://www.washingtonpost.com/world/eu-leaders-agree-to-donate-100-million-doses-of-vaccines/2021/05/25/9da2a466-bd4b-11eb-922a-c40c9774bc48_story.html.

Schwartz, Meredith Celene. *The Ethics of Pandemics*. Peterborough, Ontario: Broadview Press, 2020.

Sherman, David. *Camus*. West Sussex, UK: Wiley Blackwell, 2009.

Slater, Joanna. "India Sets Pandemic Record with More Than 400,000 New Cases; Fauci Says Crisis 'Is Like a War.'" *The Washington Post*, May 1, 2021. https://www.washingtonpost.com/world/2021/05/01/india-coronavirus/.

Slater, Joanna. "In India, the Deadliest Day for Any Country Since the Pandemic Began." *The Washington Post*, May 19, 2021. https://www.washingtonpost.com/world/asia_pacific/india-deadliest-covid-day/2021/05/19/2452925c-b89a-11eb-bc4a-62849cf6cca9_story.html.

Solomon, Robert. "Facing Death Together: Camus's *The Plague*." In *Art and Ethical Criticism*, edited by Garry L. Hagberg, 163–183. Blackwell, 2008.

Warraich, Haider J. *Modern Death: How Medicine Changed the End of Life*. New York: St. Martin's Griffin, 2018.

The Washington Post. "Coronavirus Data." Accessed November 14, 2021 and December 31, 2021. https://www.washingtonpost.com/graphics/2020/world/mapping-spread-new-coronavirus/.

WHO Coronavirus (COVID-19) Dashboard. https://covid19.who.int/. Accessed July 4, 2022, and December 31, 2021.

"WHO Director-General's Opening Remarks at the Media Briefing on COVID-19, March 11, 2020. https://www.who.int/director-general/speeches/detail/who-director-general-s-opening-remarks-at-the-media-briefing-on-covid-19—-11-march-2020.

Willsher, Kim. "Albert Camus Novel *The Plague* Leads Surge of Pestilence Fiction." *The Guardian*, March 28, 2020. https://www.theguardian.com/books/2020/mar/28/albert-camus-novel-the-plague-la-peste-pestilence-fiction-coronavirus-lockdown.

Zaretsky, Robert. "The Unwilling Guide: Camus's *The Plague*." *Social Research: An International Quarterly* 87, no. 2 (Summer 2020): 297–298. https://www.muse.jhu.edu/article/764873.

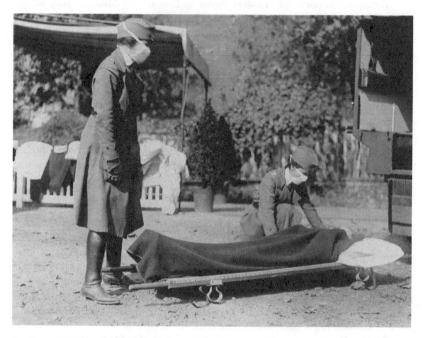

2. Demonstration of the Red Cross Emergency Ambulance Station in Washington, DC, during the influenza pandemic of 1918. F&A Archive/Art Resource, NY.

1

The Plague and the Present Moment

Steven G. Kellman

We plunder the past to flatter the present. In the 1920s, the Metaphysical poets were rescued from obscurity by T. S. Eliot, John Crowe Ransom, Allen Tate, and others who found sanction for Modernist paradox and irony in seventeenth-century aesthetics. *The Plague* has never been obscure; widely read and admired, it has remained in print since its original publication in 1947. However, seventy-three years later, Albert Camus's novel suddenly became the literary sensation of 2020, what Elisabeth Philippe in *Le Nouvel Obs* called "la Bible de ces temps tourmentés" [the Bible for these tormented times].[1] During February and March 2020, as Covid-19 became pandemic, *The Plague*—along with Boccaccio's *Decameron*, Daniel Defoe's *Journal of the Plague Year*, Ling Ma's *Severance*, and Emily St. John Mandel's *Station Eleven*—began showing up on recommended lists of pestilence books that might provide perspective on current woes. But Camus's novel was, according to Samuel Earle, "the undisputed pick of the pandemic-lit."[2]

Throughout the world, the advent of another plague created a worldwide demand for *The Plague*. It became, again, a bestseller in France, which reported a 300 percent increase in sales over 2019.[3] Sales in the United Kingdom surged by more than 3,000 percent,[4] and Japanese booksellers disposed of more copies in March 2020

---

[1] Philippe, "Coronavirus: Albert Camus," March 26, 2020.
[2] Earle, "How Albert Camus's *The Plague*," May 27, 2020.
[3] Flood, "Publishers Report Sales Boom," March 5, 2020.
[4] Abell, "It's Simply Classic Camus," May 10, 2020, 23.

Camus's The Plague. Peg Brand Weiser, Oxford University Press. © Oxford University Press 2023.
DOI: 10.1093/oso/9780197599327.003.0002

32 CAMUS'S *THE PLAGUE*

than during the previous thirty-one years combined.[5] In Italy, sales of the book tripled,[6] and in South Korea it vaulted as high as number two on one bestseller list.[7] In the crowded American market, it placed seventeenth in late March.[8] Though it is the story of a fictional epidemic in North Africa in the 1940s, *The Plague* was read as if it spoke to the global woes of 2020.

Camus would likely not have been disappointed by the reappropriation of his novel. For one thing, use of the definite article in French creates a kind of ambiguity. *Le roman*, for example, could refer either to a specific novel (*le roman que je lis à ce moment*—the novel I am reading at this moment) or else to novels in general (*je préfère le roman à la poésie*—I prefer the novel to poetry). So the title Camus chose for his 1947 novel, *La Peste*,[9] could refer to the specific pestilence that breaks out in Oran or else to plagues in general (including the one that broke out in Wuhan in late 2019 and spread globally), or to both.

Moreover, Camus prefaced his novel with an epigraph—translated into French from English—that encourages allegorical readings. Unaccountably omitted from the 1991 Viking paperback edition of Stuart Gilbert's translation, though preserved in the 1948 Modern Library edition, is a statement by Daniel Defoe: "It is as reasonable to represent one kind of imprisonment by another, as it is to represent anything that really exists by that which exists not."[10] It comes not, as might be expected, from Defoe's *A Journal of the Plague Year*, but, rather, from *Robinson Crusoe*. However, it is an invitation, *avant la page*, to read the imprisonment recounted by Dr. Bernard Rieux as also applicable to a world held captive to Covid-19. Rieux's bacterial plague is an epidemic, confined to

---

[5] Earle, "How Albert Camus's *The Plague*," May 27, 2020.
[6] Gary, "Italie: à L'Ère du Coronavirus," February 28, 2020.
[7] Seung-hyun, "*The Plague* by Albert Camus," March 15, 2020.
[8] Juris, "Apple Books Bestsellers," March 25, 2020.
[9] Camus, *La Peste*.
[10] Camus, *The Plague*, 1948, epigraph.

THE PLAGUE AND THE PRESENT MOMENT   33

a solitary quarantined city in Algeria, whereas the novel coronavirus created a pandemic that spread throughout the planet, even to Antarctica. Though Raymond Rambert sought to escape Oran and return to plague-free Paris, virtually no country on earth was safe from Covid-19 in 2020 (epidemiologists were skeptical of official claims that North Korea and Turkmenistan were each spared). Nevertheless, the range of reactions to incurable disease— including denial, hedonistic abandon, opportunism, altruism, fatalism, and despair—chronicled by Rieux—anticipates coping strategies throughout 2020 for a lethal virus for which there was as yet no vaccine.

Eight years after publishing his imaginary chronicle, Camus offered his own exegesis of what he had represented by one form of imprisonment. In an open letter to Roland Barthes, he wrote: "*The Plague*, which I wanted to be read on a number of levels, has as its obvious content the struggle of the European resistance movements against Nazism. The proof of this is that although the specific enemy is nowhere named, everyone in every European country recognized it. Let me add that a long extract from *The Plague* appeared during the Occupation, in a collection of underground texts, and that this fact alone would justify the transposition I made. In a sense, *The Plague* is more than a chronicle of the Resistance. But certainly it is nothing less."[11] The parallels might have been obvious to French readers in 1947—the sealing of borders, the sports stadium used as a holding pen for quarantined patients, like the Vélodrome d'Hiver that held captive Jews, and so on. But they are not necessarily accurate. Human beings were responsible for the Nazi atrocities, and many were held accountable. However, a plague is a natural occurrence for which no one can be assigned blame, except perhaps for failure to take measures to mitigate misfortune. Such failure was flagrant in 2020, during an ordeal that had more in common with

[11] Camus, "Letter to Roland Barthes," 339.

34 CAMUS'S *THE PLAGUE*

Camus's fictional plague in Oran than did the German occupation of Paris.

Early in the novel, as the number of infections is increasing dramatically, a meeting of local medical leaders is convened in the office of the city's Prefect. Drs. Castel and Rieux argue strenuously that all symptoms point to an outbreak of plague and that it is necessary to proclaim the truth and take urgent prophylactic measures to limit the spread. The Prefect and the other physicians, especially Dr. Richard, the chairman of the Oran Medical Association, are reluctant. Castel, who has practiced medicine for many years and in many parts of the world, has encountered such resistance before, calling it, "The usual taboo, of course; the public mustn't be alarmed, that wouldn't do at all."[12] Similarly, in 2020, the president of the United States, Donald Trump, scoffed at warnings about the dangers of a novel coronavirus that were coming from the most respected epidemiologists. On January 22, 2020, after the first Covid-19 case was reported in the United States, Trump told an interviewer "We have it totally under control. It's one person coming in from China, and we have it under control. It's going to be just fine." Two days later, he tweeted: "It will all work out well." On February 28, Trump tried to dismiss discussion of the pandemic as a politically motivated "hoax."[13] However, in a March 19 interview taped by Bob Woodward but not made public until the publication of Woodward's book, *Rage*, in September, Trump admitted that he was well aware of the severity of the public health crisis—that Covid-19 was highly contagious, airborne, and deadly—but that: "I wanted to always play it down. I still like playing it down, because I don't want to create a panic."[14]

Official denial does not last very long in Oran. The medical statistics soon become too alarming even for the lethargic Prefect, and, quarantining the entire city, he proclaims a state of plague.

---

[12] Camus, *The Plague*, 1991, 35–36. Hereafter all quotes are from this edition.
[13] Keith, "Timeline: What Trump Has Said," April 21, 2020.
[14] Woodward, *Rage*, 18.

THE *PLAGUE* AND THE PRESENT MOMENT   35

However, despite intermittent contradictory statements, Trump continued to deny the severity of a Covid-19 pandemic that, by the end of 2020, had claimed 345,000 lives in the United States, 1,810,000 worldwide.[15] The president mocked those who wore protective masks, encouraged his followers to ignore social distancing guidelines, belittled medical experts, and attacked governors and other officials who followed scientific recommendations. During the meeting with the Prefect, Rieux warns that, if appropriate measures are not taken, "there's a risk that half the population may be wiped out."[16] Covid-19 did not wipe out half the population of the United States, but a study conducted by the National Center for Disaster Preparedness at Columbia University estimated that 130,000–210,000 American lives might have been saved[17] if the president had not tried to pretend that all was well. He explained: "I'm a cheerleader for this country. I don't want to create havoc and shock and everything else."[18]

Many other world leaders were more concerned about saving lives than averting panic, and the United States ended up with a far higher incidence of Covid-19 cases and Covid-19 mortality than any other country. However, one other notable example of official denial was Brazil, whose president, Jair Bolsonaro, downplayed the disease as a "measly cold."[19] Although he himself—like Trump—contracted and recovered from the coronavirus, Bolsonaro lashed out at anyone supporting face masks, social distancing, and lockdowns. He pointedly refused to be inoculated with a Covid-19 vaccine, warning, without any evidence, that it might turn people into crocodiles, grow beards on women, and give men effeminate voices.[20] Brazil trailed only the United States in Covid-19 deaths.

---

[15] Center for Systems Science and Engineering at Johns Hopkins University.
[16] Camus, *The Plague*, 50.
[17] Redliner et al., "130,000—210,000 Avoidable Covid-19 Deaths," October 21, 2020.
[18] Keith, "Timeline: What Trump Has Said."
[19] Londoño et al., "Bolsonaro, Isolated and Defiant," June 18, 2020.
[20] Slisco, "Bolsonaro Says Vaccine Might Create 'Crocodiles,'" January 22, 2020.

36 CAMUS'S *THE PLAGUE*

Armed guards stand vigil at the gates of Oran, preventing anyone from entering or leaving the infected city. Its isolation from the rest of the world differs from the isolation—exacerbated by travel bans and lockdowns—felt throughout the world in 2020. Narrating the novel, Rieux—who will never again see his wife, who dies before the gates of Oran are reopened in a sanatorium in another town—is at pains to stress the agonizing separation felt by parted lovers. And yet he also emphasizes how the ordeal of solitude paradoxically brings everyone together, how "every one of us realized that all, the narrator included, were, so to speak, in the same boat, and each would have to adapt himself to the new conditions of life. Thus, for example, a feeling normally as individual as the ache of separation from those one loves suddenly became a feeling in which all shared alike and—together with fear—the greatest affliction of the long period of exile that lay ahead."[21]

Since disease does not care about the personal identity of its victims, "We are all in this together" became—as voiced by Rieux and others in Oran—also a mantra of the Covid-19 plague. However, the virus had a disproportionate effect on the elderly, those with preexisting conditions, and people of color. Rates of infection and mortality were much higher in nursing homes, prisons, and homeless shelters and among hospital employees, grocery store clerks, and others deemed "essential workers" than among those who enjoyed the luxury of solitary confinement to their homes. Through scofflaws such as Raoul and Cottard, Camus acknowledges that not everyone is in the plague together. Pocketing 10,000 francs for arranging to smuggle Rambert out of Oran, Raoul is in it for himself. And Cottard positively exults in the pestilence that plagues his fellow townspeople, for two reasons. A wanted criminal, he is spared arrest by police too preoccupied with the epidemic. As Jean Tarrou notes in his journal, "The plague has put an effective stop to police inquiries, sleuthings, warrants of arrest, and so forth."[22]

---

[21] Camus, *The Plague*, 67.
[22] Camus, *The Plague*, 196.

THE PLAGUE AND THE PRESENT MOMENT   37

In addition, plague presents Cottard with a lucrative opportunity for personal profit in a flourishing black market. While Rieux loses himself in the communal struggle against the plague and is so committed to the ideal of impersonality that he does not even reveal his identity as narrator until the final pages of his chronicle, Cottard is an egotist, an anti-Rieux. He exploits the misery of his fellow citizens to profit from smuggling liquor, cigarettes, and other contraband.

During the Covid-19 pandemic, many states and municipalities in the United States postponed court proceedings. Only those suspected of serious crimes were confined to jails, and some states allowed early release of convicted criminals. Like Cottard, many in trouble with the law were thus able to avoid an immediate reckoning. Nevertheless, during a lethal five-month spree in late 2020, while the public was distracted by the death toll from Covid-19, the Trump administration carried out ten executions—the most by the federal government since 1896.[23] A staunch, outspoken opponent of capital punishment, Camus—like Tarrou, who "resolved to have no truck with anything which, directly or indirectly, for good reasons or for bad, brings death to anyone or justifies others' putting him to death"—would have been appalled.[24]

Like the opportunist Cottard, two brothers in Tennessee, Matthew and Noah Calvin, bought up more than 17,000 hand sanitizers and then took advantage of a shortage to try to sell them for as much as $70 each. Faced with prosecution for price gouging, they ended up donating their supply.[25] Many others were also exploiting shortages to enrich themselves. A study by the U.S. Public Interest Research Group of listings for hand sanitizers, surgical masks, and other health products on Amazon.com found that "The prices for more than half the examined products spiked by at

---

[23] Giuliani-Hoffman, "The US Government Has Executed 10 People This Year," December 17, 2020.

[24] Camus, *The Plague*, 252–253.

[25] Nicas, "He Has 17,700 Bottles of Hand Sanitizer," March 15, 2020.

38   CAMUS'S *THE PLAGUE*

least 50% compared to the average price. At times, the cost of these products would spike 2.3 times higher than the 90-day average."[26] Moreover, when the dangers of meeting in classrooms made many schools and universities resort to online instruction, some students found that taking exams virtually rather than in person made it easier to cheat. At the Inha University School of Medicine in Incheon, South Korea, more than ninety students—83 percent of the school's freshmen and sophomores—took advantage of remote learning to cheat on online exams.[27] Similarly, despite West Point's strict honor code, more than seventy cadets at the United States Military Academy cheated on an online calculus exam.[28]

Although his longing to return to a lover in Paris tempts him to slip through the gates of Oran, Raymond Rambert is basically an honest man. A French journalist on assignment in Algeria, he finds himself trapped in the city when it is sequestered. Before Rambert accepts the situation and makes common cause with those fighting the plague, his main preoccupation is finding a way to escape, not doing his job as a journalist and reporting the story of the plague. However, Rieux makes occasional reference to newspaper and radio reports, though the mid-century world of *The Plague* is not saturated with the 24/7 deluge of information, misinformation, and disinformation made possible by the technology available in 2020. The citizens of Camus's Oran are even deprived of postal communication when, out of fear that letters might carry germs, mail delivery is suspended. And, because of unruly crowds that swarm booths, even telephone calls are prohibited.[29]

Rieux and his fellow townspeople lack access to Facebook, Twitter, WeChat, and other social media that, despite quarantines, allow residents of the twenty-first century to make instantaneous connections with others around the world. The global village

---

[26] Garber, "Price Gouging on Amazon," accessed February 19, 2021.
[27] Kang, "Med School Students in South Korea," June 3, 2020.
[28] Shanahan, "More Than 70 West Point Cadets," December 21, 2020.
[29] Camus, *The Plague*, 68–69.

THE PLAGUE AND THE PRESENT MOMENT   39

presaged by Marshall McLuhan in his 1962 book *The Gutenberg Galaxy: The Making of Typographic Man* was much more of a reality in 2020 than in the 1940s of Camus's novel.[30] Although Covid-19 caused long-distance travel to grind to a halt and schoolrooms and theaters to empty, meetings, classes, and performances resumed via Zoom. Separate solitudes were connected in a way not possible in *The Plague*. The ease of communication also multiplied rumors and false reports—touting quack remedies such as hydroxychloroquine, bleach, and oleandrin and spreading spurious reports that Covid-19 was created by China as a bioweapon or Bill Gates as a form of population control. In Camus's novel, some set fire to their houses in hopes that it would detoxify them. What in 2020 would come to be called "fake news" is spread in Camus's Oran when newspapers and radio stations initially identify the disease, erroneously, as cholera.[31] Tarrou observes that the town's newspapers "complied with the instructions given them: optimism at all costs."[32]

The "dreary evenings" in Camus's Oran lack few distractions other than to trod about "the treeless streets filled with teeming crowds of men and women."[33] Rieux reports that the sound they make is "but one vast rumor of low voices and incessant footfalls, the drumming of innumerable soles timed to the eerie whistling of the plague in the sultry air above, the sound of a huge concourse of people marking time."[34] Although some go to the cinema, because of the prohibition against imports and exports, they are doomed to watch the same film night after night after night. The cafés and restaurants of Oran remain crowded, as social distancing does not seem the prophylactic against infection enforced during the Covid-19 pandemic.

By contrast, in 2020, movie theaters, in order to limit contagion, ceased operations, but, instead of wandering endlessly through

[30] McLuhan, *The Gutenberg Galaxy*.
[31] Camus, *The Plague*, 60.
[32] Camus, *The Plague*, 237.
[33] Camus, *The Plague*, 185.
[34] Camus, *The Plague*, 185.

40 CAMUS'S *THE PLAGUE*

the streets, people could stay home and, through streaming services such as Netflix, Prime Video, Tencent, and Disney+ distract themselves with a vast treasury of video narratives. One of the more dramatic moments in *The Plague* occurs when Cottard and Tarrou seek to pass a few hours at the Municipal Opera House. A visiting company is trapped in the city and condemned to perform the same work, Cristoph Willibald Gluck's *Orfeo ed Euridice*, night after night. On the evening that Cottard and Tarrou attend, the singer playing Orpheus collapses on stage, dead of the plague.[35] In 2020, a similar event occurred at the Zanies Nashville Comedy Club in Tennessee. Comedian D. L. Hughley was in the midst of performing when he fell off a stool and collapsed on stage. Rushed to a hospital, he was diagnosed with Covid-19, but, unlike Camus's fictional tenor, Hughley survived.[36]

Mass infection is a fundamental test of character for each of Camus's characters. Cottard, Joseph Grand, Paneloux, Rambert, Rieux, Tarrou, and the others each make an ethical choice in their response to the epidemic—Cottard in his selfish pursuit of private gain, Paneloux in his determination to trust in God, Rambert in his renunciation of personal happiness in order to join the communal struggle, and Grand and Rieux in their selfless devotion to the task at hand. Tarrou, who aspires to be "a saint without God,"[37] makes it his life's mission to come to the aid of victims, wherever they are. If, as he contends, "each of us has the plague within him,"[38] plague is a metaphor for human life, and *The Plague* becomes a set of case studies in the examined life.

It would be presumptuous to generalize about how 8 billion human beings responded to the spread of Covid-19, but it is clear that there were many opportunistic Cottards, just as there were also real-life versions of the sanitary squads that Tarrou

---

[35] Camus, *The Plague*, 201.
[36] Romano, "D. L. Hughley Discusses His Collapse," July 8, 2020.
[37] Camus, *The Plague*, 255.
[38] Camus, *The Plague*, 253.

THE *PLAGUE* AND THE PRESENT MOMENT   41

organized—medical personnel, first responders, trash haulers, package deliverers, grocery workers, and others who risked (and sometimes sacrificed) their lives on behalf of others. Among the outbreaks of altruism during the pandemic would have to be counted the 250,000 Britons who volunteered with the United Kingdom's National Health Service to help those most vulnerable.[39] The most prominent analogy to Dr. Bernard Rieux, the dedicated physician who describes himself as "a conscientious witness"[40] and refuses "to play false to the facts,"[41] would have to be Dr. Anthony Fauci, the director of the National Institute of Allergy and Infectious Diseases, who refused to project false optimism about the coronavirus and debunked claims of bogus cures. Like Rieux, who tells Rambert: "I've no use for statements in which something is kept back,"[42] Fauci insisted on acknowledging the severity of the Covid-19 pandemic, even when it resulted in insults from the president of the United States and death threats from some of his followers. The prospect of violence from science deniers led many state and local health officials in the United States to give up. Barely four months into the pandemic, the National Association of City and County Health Officials reported that at least twenty-four public health officials had either resigned, retired, or been fired from their positions.[43] Facing the facts should not be controversial. "But again and again," Rieux observes, "there comes a time in history when the man who dares to say that two and two makes four is punished with death."[44]

Like Rieux, Fauci and other scientists at the Centers for Disease Control and other medical professionals throughout the world hewed to verified facts in the face of assaults on the very possibility of veracity. As both physician and narrator, Rieux is scrupulous to

[39] Godin, "'Outbreaks of Altruism,'" March 25, 2020.
[40] Camus, *The Plague*, 301.
[41] Camus, *The Plague*, 180.
[42] Camus, *The Plague*, 12.
[43] Mossburg, "Some Public Health Officials Are Resigning," June 23, 2020.
[44] Camus, *The Plague*, 132.

42 CAMUS'S *THE PLAGUE*

note how he "aimed at objectivity."[45] But Kellyanne Conway, counselor to President Trump, coined the euphemism "alternative facts" in 2017 to justify one of the thousands of falsehoods his administration tried to propagate, even during the pandemic.[46] "Truth isn't truth," declared Rudy Giuliani, Trump's personal attorney, in a startling reiteration of the classic Cretan paradox.[47] If truth is not truth, then that claim itself is false.

A traditional belief in God is inconsistent with rejection of Truth, and a majority of Americans claim to be believers, whose faith was in fact strengthened by the Covid-19 pandemic.[48] The same survey found that almost two-thirds of Americans believe that God sent the coronavirus as a message, though they disagreed about what that message was. Theodicy—the attempt to reconcile the existence of evil with an omnipotent, omniscient, and omnibenevolent Deity—is a central issue in *The Plague*, where unmerited suffering is rampant, particularly in the case of Jacques Othon, the magistrate's young son. He not only dies from the plague, but he does so after a long and agonizing struggle witnessed by Rieux, Tarrou, and Paneloux. How can the torture of that innocent child possibly be explained?

The question of why bad things happen to good people is addressed by Paneloux in the two sermons he preaches at symmetrically positioned points—Books Two and Four—of Camus's five-book novel. In the first, delivered in the city's cathedral during the "Prayer Week" proclaimed at the outset of the plague, Paneloux pronounces the epidemic an instrument of divine retribution for the sins of humanity. For Camus's priest, the plague and the universe are intelligible. Disease is the instrument of an anthropomorphized God who uses it to vent His anger and punish transgressors. "The just man need have no fear," Paneloux declares, "but the evildoer has good cause to tremble. For plague is the flail of God and the world

---

[45] Camus, *The Plague*, 180.
[46] Gajanan, "Kellyanne Conway Defends," January 22, 2017.
[47] Kenny, "Rudy Giuliani Says," August 19, 2018.
[48] Lofton and Zubrzycki, "If COVID-19 Is a Message from God," June 5, 2020.

THE PLAGUE AND THE PRESENT MOMENT   43

his threshing-floor, and implacably He will thresh out His harvest until the wheat is separated from the chaff."[49] According to a poll conducted by the Associated Press–NORC Center for Public Affairs Research at the University of Chicago, about 11 percent of Americans viewed the outbreak of Covid-19 similarly, as God's punishment for human sin.[50] Thus did televangelist Pat Robertson proclaim that the Supreme Being sent Covid-19 as a punishment for same-sex marriage and abortion, both of which he believes to be offenses against God.[51] In Africa, the Rev. Dr. Samson Olasupo A. Ayokunle, president of the Christian Association of Nigeria, also portrayed Covid-19 as divine retribution. Citing the Israelites' rebelliousness toward Moses and God in Numbers 21:4–9, he proclaimed: "We have sinned against God and he has sent to our midst a fiery serpent! I urge all believers and those who know God to call upon him day and night. The church must cry to God for mercy and Coronavirus will be a thing of the past in the name of Jesus."[52] However, according to the Anglican theologian John Milbank, the pandemic was God's response to a transgression not mentioned in Scripture—Brexit. "We have sown the Brexit win [sic] and now reap the Covid whirlwind," he tweeted. "Past generations would have seen divine judgement manifest here."[53] Various lunatic conspiracy theories (that the disease was deliberately created and/or spread by China, the United States, Bill Gates, George Soros, 5G technology, etc.) had less to do with theology than psychopathology.

Paneloux delivers his second sermon after having witnessed the excruciating death throes of the Othon child. No longer confident that God's will is intelligible, he insists that we must love what we can never understand. Paneloux reaffirms his faith *despite* the apparent injustice in innocent suffering. "My brothers," he exclaims,

---

[49] Camus, *The Plague*, 95.
[50] Lofton and Zubrzycki, "If COVID-19 Is a Message from God," June 5, 2020.
[51] Kuruvilla, "Pat Robertson Suggests," April 23, 2020.
[52] Emmanuel, "Sin, Disobedience to God," March 22, 2020.
[53] Milbank, Twitter, December 21, 2020.

44 CAMUS'S *THE PLAGUE*

"the love of God is a hard love. It demands total self-surrender, disdain of our human personality. And yet it alone can reconcile us to suffering and the deaths of children, it alone can justify them, since we cannot understand them, and we can only make God's will ours."[54] Faced with the widespread, apparently senseless suffering wrought by the coronavirus in 2020, the Jesuit priest James Martin offered a similar admission of ignorance and leap of faith: "In the end, the most honest answer to the question of why the Covid-19 virus is killing thousands of people, why infectious diseases ravage humanity and why there is suffering at all is: We don't know. For me, this is the most honest and accurate answer."[55]

For Rieux, the most honest and accurate answer is defiance. To Paneloux's suggestion that "perhaps we should love what we cannot understand," Rieux, a man of science who has no use for God, responds: "No, Father. I've a very different idea of love. And until my dying day I shall refuse to love a scheme of things in which children are put to torture."[56] For him, the plague is the result of a destructive bacillus, just as the cause of the pandemic in 2020 came to be understood through virology, not theology, as SARS-CoV-2, a positive-sense single-stranded RNA virus. Whether or not they understood the biology, many regarded Covid-19 in secular terms and attributed its spread to human agency. According to the Associated Press–NORC poll, 43 percent of Americans blamed a foreign government and 37 percent the U.S. government for the pandemic.[57]

Politics created the most salient difference between Camus's fictional plague and the real Covid-19 ordeal. The 2020 ordeal coincided with a bitterly contentious campaign for the presidency of the United States, and the virus was consistently politicized. Refusal to wear facial masks and maintain social distancing, as prescribed by medical authorities, became a mark of allegiance to President

---

[54] Camus, *The Plague*, 228.
[55] Martin, "Where Is God in a Pandemic?" March 22, 2020.
[56] Camus, *The Plague*, 218.
[57] Lofton and Zubrzycki, "If COVID-19 Is a Message from God," June 5, 2020.

THE PLAGUE AND THE PRESENT MOMENT   45

Trump, who, in defiance of health standards, held massive political rallies. He mocked his opponent, Joe Biden, for wearing masks and for limiting most of his campaign events to virtual appearances. He complained that talk about the pandemic, whose severity he consistently minimized, was an attempt by Democrats to make him look bad. The pandemic became a central issue of the presidential campaign, as Democrats repeatedly faulted Trump for bungling the government's response. After the election and even after more than 300,000 Americans had died of Covid-19, Trump attributed his defeat to exaggerated fears of an imaginary pandemic. He retweeted a video that outlined a conspiracy mounted by his enemies to undo him: "Start with a virus, import it into America, talk about it nonstop, call some governors . . . put patients into nursing homes, kill thousands, blame the president, keep blaming, blame some more."[58]

By contrast, electoral politics is not at play at all in *The Plague*. In the 1940s, in the midst of World War II, Algeria, officially considered an integral part of France, was governed by the collaborationist Vichy régime. However, the novel makes no explicit reference to the war or to representative government in Oran. The city is run by an anonymous figure referred to merely as "the Prefect." He does not play much of a role in the story other than to declare, reluctantly, the outbreak of a plague and to institute measures such as the closing of the city gates and compulsory quarantine of the infected in a football stadium. Rieux records occasional attempts at resistance, but there is no sense that any official is especially responsive to public opinion or will be held accountable at the ballot box. The Prefect is not judged by his management of the plague the way Trump, Boris Johnson, Emmanuel Macron, Angela Merkel, and other elected leaders of Western democracies were judged for their responses to Covid-19.

In the United States and other countries with a history of racial injustice, the Covid-19 pandemic also coincided with the Black Lives

---

[58] Czachor, "Trump Shares Video," December 12, 2020.

46   CAMUS'S *THE PLAGUE*

Matter movement, a reaction against the killing by police of unarmed African Americans. Many, if not most, of the hundreds of thousands who rallied in the streets of major cities to demand justice and police reform wore face masks as protection against the coronavirus. It was often noted that people of color were disproportionately infected and killed by the disease. By contrast, aside from the fact that Rambert has been dispatched by his Paris daily to "make a report on the living conditions prevailing among the Arab population, and especially on the sanitary conditions,"[59] *The Plague* ignores the most consequential political problem in Algeria, one that would erupt in a bloody revolution a decade later—the inequality between the native Arabs and the *pieds noirs*, the descendants of European settlers. Although Arabs constituted at least one-quarter of the population of Oran in the 1940s, they are entirely missing from the cast of characters in Camus's novel. When the Week of Prayer is proclaimed, it is a question of Christian, not Muslim, prayer, and it is a Roman Catholic cathedral, not a mosque, in which Rieux and his fellow townspeople assemble. All conversation is conducted in French, not Arabic.

Five years before *The Plague*, Camus published a collection of philosophical essays he called *The Myth of Sisyphus* (1942/1955).[60] In it, he appropriates the Greek figure Sisyphus, who was condemned by the gods to roll a boulder up the side of a mountain. Just before reaching the peak, the boulder rolls back down the mountainside, whereupon he is condemned to start all over again with the same meaningless task, performed for the rest of eternity. Sisyphus's futile mission, a metaphor for the absurdity of the human condition, is reenacted in many ways in *La Peste*, which makes use of the French verb *recommencer* (to begin again) again and again. Rieux's asthma patient spends his days senselessly transferring peas back and forth between two pans. Just as Rambert thinks he is on the verge of escaping from Oran, his plan falls through, and he must keep making arrangements from scratch.

---

[59] Camus, *The Plague*, 12.
[60] Camus, *The Myth of Sisyphus and Other Essays*.

THE PLAGUE AND THE PRESENT MOMENT   47

He possesses one phonograph record, of St. James Infirmary, and is reduced to playing it ten times a day—"the same thing over and over again."[61] Similarly, the same movies are shown day after day in Oran. Rieux and Grand each look to make fresh starts in their troubled marriages. After Rieux and Tarrou slip away from their grim business of fighting the plague to take a swim together, Rieux notes that "the disease had given them a respite, and this was good, but now they must set their shoulders to the wheel again."[62] Like Sisyphus, the novel ends by circling back to its start, with Rieux's determination to relive the plague by writing about it, as well as the realization that the plague bacillus will surely return some day.

As a physician, Rieux goes out every day to perform a futile task, treat a disease for which there is no cure; Dr. Castel spends much of the novel trying to develop an effective serum, but he never succeeds. The version that he tries on Othon's son may or may not have prolonged his life, in utter agony, but it does not save him, nor is there any evidence that medical intervention is responsible for the—temporary—retreat of the plague. The role of the physician in 2020 was not quite as absurd. Palliative measures helped in many cases, and in the final month of the year pharmaceutical companies began to distribute vaccines that promised to immunize the population and thereby end definitively the scourge of Covid-19. However, commentators frequently invoked Sisyphus to describe the boring and meaningless repetitiveness of life under lockdown during the pandemic. "Unlike a large stone, coronavirus is very small, and yet our struggle against it is precisely a Sisyphean task: we have no choice but to push coronavirus away, doing so over and over again, having little hope of that making a real difference, and being far from enlivened by the process,"[63] wrote Thaddeus Metz, a professor of philosophy at the University of Johannesburg. Dr. David Aronoff, an infectious disease specialist at

---

[61] Camus, The Plague, 161.
[62] Camus, The Plague, 257.
[63] Metz, "What the Myth of Sisyphus Tells Us," April 20, 2020.

48 CAMUS'S *THE PLAGUE*

Vanderbilt University, invoked the figure of Sisyphus to describe the monotony of a routine similar to Rieux's: "Every day since March, I come to work, and I push up against this boulder of Covid-19, and at the end of the day I feel like I may have accomplished something. Then I come back in the morning, and I see the boulder at the bottom of the mountain again."[64]

By doing his job day after day, Rieux is affirming the values of civility and kindness. As he tells Rambert, "the only means of fighting a plague is—common decency."[65] Ultimately, after the plague is over, Rieux reflects that "what we learn in a time of pestilence" is "that there are more things to admire in men than to despise."[66] That sanguineness was sorely tested during the Covid-19 pandemic. It is true that countless unsung acts of altruism merited admiration, but they sometimes seemed outweighed by scammers and opportunists who exploited the health crisis for personal gain and nihilists and denialists who endangered themselves and others by flouting regulations. It was a point of pride for the violent insurrectionists who stormed the U.S. Capitol on January 6, 2021, not to wear protective masks or observe social distancing.

Rieux's optimistic take on humanity was explicitly referenced in several commentaries during the pandemic. Konrad Yakabuski, for one, urged agreement with the proposition that our species offers more things to admire than despise: "Through the darkest of springs," he wrote, after quoting Rieux, "we must try to hold on to that thought."[67] Geoff Dyer expressed skepticism. "I want this to be true," he says of Rieux's observation, "but how does that square with people hoarding toilet paper and face masks?"[68] Squaring human impulses and actions with Camus's wise, enduring novel remains an urgent challenge.

---

[64] Calfas, "Why Covid-19 Is Spreading Again," October 15, 2020.
[65] Camus, *The Plague*, 163.
[66] Camus, *The Plague*, 308.
[67] Yakabuski, " 'There Is More to Admire in Men Than to Despise,' " March 19, 2020.
[68] Dyer, "The Existential Inconvenience of Coronavirus," March 23, 2020.

THE PLAGUE AND THE PRESENT MOMENT   49

Works Cited

Abell, Stig. "It's Simply Classic Camus." *The Sunday Times*, May 10, 2020.

Calfas, Jennifer. "Why Covid-19 Is Spreading Again: Fatigue, Colder Weather, Eased Restrictions." *Wall Street Journal*, October 15, 2020. https://www.wsj.com/articles/why-covid-19-is-spreading-again-fatigue-colder-weather-eased-restrictions-11602759601.

Camus, Albert. "Letter to Roland Barthes on *The Plague*." *Lyrical and Critical Essays*. Edited by Philip Thody, 338–341. Translated by Ellen Conroy Kennedy. New York: Vintage, 1970.

Camus, Albert. *The Myth of Sisyphus and Other Essays*. Translated by Justin O'Brien. Alfred A. Knopf, 1955. [*Le Mythe de Sisyphe*. Paris: Gallimard, 1942.]

Camus, Albert. *La Peste*. Paris: Gallimard, 1947.

Camus, Albert. *The Plague*. Translated by Stuart Gilbert. New York: Modern Library, 1948.

Camus, Albert. *The Plague*. Translated by Stuart Gilbert. New York: Vintage, 1991.

Center for Systems Science and Engineering at Johns Hopkins University. "COVID-19 Dashboard." https://gisanddata.maps.arcgis.com/apps/opsdashboard/index.html#/bda7594740fd40299423467b48e9ecf6.

Czachor, Emily. "Trump Shares Video Suggesting COVID Pandemic Created to Make Him Look Bad, Lose Election." *Newsweek*, December 12, 2020. https://www.newsweek.com/trump-shares-video-suggesting-covid-pandemic-created-make-him-look-bad-lose-election-1556243.

Dyer, Geoff. "The Existential Inconvenience of Coronavirus." *The New Yorker*, March 23, 2020. https://www.newyorker.com/magazine/2020/03/23/the-existential-inconvenience-of-coronavirus.

Earle, Samuel. "How Albert Camus's *The Plague* Became the Defining Book of the Coronavirus Crisis." *The New Statesman*, May 27, 2020. https://advance-lexis-com.libweb.lib.utsa.edu/api/document?collection=news&id=urn:contentItem:600N-R1X1-DYX2-C0MV-00000-00&context=1516831.

Emmanuel, Dumebi. "Sin, Disobedience to God Responsible for COVID-19." *Politics Nigeria*, March 22, 2020. https://politicsnigeria.com/sin-disobedience-to-god-responsible-for-covid-19-can/.

Flood, Alison. "Publishers Report Sales Boom in Novels about Fictional Epidemics." *The Guardian*, March 5, 2020. https://www.theguardian.com/books/2020/mar/05/publishers-report-sales-boom-in-novels-about-fictional-epidemics-camus-the-plague-dean-koontz.

Gajanan, Mahita. "Kellyanne Conway Defends White House's Falsehoods as 'Alternative Facts.'" *Time*, January 22, 2017. https://time.com/4642689/kellyanne-conway-sean-spicer-donald-trump-alternative-facts/.

50 CAMUS'S THE PLAGUE

Garber, Adam. "Price Gouging on Amazon during the Coronavirus Outbreak." *PIRG Consumer Watchdog*. https://uspirgedfund.org/sites/pirg/files/resources/Revised%20US%20PIRG%20Coronavirus%20Price%20Gouging%20Factsheet.pdf.

Gary, Nicolas. "Italie: à L'Ère du Coronavirus, La Peste de Camus Devient un Best-seller." *Actualitté*, February 28, 2020. https://actualitte.com/article/8811/reseaux-sociaux/italie-a-l-ere-du-coronavirus-la-peste-de-camus-devient-un-best-seller.

Giuliani-Hoffman, Francesca. "The US Government Has Executed 10 People This Year—The Most Since 1896." *CNN Politics*, December 17, 2020. https://www.cnn.com/2020/12/17/politics/federal-death-penalty-2020-trnd/index.html.

Godin, Mélissa. "'Outbreaks of Altruism.' 250,000 People in U.K. Volunteer to Help Vulnerable, Amid Growing Coronavirus Crisis." *Time*, March 25, 2020. https://time.com/5809624/250-000-volunteer-nhs-covid-19/.

Juris, Carolyn. "Apple Books Bestsellers March 22, 2020." *Publishers Weekly* 267, no. 13 (March 25, 2020). https://www.publishersweekly.com/pw/by-topic/digital/content-and-e-books/article/82822-apple-books-category-bestsellers-march-22-2020.html.

Kang, Heejin. "Med School Students in South Korea Caught Cheating on Online Exams during Coronavirus Pandemic." *ABC News*, June 3, 2020. https://abcnews.go.com/International/med-school-students-south-korea-caught-cheating-online/story?id=71043491.

Keith, Tamara. "Timeline: What Trump Has Said and Done About the Coronavirus." *NPR.org*, April 21, 2020. https://www.npr.org/2020/04/21/837348551/timeline-what-trump-has-said-and-done-about-the-coronavirus.

Kenny, Caroline. "Rudy Giuliani Says 'Truth Isn't Truth.'" *CNN Politics*, August 19, 2018. https://www.cnn.com/2018/08/19/politics/rudy-giuliani-truth-isnt-truth/index.html.

Kuruvilla, Carol. "Pat Robertson Suggests Same-Sex Marriage, Abortion among Reasons for COVID-19." *Huffington Post*, April 23, 2020. https://www.huffpost.com/entry/pat-robertson-covid-19_n_5ea0b4abc5b67cf2adbd78ee.

Lofton, Kathryn, and Geneviève Zubrzycki. "If COVID-19 Is a Message from God, What's the Message? *Hartford Courant*, June 5, 2020. https://www.courant.com/opinion/op-ed/hc-op-lofton-beyerlein-nirenberg-zubrzycki-god-covid-0605-20200605-fijukv2szrezxixdol4b2ouw6e-story.html.

Londoño, Ernesto, Manuela Andreoni, and Letícia Casado. "Bolsonaro, Isolated and Defiant, Dismisses Coronavirus Threat to Brazil." *New York Times*, June 18, 2020. https://www.nytimes.com/2020/04/01/world/americas/brazil-bolsonaro-coronavirus.html.

THE PLAGUE AND THE PRESENT MOMENT 51

Martin, James. "Where Is God in a Pandemic?" *New York Times*, March 22, 2020. https://www.nytimes.com/2020/03/22/opinion/coronavirus-relig ion.html.

McLuhan, Marshall. *The Gutenberg Galaxy: The Making of Typographic Man.* Toronto: University of Toronto Press, 1962.

Metz, Thaddeus. "What *The Myth of Sisyphus* Tells Us about the Coronavirus." *The National Interest*, April 20, 2020. https://nationalinterest.org/blog/buzz/ what-myth-sisyphus-tells-us-about-coronavirus-144902.

Milbank, John. Twitter. December 21, 2020. https://mobile.twitter.com/johnm ilbank3/status/1340919034347458563.

Mossburg, Cheri. "Some Public Health Officials Are Resigning amid Threats during the COVID-19 Pandemic." *CNN US*, June 23, 2020. https://www. cnn.com/2020/06/22/us/health-officials-threats-coronavirus/index.html.

Nicas, Jack. "He Has 17,700 Bottles of Hand Sanitizer and Nowhere to Sell Them." *The New York Times*, March 15, 2020. https://www.nytimes.com/ 2020/03/14/technology/coronavirus-purell-wipes-amazon-sellers.html.

Philippe, Elisabeth. "Coronavirus: Albert Camus avait Vraiment Tout Prédit, Étape par Étape." *L'Obs*, March 26, 2020. https//www.advance-lexis-com. libweb.lib.utsa.edu/api/document?collection=news&id=urn:contentI tem:5YHF-PBY1-F12R-94F5-00000-00&context=1516831.

Redliner, Irwin, Jeffrey D. Sachs, Sean Hansen, and Nathaniel Hupert. "130,000–210,000 Avoidable Covid-19 Deaths—And Counting—In the U.S." October 21, 2020. https://ncdp.columbia.edu/custom-content/uplo ads/2020/10/Avoidable-COVID-19-Deaths-US-NCDP.pdf.

Romano, Nick. "D. L. Hughley Discusses His Collapse and COVID-19 Diagnosis with Anthony Anderson." *MSN Entertainment*, July 8, 2020. https://www.msn.com/en-us/tv/news/dl-hughley-discusses-his-collapse-and-covid-19-diagnosis-with-anthony-anderson/ar-BB16udI8.

Seung-hyun, Song. "*The Plague* by Albert Camus Makes Bestseller List." *The Korea Herald*, March 15, 2020. http://www.koreaherald.com/view.php?ud= 20200315000236.

Shanahan, Ed. "More Than 70 West Point Cadets Are Accused in Cheating Scandal." *The New York Times*, December 21, 2020. https://www.nytimes. com/2020/12/21/nyregion/west-point-cheating.html.

Slisco, Aila. "Bolsonaro Says Vaccine Might Create 'Crocodiles' as Brazil Sees Second Most COVID Deaths." *Newsweek*, January 22, 2020. https://www. newsweek.com/bolsonaro-says-vaccine-might-create-crocodiles-brazil-sees-second-most-covid-deaths-1556090.

Woodward, Bob. *Rage.* New York: Simon & Schuster, 2020.

Yakabuski, Konrad. "'There Is More to Admire in Men Than to Despise': '*The Plague*' Is Essential Reading for a Pandemic." *The Globe and Mail*, March 19, 2020. https://www.theglobeandmail.com/opinion/article-there-is-more-to-admire-in-men-than-to-despise-the-plague-is/.

3. Edvard Munch, *Muerte En La Habitacion*—1893—Expresionismo. National Gallery, Oslo, Norway. Photo: Album / Art Resource, NY. © 2022 Artists Rights Society (ARS), New York.

2

Present in Effacement

The Place of Women in Camus's Plague and Ours

Jane E. Schultz

One year before Camus published *The Plague*, he wrote during a trip to the United States, "*Peste*: c'est un monde sans femmes et donc irrespirable" ["*Plague*: it's a world without women and thus unbreathable"].[1] "Unbreathable" is a peculiar word choice in French or English, even if we acknowledge the juxtaposition of physical restrictions during plagues to suffocation. Written at the end of World War II, the novel's celebration of male solidarity figures as a postwar legacy. *The Plague* has also been read as an allegory about totalitarianism.[2] But why, we might ask, did Camus associate the airlessness of plagues with the absence of women? Plagues kill men as readily as they kill women, being biomedical freaks of nature that have not historically discriminated by gender. Interpreted metaphorically, the meaning shifts to emphasize gender disparity resulting from the absence of women as a sterilizing agent in a plague-ridden world. In the woman-loving world that Camus embraced, despite the critique of his oeuvre for its "blindness to questions of gender and sexuality,"[3] a plague becomes a metaphorical space without women. How, then, does the absence of women relate to the plague on the ground in Oran, and where have the

---

[1] Camus, *Journaux de Voyage*, 42. Quoted in Gray, "Layers of Meaning in *La Peste*," 169.
[2] Isaac, *Arendt, Camus, and Modern Rebellion*, 49.
[3] Isaac, *Arendt, Camus, and Modern Rebellion*, 19.

Camus's The Plague. Peg Brand Weiser, Oxford University Press. © Oxford University Press 2023.
DOI: 10.1093/oso/9780197599327.003.0003

54 CAMUS'S *THE PLAGUE*

women gone as men assume management duties? What finally can Camus's fictional plague reveal to us about the dilemmas besetting health care workers in today's Covid-19 pandemic?

I answer these questions by first exploring the novel's depictions of gender imbalance and gender flattening during the plague; and second, by suggesting that the absence of women in Oran replicates the dynamic of uneven power relations among physicians, their subordinates, and patients in medical discourse—one source of the current pandemic's professional malaise. Camus's mid-century tale equates a public health catastrophe with a rent in the social fabric that consigns women to a narrative hinterland and places men at the center of a heroic one. Oran's plague blankets its citizens in exile from their North African culture (represented by the port's closed face to the sea), an alienation that critics have understood in both colonial and postcolonial terms.[4] If women in *The Plague* are exiled from the rhythms of daily living as well as from an Arabic culture dominated by French language and traditions,[5] then they experience a double exile. Camus depicts them as people without local or political agency who cannot alter their community's fortunes, making exile not simply physical but also obstructing their access to citizenship. The women we glimpse are often aged, replaceable, generally immobile, and usually nameless, like the Spanish mother of the Gonzales brothers (who, reminiscent of Camus's own mother, is another level removed from the French/Algerian world): a "wrinkled," "dried-up little wisp of a woman."[6] They are forgettable charwomen and waitresses who serve as occupational placeholders; or the graphically expendable women whom the doctor encounters "screaming in agony" as the plague overcomes

---

[4] Marx-Scouras critiques the charge of colonialism; LeBlanc and Jones propose a postcolonial narrative at work in *The Plague*.

[5] Margerrison contends that three-quarters of Oran's citizens were of European descent, making the Algerian port far less vulnerable to colonial politics than some have suggested. See "Algeria's Others," 32.

[6] Camus, *The Plague*, 202, 204.

PRESENT IN EFFACEMENT   55

them.[7] Young women are quickly dispatched, such as Dr. Rieux's tubercular wife, who leaves for a sanatorium in the first chapter and whose inability to hear her husband's parting words prove ill omens of the incipient contagion.[8] Even the parcel-wielding women, waiting silently outside the barracks hospital in tableau vivant, serve more as a choric element of setting than as actors with the means to ameliorate suffering.[9]

Other women in *The Plague* are not physically embodied and merit notice primarily as symbolic figures. Rambert's far-off lover who, like Rieux's wife is never named, registers as an object of desire whom he fears will age too soon.[10] Joseph Grand's literary muse, the equestrian maiden who inhabits the continually revised opening sentence of his masterpiece, is neither named nor embodied. Similarly, Grand's estranged wife, Jeanne, does not assume a bodily shape in the novel's pages, although he has pinned his hopes for reconciling with her on the perfection of his invention of the disembodied maiden. Altogether the plague creates conditions whereby women lack the individuality and interiority characteristic of human beings. Indeed, most have gone underground rather like the spat-upon cats, which, one critic laments, has made them seem "immune from suffering or death."[11]

Though scholars observe that Camus's female characters have been "denied the possibility of action, and thus of rebellion" and are essentially "absent, robotic, battered, or dead,"[12] these conclusions strike me both as too dismissive and undercontextualized. Granted, the *fraternité* of Rieux, Tarrou, Paneloux, Grand, Rambert, and Othon fight the plague. Their relation to female characters is tangential to their struggle, highlighting the men's homosocial bonds

[7] Camus, *The Plague*, 51.
[8] Camus, *The Plague*, 11.
[9] Camus, *The Plague*, 146.
[10] Camus, *The Plague*, 150.
[11] Margerrison, *Ces Forces Obscures de l'Âme*, 141.
[12] Bartlett, *Rebellious Feminism*, 13; and Allen, "An Introduction to Patriarchal Existentialism," 73.

56   CAMUS'S *THE PLAGUE*

and removing the women even further from the sphere of narration.[13] Anthony Rizzuto has cautioned that "if Camus were to accept women as anything other than object, then the whole notion of fraternity would disintegrate."[14] Contrary to those who believe that objectification renders Camus's women civically ineligible in a kind of zero-sum game, I suggest that their work guarantees them a role to play—whether it is as bedside attendants or as bulwarks of familial cohesion.[15] If we seek to understand their movements beyond the framing lens of Camus's prose, then such women do not threaten male solidarity because of their secondary narrative status. Characters like Mesdames Rieux and Othon, for example, keep the *fraternité* upright and functioning, not as "stand-by-your-man" women but as steadfast models of diligence and persistence who ask no recognition and seek through domestic practice to re-order the chaos of plague time. That they are *not* agents of rebellion, a role that men play in much of Camus's work, does not preclude them from exhibiting heroism.

Given Camus's evolution as a thinker who believed that human progress was achievable in a collaborative civic realm, the novel's women are essential to his vision, even though they often appear on the margins.[16] I mean no apology for Camus, but rather that taken in the context of the war and postwar periods, his beleaguered representation of women may be understood as patriarchal blindness. In referencing *The Plague*, Camus told Roland Barthes that his oeuvre moves from "an attitude of solitary revolt to the recognition of a community whose struggles must be shared."[17] Rieux enunciates that vision when he says that the plague "[has] helped men to rise

---

[13] Margerrison has also noted the homosociality of the plague fighters. See *Ces Forces Obscures de l'Âme*, 160.

[14] Rizutto, *Camus: Love and Sexuality*, 58.

[15] Bartlett, *Rebellious Feminism*, 14. See also Marx-Scouras, "Portraits of Women, Visions of Algeria," 138.

[16] Margaret Gray observes that Camus privileges collective action over personal achievement—a choice that implies gender solidarity. See Gray, "Layers of Meaning in *La Peste*," 167.

[17] Quoted in Isaac, *Arendt, Camus, and Modern Rebellion*, 99.

above themselves," a statement predicated on faith that men and women will cooperate when facing such catastrophes.[18] The doctor's use of the generic "men" for humanity suggests the conventional nomenclature of the nineteenth and twentieth centuries, but even if Rieux (and Camus) had men in mind when observing moral improvement, readers have no reason to categorically exclude women. Camus's position (and Rieux's by extension) may strike today's readers as naive, given the social and political fracturing of public opinion regarding Covid-19. That said, we err by not perceiving the integral roles that women play in maintaining domestic order, in nursing, and in keeping Oran's professional elite in check.

Contexts in Nursing and Medicine

Nevertheless, it is puzzling that the plague in Oran screens and shrouds women's activities, given the medical world's increasing dependence on women throughout the twentieth century. Considered alongside the pandemic of 2020–2022, Camus's version differs not only in its emphasis on masculine plague fighters but also in its representation of community solidarity, a tacit agreement that plague is a medical disaster galvanizing support between frontline workers and the public—an assumption that cannot be made globally or nationally today. Camus's delimitation of women in *The Plague* is not an exception to the fictional conventions of masculine struggle in his era. Writers from Andre Malraux and George Orwell to Ernest Hemingway and Norman Mailer created similarly male-identified spaces governed by the politics of the gaze—a narrative practice that obscures female perspective and animus via objectification.[19]

---

[18] Camus, *The Plague*, 125. Laura Marris echoes that view in recognizing Camus's valuing of "shared consciousness as a healing force" and of "a global collectivity" that had the power to vaccinate people against the uglier aspects of nationalism.

[19] Film scholar Laura Mulvey first described the male gaze in visual culture in her 1975 essay "Visual Pleasure and Narrative Cinema." Feminist critics have found wide applicability for the concept in their analyses of point of view and of characterization.

58   CAMUS'S *THE PLAGUE*

Camus's plague world utilizes this dynamic, making the scarcity of the novel's women a problem of literary representation. But more unfortunate is that the minimizing language depicting female characters also minimizes their historical visibility; Camus does not see and thus does not reflect his era's ample supply of women in health care. My attempt to understand the bridge between his vision and the Covid-19 pandemic does not finally reside in the author's "disappearing" women from the text but in how references to them provide a context for reading the stresses on female health care professionals in the current pandemic. Women's marginality in the novel sets the stage for modern medical workers' chief complaint: that their work has not been visible to the public nor valued as it should be. In this sense, the novel's description of a health care crisis and a medical community's response to it mediate a crucial prehistory of the professional dilemmas that face today's practitioners.

The irony of Camus's rendering of a plague vis-à-vis the ongoing one should not be lost on us. Camus filters an understanding of the bubonic and pneumonic stages of Oran's plague through a male physician's perspective, which sets in motion the clinical objectification long associated with medical observation. Rieux understandably believes that the epidemic calls for heroic measures, a style of practice in Western medicine that granted physicians a discursive authority to act and speak as subjects of the medical encounter, an approach that disadvantages prognosis and removes patients from active roles in their care.[20] This authoritative mindset has facilitated Rieux's observation of Oran's women through the wrong end of a telescope; that is, at a distance and with little clarity in contrast to the way he perceives the community's men.[21] His team reconstitutes the pieces of civil society, with Castel and Richard representing medicine; Grand, civil service; Othon, the

---

[20] See Hunter's *Doctors' Stories*; and Dornan et al., "Medical Teachers' Discursive Positioning of Doctors in Relation to Patients."

[21] Coincidentally, Camus uses the same analogy for Tarrou's tendency to understate; Camus, *The Plague*, 24.

PRESENT IN EFFACEMENT   59

law; Rambert, the press; Paneloux, religion; and Tarrou, philosophy, but domestic concerns do not pierce this rubric. Oran's men are praised for their voluntarism in burial details, while the renegade Cottard earns more notice that any single woman character. Rieux's mother, arguably the most exemplary woman in *The Plague*, is not depicted as integral to the unfolding dramas of diagnosis, treatment, death, or burial. Indeed, as Christine Margerrison's brilliant work on gender and myth in the novel has concluded, Camus's idealization of the maternal literally places Madame Rieux *hors du combat*[22] in comparison to the male plague fighters. We perceive her and other women as remote, understated, even diffident. On the other hand, Camus holds up the doctor and his team for admiration.[23] This apparent lack of regard for women counts as a failing of Rieux-the-physician but not of Rieux-the-narrator. An identity hidden from readers throughout the novel, Rieux-the-narrator focuses on the fog of apathy threatening the autonomy of community members who are increasingly removed from one another's orbit, thus paying little heed to gender distinctions.[24]

Camus was not oblivious to the work of nursing when he wrote *The Plague*. Indeed, one of the central characters in *L'Étranger* (1942) is Meursault's nurse, whose role in the earlier novel begs for greater critical attention.[25] As early as the 1870s, European and American schools of nursing began to staff hospitals with women to take care of patients. In the 1940s, the decade of *The Plague*'s composition, women were already a dominant force in nursing, as caregivers in the field and administrators of the profession, especially in the wake

---

[22] Margerrison, *Ces Forces Obscures de l'Âme*, 133. Literally "beyond the fray" in French.

[23] Clay Jenkinson labels Rieux "unheroic" because of his selflessness, but I see it differently. Despite the absurdity of the environment in which Rieux finds himself, his persistence and tirelessness constitute heroism to my mind. See Jenkinson's "Why We Should Be Reading Albert Camus during the Pandemic."

[24] Baker, "Doctors as Rebels," 151.

[25] Marx-Scouras observes that even though such women are not usually protagonists, they have helped to shape Camus's philosophy. See "Portraits of Women, Visions of Algeria," 131.

60 CAMUS'S *THE PLAGUE*

of their World War II recruitment.[26] Though long denied entry to schools of medicine and unwelcome when they achieved admission, women also sought medical degrees in increasing numbers after the war. They currently constitute 36 percent of physicians in the United States, some of whom have played prominent roles in Covid-19 vaccine development. A 2018 study found that 60 percent of physicians aged thirty-five and under are women.[27] Women still outnumber men as frontline health workers who assume the greatest risk of contagion, not so much because medical cultures have evolved to place them in physicians' roles but because nurses and other low-status workers in hospital and home care systems have been women.[28] True, men now make up 12 percent of working nurses and 11.4 percent of those enrolled in bachelor of science in nursing programs, making the profession less female-dominated than in the past.[29] But the traditional gendering of nursing as women's work would have made women the default for hospital attendance by the 1940s, whether in a postwar military setting or in a modern Algerian city locked in the clutches of an epidemic.

Well before the nineteenth century, the connection of women to nursing and health care struck deep roots in the Francophone world. Catholic religious orders that specialized in nursing took charge of sick houses as early as the sixteenth century. Daniel Defoe documented the prevalence of women attending the stricken a century later. His *Journal of the Plague Year* (1721) chronicles their movements in the 1665 bubonic plague, which decimated nearly a quarter of London's inhabitants in eighteen months, including many who stepped up to nurse. Although these references suggest just how foundational women have been for hundreds of years in attending the sick and infirm, the last two decades have witnessed

---

[26] See D'Antonio's discussion of Black women's exclusion from military and hospital roles, despite an under-enrolled nursing force in chapter 6 of *American Nursing*.

[27] Report of the American Association of Medical Colleges, February 2, 2021. See also "Last Word: Thank You;" and Johnson, "The Future of Healthcare Is Female."

[28] Hallarman, "Honor Home Health Workers."

[29] See "Male Nursing Statistics," August 8, 2019.

PRESENT IN EFFACEMENT 61

a critical nursing shortage, forcing countries like the United States and Great Britain to import nurses from Asia;[30] the shortage has also created burnout conditions for those in understaffed institutions and training schools. The Covid-19 pandemic has brought the undersupply of nurses to a boiling point, unleashing bidding wars between hospital administrators and convincing seasoned practitioners to retire early. Inevitably, the shortage has led to workplaces where nurses experience continual stress, a complicating factor in patient—and practitioner—health.[31]

This professional debacle has not occurred in a vacuum. Long before physicians organized to galvanize their power in the mid-nineteenth century, medical work was sex segregated. The qualities believed to be central to good doctoring were defined as inherently masculine ones (like courage, logic, physical strength, scientific aptitude, and objectivity), whereas good nursing was the province of every woman in a domestic context.[32] When professionally trained nurses entered practice as "the physician's hand,"[33] a phrase that resonated with their patriarchally limned status in health care institutions, the qualities to which ideal nurses could aspire were little different from those that had characterized female domesticity: moral purity, gentleness, submissiveness, emotional intelligence, and obedience.[34] Elizabeth Bartlett has alluded to this sex-specific dynamic in *The Plague*: "If Camus is guilty of anything here, it is of using predominantly female characters to represent

[30] See, for example, Alonso-Garbayo and Maben, "Internationally Recruited Nurses from India and the Philippines in the United Kingdom"; and Dimaya et al., "Managing Health Worker Migration."

[31] See, for example, Jacobs, "As Delta Rises, Nurse Shortage Imperils Patients," August 22, 2021; and "Proposed 1% Pay Hike Shows U.K. Government Doesn't Value Us," March 17, 2021. Members of Britain's Royal College of Nursing asked for a 12.5 percent pay increase. Mental health nurse Matt Tasey said, "The pay is not worth the stress."

[32] On the relationship of gender to medicine, see Warner, *The Therapeutic Perspective*; and Morantz-Sanchez, *Sympathy and Science*.

[33] Melosh's coinage shows nurses struggling to establish professional autonomy. See *The Physician's Hand*, 6–7.

[34] Nursing histories take up these issues, for example, Susan Reverby's *Ordered to Care* and Anne Summers's *Angels and Citizens*.

62 CAMUS'S *THE PLAGUE*

nurturing, compassion, caring, embodiment; while using predominantly male characters to represent action, logic, [and] adherence to abstract principles of justice."[35] The idealization of masculine and feminine qualities related to health care roles has created turbulence throughout the twentieth century, and only recently, as the medical professions have become less sex-segregated, have the characteristics of good practice begun to lose their gendered associations.[36]

Despite the gradual erosion of gender-based beliefs linked to professional conduct, physicians' authoritative subjectivity has remained entrenched. Medical humanists have observed how the twentieth century's growing genre of illness narratives captures this tension, where a physician's voice, imitating the narration of clinical encounters, monopolizes the story line and does not engage the patient's perspective.[37] The patient is not the only one silenced. An entire constellation of medical stories chronicles surgical egotism at the expense of predominantly female support staff.[38] The physician controls the narrative of patient care through an assumption of expertise that often occludes the labors and insights of nurses, aides, or other witnesses. Not surprisingly, female medical students and physicians find collegiality wanting from their male associates, whose traditional communication strategies convey exclusivity instead of a more collective approach to medical problem-solving.[39] Male physicians have not played a categorically malevolent role at the top of the medical food chain but have often been blind to their professional privilege and thus not obligated to consider how language and conduct may paper over other crucial perspectives; how a fuller understanding of the human medical condition emerges when they surrender privilege

---

[35] Bartlett, *Rebellious Feminism*, 17.

[36] Sandelowski's *Devices and Desires*, for example, explores how nurses' technological training moved them away from traditional nursing values.

[37] See, for example, Jurecic's *Illness as Narrative*; and Hunsaker Hawkins's *Reconstructing Illness*.

[38] See, for example, Brown's *The Shift*; and Tarkan's "Arrogant, Abusive and Disruptive—and a Doctor."

[39] See, for example, Hamilton, "Surgical Strike."

PRESENT IN EFFACEMENT   63

and listen to a broader range of voices. Camus himself employs the voice of medical authority via Rieux and Tarrou, who frame the story as an account of men's work to banish an unpredictable virus.

Oran's Women of the Plague

This narrative pattern explains why Oran's women are depicted as secondary characters in contending with the plague. At the same time, they do not demur from assuming difficult, potentially deadly, assignments despite the growing morbidity of the epidemic—like the women of Defoe's chronicle who give little thought to the risk they incur. In Oran they are present at bedsides and subject to quarantine. One of these, Madame Othon, faces additional quarantine and nursing obligations when her son Jacques is stricken, forcing her to act without the aid of her husband, who is billeted at the city's quarantine camp. As the child dies, the distressed Rieux is unable to look directly at Madame Othon, signaling the broken communication between physician and nurse. She has already nursed and lost her mother to the plague, and it is not unlikely that she has unwittingly spread the disease to her child—an inference that Camus does not make but that Covid-19-conscious readers may connect symbolically with women's storied impurity. The women who take charge at home, like Rieux's mother, who is herself susceptible to disease given her age and proximity to a practicing physician (and to Tarrou whom she nurses), do so silently and without public notice. Camus writes that the two often communicate through silence and only occasionally with words. Madame Rieux's seamless ministrations leave almost no physical trace of animus, sound, or discomfiture on her son as she tends to his daily needs in the darkened apartment, a place where she "seemed no more than a darker patch of shadow"; this ominous reference traces Tarrou's mournful report of his own mother: "I can't say she died. She only effaced herself a trifle more than usual, and when I looked round

64 CAMUS'S *THE PLAGUE*

she was no longer there."[40] Despite her service at Tarrou's bedside, he "sees" only his own mother's demise in Madame Rieux's attentions; in the effacement of one, he effaces the other.

In another instance, Rieux and his mother dialogue about the newly contagious pneumonic variant that has swept the town (a development analogous to the Delta and Mu variants of Covid-19), and ever-steady and serene, she declares that there is little left to fear at her advanced age, in effect squelching an appropriately human reaction during an epidemic.[41] While this testimonial issues from Madame Rieux herself, readers must recognize that Dr. Rieux's narration of their conversation creates the hagiographic recollection. Content to mark time in her son's absence, as he reminds us, she values the care she can render and does not regret moments of inactivity—a wisdom calculated to sustain life and undergird survival despite the risk of contagion. That risk has already been discussed when Tarrou urges the doctor to establish a corps of male sanitary workers, and Rieux observes, "I take it you know that work of this kind may prove fatal to the worker."[42] He never makes a similar statement about the risk incurred by women who nurse.

Madame Rieux can be considered the most visible of the novel's women and mothers, even while sheltered in domestic precincts. Similarly situated caregivers earn scorn and dismissal. The "pious old lady" who takes in Father Paneloux during his final illness finds him recalcitrant and unwilling to see a doctor. Camus's characterization satirizes her as shrill and sanctimonious; she has blanketed the furniture in the priest's bedroom with crochet covers, and she flings a "sour 'Good night'" at him after they quarrel about scripture.[43] The narrator explains that the subsequent account of Paneloux's illness comes from the lady's testimony, even though he is quick to undermine her account. She reports of the clergyman's

---

[40] Camus, *The Plague*, 288, 277.
[41] Camus, *The Plague*, 123.
[42] Camus, *The Plague*, 125.
[43] Camus, *The Plague*, 230.

PRESENT IN EFFACEMENT   65

residence with her that she "most politely (as she put it)" urged him to see a doctor. The narrator's parenthetical insertion questions her intention and the reader's trust in her earnestness. When Paneloux rejects her second offer of medical aid, the lady states that she has no anxiety about her own risk of contagion but feels obliged to do right by him "(according to her account)," another dubious insertion by the narrator.[44] After being rebuffed a third time and observing Paneloux's physical decline, she summons the doctor. It is only when medical authority is engaged that the priest agrees to be moved. Although a timely consultation might have prolonged his life, this superannuated dame is dismissed from the text without further mention. The narrator finds her a deficient nurse despite her conscientious efforts to intervene. This vignette projects the germs of professional discord in the male patient's lack of respect for his caregiver. Though the ever- modest and unassuming Dr. Rieux does not berate the lady, we notice the preemptive application of his authority in a dynamic reminiscent of interactions between physicians and their less powerful colleagues.

We see other examples of nursing in *The Plague*, but Camus seldom uses the word "nurse." The woman who accompanies Rieux's wife to the sanatorium is called "nurse," though we do not witness the performance of her duties. Similarly, we see just one reference to Madame Othon's "nursing her mother."[45] He mentions nurses one other time, when late in the novel we find the description of a procedure in which "two nurses" restrain a patient awaiting Dr. Rieux's lancet.[46] In fact, the doctor and his medical colleagues fill their days seeing patients whom we seldom see and working on a serum to arrest the virus. We learn little about the organization of hospital space and who staffs it, except for the antiseptic anteroom Rieux has installed to receive patients, with its lake

---

[44] Camus, *The Plague*, 231.
[45] Camus, *The Plague*, 231.
[46] Camus, *The Plague*, 208.

of cresylic acid and brick island.[47] His brief references to trained nurses imply that Camus envisions nursing generically, as work which women are best suited to perform, regardless of accreditation or circumstance. Characters who tend the sick, but are not called nurses, might easily escape readers' notice. Madame Michel, the concierge's wife, watches at his sickbed before the word "plague" has ever been uttered, and mothers who "wail" when they see the "fatal stigmata" on children's bodies, like Madame Loret, beg the doctor to let them be nursed at home.[48] Late in Part Three, with the death rate soaring, the "necropolis" of Oran has been reduced to a flattened temporality of present moments. Without any sense of a past or a future, the people "[drink] their beer [and nurse] their sick."[49] The conjunction of these two activities dismisses the importance of nursing. Like automatons, the people are reduced to nourishing themselves and others with little forethought.

Gender Flattening

In this temporally debased and airless environment, the quality Camus has metaphorically associated with the absence of women, gender differentiation also erodes, as the qualities that have ordered the lives of women and men no longer have utility. We see this erosion foreshadowed in the necessity of burying men and women together in mass graves when the number of deaths prevents sex-segregated burial, a practice "the authorities [had formerly] set great store by."[50] This undoing of gender distinction, "this last remnant of decorum," has implications not only for the women characters but

---

[47] Camus, *The Plague*, 89.

[48] Camus, *The Plague*, 90.

[49] Camus, *The Plague*, 171, 184. Margaret Gray has also observed the oppression of Oran's "eternal present," which Dr. Rieux acknowledges by proclaiming that "nothing was left us but a series of present moments," 182. See "Layers of Meaning in *La Peste*," 167.

[50] Camus, *The Plague*, 176.

PRESENT IN EFFACEMENT   67

for men as well.[51] Dr. Rieux, who has done perhaps more than any other to assuage death, questions his own masculine fortitude in moments of self-doubt. He fears that he has done too little to save lives and that his efforts have been futile, work that "could hardly be reckoned a man's job."[52] As Margaret Gray puts it, "For all the mastery and control, the restraint and discipline of Rieux's narrative, for all the healing he *is* able to accomplish, he nevertheless remains vulnerable, human, and thus one of us: confronting circumstances that overwhelm and engulf him, but to which he refuses to succumb."[53] Previously animated by a sense of masculine achievement, Rieux perceives a shift in his role as physician to a more neutral gear, a shift that contaminates the practice of medicine itself. Instead of the heroic, male-defined medical work of saving lives, Rieux now asks whether any physician in Oran can perform "an activity worthy of his manhood."[54] Moving outside the frame of gender, a sign of the social disarray to which Oran now concedes, citizens go through the motions of daily living with narrowing blinders, oblivious to the self-doubt that plagues their physicians.

It is useful to note that the disutility of practitioners' labors does not inaugurate a reconfiguration or a rebalancing of the gender system, where women step into the void left by men's futile efforts. In other words, the plague "unmans" all of Oran's citizens in the sense that it deprives them of fortitude and empties them of prospects—including women whom the masculine narrative lens has represented in supporting roles at best.[55] Devoid of the structures of gender to order social difference, the characters' relations to power also change. We have seen how Dr. Rieux's affection for his wife and Rambert's for his Parisian mistress serve as

[51] Camus, *The Plague*, 175.
[52] Camus, *The Plague*, 193.
[53] Gray, "Layers of Meaning," 172.
[54] Camus, *The Plague*, 193.
[55] The *Oxford English Dictionary* definitions of "unman" include these senses of the verb, which does not require specific reference to people who identify as men. See the *OED*, vol. II, 266–267.

68   CAMUS'S *THE PLAGUE*

anodyne. These absent women can be regarded as more symbolically powerful late in the novel than early on. Rieux's increasing anxiety about his inability to oversee his wife's care makes her even more valuable to him. Though she does not suffer from the plague, their long separation instills regret that "he might have helped [her] to make a good recovery"—language that suggests his own declining agency.[56] Rambert's about-face to stay in Oran enacts a slightly different form of regret. He recognizes that "if he went away, he would feel ashamed of himself, and that would embarrass his relations with the woman he loved."[57] Thus, it is not exactly the love of a woman he seeks, when keeping her at an idealized distance keeps him on task, but the sort of self-love and self-respect that obtains from working collectively in a cause with others. In other words, he desires to become better—indeed "to rise above [himself]"—so he might be worthy of the Parisienne. Though references to both women dissipate throughout the novel, their absence allows them to retain a powerful hold on their plague-fighting men.

Margerrison's study of *The Plague* illuminates how deeply the myth of Orpheus and Eurydice saturates the novel's gendered values of characterization. In addition to the embodied but absent women who manage to escape the gender-flattening scythe of the late-stage plague (young Madame Rieux, Rambert's lover, Grand's Jeanne), the operatic performance of Christoph Gluck's *Orphée et Eurydice* reveals how the idealization of the feminine leads to a form of erasure, of "symbolic [petrification]."[58] Unable to save Eurydice because of an errant faith, Orpheus leaves her behind in Hades, which enables him to continue singing *about* her but not *to* her, a reminder that dialogue in *The Plague* is reserved primarily for men while women inhabit spaces of silence and nonverbal gesture. For the mythological Eurydice, there are only sulfur fumes, of course, but

[56] Camus, *The Plague*, 191.
[57] Camus, *The Plague*, 209.
[58] Margerrison, *Ces Forces Obscures de l'Âme*, 151–154, 150. Margerrison writes "petrefaction."

PRESENT IN EFFACEMENT 69

paradoxically she lives eternally in Orpheus's verses, always there to lend a hand to an aspirational hero, notwithstanding her death and abandonment. She has endured a "problematical trajectory from the concrete to the abstract," but this abstraction places her in a realm beyond "human life itself," an "unbridgeable" chasm that reinforces men's "experiential development in the real world and the stasis of women, outside of history."[59] The epic features of this Western patriarchal myth are undermined in the novel's tragicomic sidebar when the actor playing Orpheus falls off the stage, the latest victim of the plague. In an unanticipated collision between art and life, the embodied women of Oran confront the plague's horror and flee the theater, leaving behind the trappings of their elegant night out, like so many orphans without families to return to. Neither they nor the powerful symbol of Eurydice exits the stage unscathed.

Coda

In a study considering the intersections of class, race, gender, and colonialism in *The Plague* and their impact on the evolution of Covid-19, Ahmed Kabel and Robert Phillipson observe that the pandemic has merely "intensified" forms of structural inequality "that condemn the marginalized to loss of agency, social apartheid, and disposability."[60] In attempting to show how the accretion of inequalities over time wreaks havoc on any population in the midst of a public health or environmental disaster, they note that "Covid feeds on the ruins of structural and embodied racism."[61] The authors take Camus to task for his blindness to the colonial dynamics that shaped his perspective and thus "mask" how violence and domination undergird

---

[59] Margerrison, *Ces Forces Obscures de l'Âme*, 139, 148. Margerrison also notes that Camus's version of the myth "suggests a dismissal and surpassing of Eurydice," 151.

[60] Kabel and Phillipson, "Structural Violence and Hope," 3.

[61] Kabel and Phillipson, "Structural Violence and Hope," 12. They also note that structural violence brings about "linguicide, memoricide, historicide, and culturicide," 13.

70 CAMUS'S *THE PLAGUE*

the trajectories of plagues, and by extension the plague of Covid-19. They call his elision of the colonial backdrop of Algeria "morally indefensible,"[62] a charge that resembles Camus's failure to recognize his novel's women as a miscarriage of justice upon a modern world that has placed female health care workers in positions of danger and vulnerability. Camus's identity as an Algerian of European extraction, one for whom Algeria was home, makes his avoidance of colonial politics in *The Plague*—and their implications for women's subordination— disconcerting. What looks initially like Camus's blindness to the concerns of the subaltern might also reveal itself as his inclination to inhabit his home culture without drawing punitive or critical inferences to it. Other authors managed to articulate the violence of colonial occupation before Edward Said and others launched the late twentieth-century critique of Western colonialism.[63] By the same token, we can chastise Camus for his patriarchal take on women in *The Plague*, even though the structural imperatives of gender as a category of human experience were not fully theorized until the 1970s. Simone de Beauvoir's *The Second Sex* was not published until 1949, but she and Camus locked horns earlier over his patriarchal parochialism and its minimization of the feminine.

We criticize authors for what they might not have known, or have not yet learned, to show how the seeds of cultural crises have been sown in earlier epistemologies. In this light, Kabel and Phillipson offer trenchant analysis on what causes the very gaps in knowledge that construct the inequalities which social privilege immunizes against. As one commentator has argued, the leveling language leveraged on behalf of a well-heeled public encountering Covid-19 effaces socioeconomic realities that severely burden underserved populations in "the soporific narrative of the great equalizer."[64] As

---

[62] Kabel and Phillipson, "Structural Violence and Hope," 5–6.

[63] Said's *Culture and Imperialism* foregrounds the Western colonial enterprise against a backdrop of non-Western cultures.

[64] As Carol Hay puts it, "Social privilege continues to structure the narratives many people use to process life under the pandemic, even while material conditions are much

PRESENT IN EFFACEMENT 71

critics of this leveling, or the contention that social differences are immaterial and inconsequential, Kabel and Phillipson remind us that the pandemic has "laid bare the politics of work by uncovering the tension between value and social contribution," a subject with which the current female health care force is all too familiar.[65] The bedside work of nurses earns neither the social nor the economic rewards of pharmaceutical companies which, while they have produced vaccines that appear to arrest the spread of the Covid-19 virus, have also brought tragedy upon a gullible public in the arena of opioid distribution. The invisibility of real women doing real work in *The Plague* must be compared to the invisibility of pandemic workers, who, despite yard signs praising their frontline heroism, must risk their own lives on understaffed and underpaid shifts. The rhetoric of collectivity, the sense that we're all in this together, fighting hard—a rhetoric that punctuates Camus's novel, even if only characterized by masculine action—desensitizes us to the real differences between comfortable suburbanites, for example, and those who are food insecure.

By this measure, the conclusion of *The Plague* in which Camus writes, "The first thrill of hope had been enough to shatter what fear and hopelessness had failed to impair" is "deeply problematic," according to Kabel and Phillipson.[66] With the benefit of critical hindsight, they reckon the novel "tainted by a cynical sentimentalism" that endows hope with the power to neutralize fear and despair.[67] A more benevolent voice regards *The Plague* as "a serum for the future" whose need the author long ago anticipated.[68] Camus's view, a testament to the endurance of the human spirit and will,

worse for those not in charge of these narratives." See Hay, "How Privilege Structures Pandemic Narratives," 7; and Kabel and Phillipson, "Structural Violence and Hope," 16.

[65] Kabel and Phillipson, "Structural Violence and Hope," 9.
[66] Camus, *The Plague*, 273; and Kabel and Phillipson, "Structural Violence and Hope," 13.
[67] Kabel and Phillipson, "Structural Violence and Hope," 14.
[68] Marris, "Camus's Inoculation against Hate."

72 CAMUS'S *THE PLAGUE*

was a triumphal anthem celebrating Western values of strength, ingenuity, and manhood—qualities implicit in the power of patriarchy and thus poised on the shaky ledge of exclusivity. If in retrospect that view is not as expansive as Camus believed it to be, then how can he help us negotiate the medical challenges we now face? Because it is a fiction, Oran's plague ends on the seasonal plan, just a year after the city gates close. Our modern one (and any to come) rages on, unpredictably, all over the world without a promised terminus. Those trying to arrest its spread in care capacities not only cannot know what each day will bring in hospitals that variants-yet-to-be-named have clogged with new cases; they also cannot know when or how or if the pandemic will end—despite the biological Valhalla of herd immunity to which we aspire. Camus might not have bequeathed the intellectual tools to survive a plague, but his schemes of narration and characterization offer a calculus of institutional improvement, of metaphysical progress, by imposing a cautionary tale upon readers. The tale communicates that if we truncate an understanding of the complexities of gender, then a fiction in which roughly half of the characters "[stand] outside of events" is only that: a fiction that buries human possibility as readily as bodies awaiting interment.[69]

In the plague of Camus's imagination, the narrative distance of women places them beyond the orbit of life-saving activity, even as they perform in the shadows. What we regard at the end of the novel, as a flattening altogether of gender differences, further emphasizes the dehumanization of the population—both women and men. But when Camus's plague ends, we see through a masculine lens that tallies the morbidity stats for the men only. Rambert enters a strange new world of romance, Tarrou and Paneloux have succumbed, and Rieux has lost the opportunity for "a fresh start" with his wife. The women, first remote and later flattened beyond

---

[69] Margerrison, *Ces Forces Obscures de l'Âme*, 135–136.

gender distinction, become a metaphor for plague in a way not at first perceived. Their representation as a backdrop equivalent to the setting has simply evaporated. In their effacement, we read the legend of Covid-19 workers, whose presence in health care systems registers too negligibly in the cacophony of public opinion. The faulty assumption that disadvantages and inconveniences are equally felt by all who labor under Covid-19's regime shrouds what nurses and health care workers have been telling us since they organized their profession: that their toil must be valued for its hands-on connection to suffering, for its emissary of the living body and its envoy to death, and for its visible, embodied presence, regardless of the patient's proclivities or circumstances. It is not surprising that Camus was blind to understanding the discursive properties of healing in his attempt to channel the experience of a solitary physician, though it is a pity that he did not.

Works Cited

Allen, Jeffner. "An Introduction to Patriarchal Existentialism." In *The Thinking Muse: Feminism and Modern French Philosophy*, edited by Jeffner Allen and Iris Marion Young, 70–84. Bloomington: Indiana University Press, 1989.

Alonso-Garbayo, Álvaro, and Jill Maben. "Internationally Recruited Nurses from India and the Philippines in the United Kingdom: The Decision to Emigrate." *Human Resources for Health* 7 (2009): 1–11.

Baker, Christopher. "'Real Rebellion Is a Creator of Values': Doctors as Rebels in Ibsen's *An Enemy of the People* and Camus's *The Plague*." In *Critical Insights: Rebellion*, edited by Robert C. Evans, 141–157. Ipswich, MA: Salem Press, 2017.

Bartlett, Elizabeth Ann. *Rebellious Feminism: Camus's Ethic of Rebellion and Feminist Thought*. New York: Palgrave Macmillan, 2004.

Beauvoir, Simone de. *The Second Sex*. New York: Bantam, 1949.

Brown, Theresa. *The Shift: One Nurse, Twelve Hours, Four Patients' Lives*. Chapel Hill: University of North Carolina Press, 2015.

Camus, Albert. *Journaux de Voyage*, edited by Roger Quilliot. Paris: Gallimard, 1978 (English translation 1987).

Camus, Albert. *The Plague*. Translated by Stuart Gilbert. New York: Vintage, 1991.

74 CAMUS'S THE PLAGUE

D'Antonio, Patricia. *American Nursing: A History of Knowledge, Authority, and the Meaning of Work.* Baltimore: Johns Hopkins University Press, 2010.

Defoe, Daniel. *A Journal of the Plague Year* (1721). New York: Oxford Classics, 1999.

Dimaya, Roland, Mary K McEwen, Leslie A Curry, and Elizabeth H Bradley. "Managing Health Worker Migration: A Qualitative Study of the Philippine Response to Nurse Brain Drain." *Human Resources for Health* 10 (2012): 47–54.

Dornan, Tim, Selina R. Bentley, and Martina Kelly. "Medical Teachers' Discursive Positioning of Doctors in Relation to Patients." *Medical Education* 54, no. 7 (July 2020): 628–636.

Gray, Margaret E. "Layers of Meaning in *La Peste*." In *The Cambridge Companion to Camus*, edited by Edward J. Hughes, 165–177. New York: Cambridge University Press, 2007.

Hallarman, Lynn. "Honor Home Health Workers." *The New York Times*, August 15, 2021, Sunday Review, 7.

Hamilton, Joan. "Surgical Strike." *Stanford Magazine*, September/October 1998, pp. 58–61.

Hawkins, Anne Hunsaker. *Reconstructing Illness: Studies in Pathography.* West Lafayette, IN: Purdue University Press, 1999.

Hay, Carol. "How Privilege Structures Pandemic Narratives." Special Issue on "Feminist Responses to Covid-19 and Pandemics." *APA Newsletter* (Feminism and Philosophy) 20, no. 1 (September 2020): 7–12.

Hunter, Kathryn Montgomery. *Doctors' Stories: The Narrative Structure of Medical Knowledge.* Princeton, NJ: Princeton University Press, 1991.

Isaac, Jeffrey C. *Arendt, Camus, and Modern Rebellion.* New Haven, CT: Yale University Press, 1992.

Jacobs, Andrew. "As Delta Rises, Nurse Shortfall Imperils Patients." *The New York Times*, August 22, 2021, Section A, p. 1.

Jenkinson, Clay S. "Why We Should Be Reading Albert Camus during the Pandemic." *Governing* (May 15, 2020). https://www.governing.com/templa tes/gov_print_article?id=570507341.

Johnson, Megan. "The Future of Healthcare Is Female." *Athenal Health*, February 14, 2018. https://www.athenahealth.com/knowledge-hub/pract ice-management/healthcare-future-female.

Jurecic, Anne. *Illness as Narrative.* Pittsburgh: University of Pittsburgh Press, 2012.

Kabel, Ahmed, and Robert Phillipson. "Structural Violence and Hope in Catastrophic Times: From Camus's *The Plague* to Covid-19." *Race and Class* 62, no. 4 (2021): 3–18.

"Last Word." *Ms. Magazine*, Summer 2021, 48.

LeBlanc, John Randolph, and Carolyn M. Jones. "Space/ Place and Home: Prefiguring Contemporary Political and Religious Discourse in

PRESENT IN EFFACEMENT 75

Albert Camus's *The Plague*." In *Critical Insights: Albert Camus*, edited by Steven G. Kellman, 201–230. Pasadena, CA: Salem Press, 2012.

"Male Nursing Statistics." August 8, 2019. https://www.statisticstats.com/health/male-nursing-statistics/.

Margerrison, Christine. "Algeria's Others." In *Critical Insights: Albert Camus*, edited by Steven G. Kellman, 31–47. Pasadena, CA: Salem Press, 2012.

Margerrison, Christine. *Ces Forces Obscures de L'Âme: Women, Race and Origins in the Writings of Albert Camus*. Boston: Brill, 2008.

Marris, Laura. "Camus's Inoculation against Hate." *The New York Times Book Review*, August 9, 2020, p. 13.

Marx-Scouras, Danielle. "Portraits of Women, Visions of Algeria." In *The Cambridge Companion to Camus*, edited by Edward J. Hughes, 131–144. New York: Cambridge University Press, 2007.

Melosh, Barbara. *The Physician's Hand: Work Culture and Conflict in American Nursing*. Philadelphia: Temple University Press, 1982.

Morantz-Sanchez, Regina. *Sympathy and Science: Women Physicians in American Medicine*. New York: Oxford University Press, 1985.

Mulvey, Laura. "Visual Pleasure and Narrative Cinema." *Screen* 16, no. 5 (October 1975): 6–18.

Ofri, Danielle. *What Patients Say, What Doctors Hear*. Boston: Beacon Press, 2017.

"Proposed 1% Pay Hike Shows U.K. Government Doesn't Value Us." Morning Edition, National Public Radio, March 17, 2021. https://www.npr.org/2021/03/17/978065817/proposed-1-pay-hike-shows-u-k-government-doesnt-value-us-nurse-says.

Report of the American Association of Medical Colleges. February 2, 2021. https://www.aamc.org/news-insights/nation-s-physician-workforce-evolves-more-women-bit-older-and-toward-different-specialties.

Reverby, Susan. *Ordered to Care: The Dilemma of American Nursing, 1850–1945*. New York: Cambridge University Press, 1987.

Rizzuto, Anthony. *Camus: Love and Sexuality*. Gainesville: University Press of Florida, 1998.

Said, Edward. *Culture and Imperialism*. New York: Knopf, 1993.

Sandelowski, Margarete. *Devices and Desires: Gender, Technology, and American Nursing*. Chapel Hill: University of North Carolina Press, 2000.

Summers, Anne. *Angels and Citizens: British Women as Military Nurses, 1854–1914*. New York: Routledge, 1988.

Tarkan, Laurie. "Arrogant, Abusive and Disruptive—and a Doctor." *The New York Times*, December 2, 2008. https://www.nytimes.com/2008/12/02/health/02iht-02rage.18316569.html.

Warner, John Harley. *The Therapeutic Perspective: Medical Practice, Knowledge, and Identity in America, 1820–1885*. Cambridge, MA.: Harvard University Press, 1986.

4. Chris Mora of California sits silently amid an art installation "In America: Remember," which features flags representing every death from Covid-19 in the United States on the National Mall in Washington, DC, on September 24, 2021. Photo by Craig Hudson. Artwork by Suzanne Brennan Firstenberg.

3

The Meaning of a Pandemic

Andrew Edgar

Introduction

At the end of Albert Camus's novel *The Plague*, an old man—a patient of the narrator, Rieux—asks, "what does it mean 'the plague'?" [Mais qu'est-ce que ça veut dire, la peste?]. The old man seemingly treats this as a rhetorical question, for which there is no answer except: "Just life, no more than that" [C'est la vie, et voilà tout].[1] This chapter will propose that this question—as to the meaning of the plague—lies at the core of the novel. The initial experience of plague and pandemic is that of absurdity, and as such an exemplification of what Camus, in *The Myth of Sisyphus*, had termed "the absurd."[2] That is to say that a plague, and by implication the Covid-19 pandemic, is a seemingly meaningless disruption of the habits of everyday life.

This chapter treats the issue of a plague's or a pandemic's "meaning" as a problem as to how the experience of plague can be integrated into our already existing expectations as to how the world works and the sort of entities we might encounter in that world. Such expectations and frames of interpretation allow us, as competent social agents, to go on meaningfully, interacting with the physical world and our fellow human beings. Yet pandemics and plagues disrupt our expectations. They do not easily fit into

---

[1] Camus, *The Plague*, 307.
[2] Camus, *The Myth of Sisyphus*.

Camus's The Plague. Peg Brand Weiser, Oxford University Press. © Oxford University Press 2023.
DOI: 10.1093/oso/9780197599327.003.0004

78 CAMUS'S *THE PLAGUE*

preexisting interpretative schema and thus confront us as meaningless. We do not know how to go on. Camus will be interpreted as presenting, in *The Myth of Sisyphus*, the experience of the absurd as something that is disruptive in this manner, and in *The Plague* as taking the experience of pestilence as exemplary of the absurd.

The Plague will, nonetheless, be presented as a critical engagement with the earlier *Myth*. *The Plague* avoids the somewhat abstract invocation of absurdity found in *Myth*. Instead, the novel stimulates reflection in terms of a far more concrete and immediate experience and thereby offers a different, and morally more satisfactory, account as to how humans respond to the absurd. It does so by imagining the actions of ordinary citizens within the plague-afflicted town of Oran.[3]

In the first substantial section of this chapter, Camus's account of the absurd, as presented in *Myth*, will be rehearsed. The second seeks to explore the epistemology that is implicit to this account and to articulate Camus's relationship to phenomenology, and particularly to Heidegger. Here a key argument will be put forward that Camus's original position on the absurd relies on a problematic assumption as to the way in which particular experiences can be represented. The third section turns to *The Plague* itself. Camus will be presented as offering, despite his overt intentions, the outline of a phenomenology of the experience of plague. This he does by reflecting on the problem of how the plague, as an experience of the absurd, can be represented and narrated. It will be suggested that the problem of representation is fundamental to this interpretation of *The Plague*, and in understanding how particular experiences are

---

[3] Reading *The Plague* alongside *The Myth of Sisyphus* runs somewhat against the grain of the typical periodization of Camus's work (see, for example, Gray, "Layers of Meaning," 165), whereby the *Myth of Sisyphus* (published in 1942) is grouped with the novel *The Stranger* (also 1942), while *The Plague* (published 1947) is understood as the beginning of a new phrase of Camus's work, leading to *The Rebel* (of 1952). Further, my reading of *The Plague* puts to one side Camus's own suggestion that the novel should be read as an allegory of the Nazi occupation of Paris (Gray, "Layers," 165). Mine is a stubbornly literal reading—*The Plague* is a novel about a plague.

THE MEANING OF A PANDEMIC   79

integrated with general expectations (in terms of what is known as the "hermeneutic circle"). This serves to articulate the conditions through which the particular, disruptive experience of the plague can be integrated meaningfully into the expectations of the citizens of Oran—and by implication, how we might respond to Covid-19. The final section of the chapter will draw out the consequences that this reading of Camus has for our understanding of Covid-19.

The Absurd

For Camus, absurdity lies in the tension between humanity's expectation and need that the world be intelligible from its perspective, and "the unreasonable silence" of that world.[4] Even if the world is then "unreasonable," it is not, of itself, absurd. It is merely that it does not yield the sort of unity and meaning—any sort of universal and certain guidance to how we should lead our lives—that our human minds require and expect of it.[5]

Typically, humans are unaware of absurdity. The habits of everyday life and the occupation of social roles serve to conceal absurdity.[6] Camus glibly comments that "we get into the habits of living before we get into the habits of thinking,"[7] so that the question of the absurd does not arise. Indeed, in his essay "The Minotaur, or The Stop in Oran," Camus presents the town of Oran—the setting of *The Plague*—as the epitome of a town governed by habit.[8] Further, humans can actively renounce absurdity by destroying either pole of the relationship between the world and humanity upon which it rests. Such renunciation would entail either literal or "philosophical" suicide.[9] Thus, Camus begins *Myth*, famously,

---

[4] Camus, *The Myth of Sisyphus*, 32.
[5] See Camus, *The Myth of Sisyphus*, 26 and 31f.
[6] See Camus, *The Myth of Sisyphus*, 57.
[7] Camus, *The Myth of Sisyphus*, 15.
[8] Camus, *The Myth of Sisyphus*, 139–163; see also Camus, *The Plague*, 5–7.
[9] Camus, *The Myth of Sisyphus*, 32ff.

80 CAMUS'S *THE PLAGUE*

with the question of suicide. Having become aware of the absurd, one destroys oneself, as one pole of the relationship, in an attempt to erase it. Philosophical suicide, conversely, entails an illusory understanding of the world that denies its absurdity and silence (and thus, in effect, destroys the silent world, by forcing it to speak). The world may be construed as being intelligible, and indeed as supportive of human purposes and needs, for example by seeing it as a manifestation of divine will and providence—as the priest Paneloux preaches in his first sermon in *The Plague*[10]—or even as yielding evidence of progress to a more just society in which people will be free.[11] Camus laments those who have died "for the ideas or illusions that give them a reason for living."[12] He rejects both forms of suicide as failing to engage with the struggle that knowledge of the absurd, and thus a life free of illusion, demands.

The problem of suicide indicates that some people have the insight necessary to recognize absurdity. For some, the unthinking and habitual "chain of gestures" that governs the mechanical rhythm of our lives is broken: "Rising, tram, four hours in the office or factory, meal, tram, four hours of work, meal, sleep and Monday, Tuesday, Wednesday, Thursday, Friday and Saturday, according to the same rhythm—this path is easily followed most of the time. But one day the 'why' arises and everything begins in that weariness tinged with amazement." The stage set collapses.[13] In an experience that Camus compares to Sartre's notion of "nausea,"[14] life appears pointless: "A man is talking on the telephone behind a glass partition; you cannot hear him but you see his incomprehensible dumbshow: you wonder why he is alive."[15]

---

[10] Camus, *The Plague*, 94f.
[11] See Camus, *The Myth of Sisyphus*, 56.
[12] Camus, *The Myth of Sisyphus*, 11.
[13] Camus, *The Myth of Sisyphus*, 19.
[14] Sartre, *Nausea*.
[15] Camus, *The Myth of Sisyphus*, 21.

THE MEANING OF A PANDEMIC   81

What is entailed in this weariness and amazement is a recognition of how habitual life places one in time. As Camus presents this, one habitually lives in the future: " 'tomorrow', 'later on', 'when you have made your way', 'you will understand when you are old enough.' "[16] Humans exist in an arc of time where the justification of their existence lies permanently in the future, including, for the religious, the promise of the afterlife.[17] In becoming aware of the absurd, one's relationship to time—the temporality of human existence—is disrupted. Habitually, the human being understands the present moment, and the potential for action that is contained in that moment, in terms of both future possibilities that one may want to realize, and past actions, that cumulatively shape a sense of a continuing self. The absurd separates the human agent from their past and their future. The life of the person who is aware of absurdity—the absurd person [l'homme absurde]—thus lives in the present.

The life of the absurd person is characterized—by Camus—through a series of seeming paradoxes. Such a person must live without hope (for the future is irrelevant and its promises of meaning and reconciliation illusory), but without despairing; they must reject the absurd, but not renounce it (through literal or philosophical suicide); finally they must live in conscious dissatisfaction with the absurd (finding no positive value in it), but not succumb to immature unrest, for their response must be disciplined.[18] In sum, such a person lives in a permanent revolt against the absurd.[19]

At root, the absurd person, living outside the habitual experience of time, immerses themselves in the immediacy of their current experiences. Crucially, they pursue experiences, Camus argues, not for their quality, but rather for their quantity and variety, and thus in an "ethic of quantity."[20] Camus illustrates this

[16] Camus, The Myth of Sisyphus, 19.
[17] Camus, The Myth of Sisyphus, 21 and 15.
[18] Camus, The Myth of Sisyphus, 34–35.
[19] Camus, The Myth of Sisyphus, 53. See Foley, Albert Camus, on the centrality of the concept of "revolt" to Camus's writings.
[20] Camus, The Myth of Sisyphus, 59.

82 CAMUS'S *THE PLAGUE*

"ethic of quantity"[21] through a series of character sketches: Don Juan pursuing many women, albeit, in Camus's account, retiring to a life of contemplation; the actor dispersed into many roles; the conqueror or adventurer whose achievement lies primarily in overcoming the self rather than others; and finally the creative artist, who all importantly writes with no idea to the future or posterity.[22] All live in full awareness of the limitations of the human condition and its fleeting nature. Yet this is also, seemingly, the character of Tarrou, when he first appears in *The Plague*. He has only recently arrived in Oran, so has no past, and spends his days on the beach or dancing.[23]

The Phenomenology of Absurdity

While Camus claims that he is not a philosopher,[24] there are a number of epistemological and ontological assumptions underlying his characterization of the absurd. His ontology is at root dualist, setting the human subject in opposition (indeed hatred)[25] against the world as object. An epistemological consequence of this sundering—complementing the assumption that the world is not ordered to be in accord with human affairs—is the recognition that this world is not immediately knowable by humans.

Our estrangement from the world entails that our supposed knowledge of it (expressed, for example, in the natural sciences) is merely hypothetical, or more problematically, it is expressed in metaphors and images that would seek to make the world comprehensible in human terms.[26] Science constructs a world that

---

[21] Foley, *Albert Camus*, 12.

[22] Camus, *The Myth of Sisyphus*, 66ff.

[23] Camus, *The Plague*, 24.

[24] Camus said, in an interview with *Servir* in 1945: "I am not a philosopher, because I don't believe in reason enough to believe in a system" (Foley, *Albert Camus*, 173).

[25] Camus, *The Myth of Sisyphus*, 26.

[26] Camus, *The Myth of Sisyphus*, 25.

THE MEANING OF A PANDEMIC 83

panders to human needs and limitations, and as such, is itself a form of "philosophical suicide," and thus to be rejected. At his most radical, Camus argues that all we know for certain are our immediate sensory experiences. Camus refuses to sanction any inference from such personal experience to "true" (which is to say certain) knowledge.[27]

Camus's epistemology explains his relationship to phenomenology. He finds that his own conception of absurdity is compatible with Husserl's notion of intentionality, where intentionality is the assumption that consciousness is always consciousness of something.[28] This entails that the initial concern of phenomenology is with a description of the contents of consciousness, and hence immediate sensory experiences, while making no assumptions as to the reality of anything existing beyond those experiences. Further, such experiences have no structure or hierarchy. "The rose petal, the milestone, or the human hand are [sic] as important as love, desire, or the laws of gravity."[29] Phenomenology offers merely a description of the isolated particulars that make up experience, with no sense of an overarching or unifying whole.[30] Thus, at this stage in the phenomenological method, there is no pandering to the human need for intelligibility and unity. Camus only objects to Husserl's phenomenology when a grounding universal, and thus a structure, is reintroduced, in what is known as "eidetic reduction." As Camus presents this, Husserl illegitimately goes beyond experience, in pursuit of "the 'essence' of each object of knowledge," in the form of "extra-temporal essences."[31]

Apart from Husserl, the other phenomenologist with whom Camus engages is Heidegger, and in particular his *Being and Time*. Superficially Heidegger's concern with anxiety, precisely insofar as

[27] Camus, *The Myth of Sisyphus*, 24.
[28] Camus, *The Myth of Sisyphus*, 44, 46–47. Camus was clearly reading the first volume of Husserl's *Logical Investigations*.
[29] Camus, *The Myth of Sisyphus*, 30.
[30] Camus, *The Myth of Sisyphus*, 44–45.
[31] Camus, *The Myth of Sisyphus*, 45.

84 CAMUS'S *THE PLAGUE*

it appears to bring to consciousness the meaninglessness and fin-itude of human existence, has some appeal to Camus.[32] Indeed, the experience of anxiety disrupts one's unthinking absorption in the habitual, or what Heidegger characterizes as "the They."[33] This is somewhat akin to Camus's own characterization of the habitual character of everyday life;[34] yet, according to Camus, Heidegger presents anxiety merely as an awareness of loss.

For Heidegger, as Sherman argues,[35] anxiety and an awareness of the absurd do not end inquiry or the search for explanation, as they do for Camus, but rather prompt it. Heidegger's absurd [*widersinnig*] is merely that which is "unmeaning" [*unsinniges*][36]— it is a disruptive stimulus to reflection, rather than a character-ization of the human condition. Heidegger's absurd poses the individual human with a challenge as how to incorporate this ab-surd particular into, what Camus might see as, our preexisting ex-pectations of a unified and intelligible world.

Camus may be seen to be at odds with Heidegger on two core is-sues. First, his subject-object dualism, such that the human subject stands in a relationship of opposition to the world, is questioned by Heidegger.[37] Heidegger's conception of "being-in-the-world"[38] entails that humans, characterized as *Dasein*,[39] are always al-ready practically engaged in their world. *Dasein* is such that it is at once "thrown" into the world, and thus as much subject to the contingencies and threats of the natural world as any other animal or object (and is thus "there"—*Da*); and yet is uniquely aware of its own existence, for its "Being is an issue for it,"[40] which is to say that

---

[32] Camus, *The Myth of Sisyphus*, 28–29.
[33] Heidegger, *Being and Time*, 149ff.
[34] Camus, *The Myth of Sisyphus*, 29.
[35] Sherman, "Absurdity."
[36] Heidegger, *Being and Time*, 193.
[37] Sherman "Absurdity," 273.
[38] See Heidegger, *Being and Time*, 33.
[39] "Dasein" literally translates as "there-being," but is a semi-technical term in German philosophy, used for example by Leibniz and Kant, meaning "existence."
[40] Heidegger, *Being and Time*, 32.

THE MEANING OF A PANDEMIC 85

it must reflect and decide how it will live its life—and indeed, what sense it is to make of the world within which it has its Being [*Sein*].

Thus, while Camus sees the absurd person as surrendering to contingent existence (by merely being "there"), from which no true knowledge can come, Heidegger sees knowledge as an outcome of reflection and practical engagement. Subject-object dualism is a false abstraction from the more fundamental practical unity of *Dasein*.

Second, Camus, as noted above, presents the experience of absurdity as taking the absurd person out of habitual temporality. Camus's rejection of a passive faith in a future, in which everything will become intelligible, is echoed by Heidegger in his rejection of what he terms "expectation." Yet Heidegger offers an alternative relationship to the future, that of "anticipation."[41] This takes account of *Dasein's* finitude and mortality, actively projecting a meaningful future for itself, grounded in both its present and its past. This entwining of present with the past and future—temporality [*Zeitlichkeit*]—is the very meaning of *Dasein*.[42] Temporality is not time [*Zeit*], for time is merely the quantitative movement of the clock: a series of discrete "nows," as experienced by the absurd person. Temporality, in contrast, is that through which *Dasein* gives meaning to its being. Thus, again, Heidegger's position is the reverse of Camus's. Camus's contraction into the present, in an ethic of quantity,[43] is an abstraction from what Heidegger sees as the more fundamental "temporality"—Camus rejects temporality in favor of time.

Camus accepts a meaningless existence. Heidegger, in contrast, demands that *Dasein* should strive to give meaning to its existence. Put otherwise, Camus assumes that the only option open to humans is to represent the particular details of their sensuous experience,

---

[41] Heidegger, *Being and Time*, 387–388.
[42] Heidegger, *Being and Time*, 38.
[43] Camus, *The Myth of Sisyphus*, 59.

86   CAMUS'S *THE PLAGUE*

and indeed that the particular detail can be represented, truthfully, in isolation. The only universal that he can envisage is something akin to the grounding essence proposed by Husserl, and which he rejects as an illegitimate inference from experience. Heidegger offers an alternative, by appealing to hermeneutics: the interpretative process through which *Dasein* creates an ever-changing understanding of experiences. The general is not Husserl's given universal, but an assumption of a whole within which the particular detail acquires meaning. Crucially, the understanding of both particular and the general whole continually change and develop, as each is reinterpreted in the light of the other. This is the "hermeneutic circle." It is this circular relationship between particular and general to which Camus, in *Myth*, is blind (although, as will be argued below, it lies at the core of *The Plague*).

Heidegger alludes to this circular process in his account of the absurd. Typically, the objects that we experience in the world are what Heidegger calls "ready to hand." That is to say that we understand what they are and how to use them almost without thought, so familiar are they to us. In order for this to be possible, we must possess, Heidegger argues, some "fore-conception" of the objects and materials, akin to the hermeneutic presumption of a whole.[44]

A particular object or experience, in isolation, has no meaning. It has meaning only as it is assimilated into the more general fore-structure. The particular object is thus grasped in what Heidegger calls the "as-structure of interpretation."[45] That is to say, that the broader fore-structure, that is shaped by *Dasein's* practical engagement with the world, facilitates the grasp of, say, a forest *as* timber, or a mountain *as* quarry.[46] The absurd—the unmeaning—is the particular that does not fit into the fore-structure, and so we cannot make sense of our experience of it. It is, in Heidegger's terminology,

---

[44] Heidegger, *Being and Time*, 191.
[45] Heidegger, *Being and Time*, 192.
[46] See Heidegger, *Being and Time*, 100.

THE MEANING OF A PANDEMIC   87

"present-at-hand." All importantly, the absurdity of the particular challenges the general fore-structure. Just as an incomprehensible sentence or paragraph in a book may indicate that our presumption as to the nature of the book as a whole is inappropriate, so the absurd suggests that our fore-structure requires revision. Heidegger thereby rejects Husserl's reliance, in eidetic reduction, on grounding. Neither the general fore-structure nor the particular as-structure—neither the prejudgment of the whole nor the interpretation of the detail—is primary and grounding. There is rather a perpetual circular play between the two. Camus is seemingly unaware of this alternative to eidetic reduction, and so, in *Myth*, is left with the representation of particulars (in an ethic of quantity, in contrast to the qualitative meaning that Heidegger seeks).

The Plague

The experience of plague—and by implication, the Covid-19 pandemic—gives rise to the feeling of absurdity. That is to say that it is an explicit form of the relationship between the human subject that longs for intelligibility and a silent world. "A pestilence isn't a thing made to man's measure."[47] The plague can only be grasped through epidemiology and statistics. Tarrou remarks: "They fancy they are scoring off it, because a hundred and thirty is a smaller figure than nine hundred and ten."[48] For Rieux, "The only thing left to us is accountancy!"[49] Similarly, as the plague begins to recede, a doctor remarks "the graph's good today."[50] The very duration of the plague—the passing of time—is grasped largely in terms of the mortality statistics.

[47] Camus, *The Plague*, 37.
[48] Camus, *The Plague*, 113.
[49] Camus, *The Plague*, 207.
[50] Camus, *The Plague*, 235.

88 CAMUS'S *THE PLAGUE*

The plague interrupts the habits of everyday life, so that citizens' free movement is curtailed, the economy disrupted, and the threat of sudden death becomes pervasive.[51] The plague encourages, or indeed forces, the citizens of Oran to adopt the attitudes of the absurd person. The image of physical separation from the outside world and from loved ones, characterized as a form of exile, suggests a more fundamental temporal separation. The citizens of Oran are separated from their past and future. They may be "reduced to [their] past alone," but that past can no longer influence how they live in the present or allow projection into the future. They give up attempts to live in terms of the future, for no one knows how long the plague will last.[52] Faith in the future, and thus hope, becomes idiotic.[53] Temporality is thus replaced by a form of quantitative "time." Some (younger) citizens even seem to embrace a hedonistic "ethic of quantity": Tarrou speculates on the possibility of "saturnalia of Milan" beside the graves.[54]

Yet, while the plague is readily associated with the absurd as it is presented in *The Myth of Sisyphus*, Camus may be seen to be moving, significantly, away from his earlier position. Explicitly, he responds to Roland Barthes's critical comments on the novel by noting: "If there is an evolution from *The Outsider* to *The Plague*, it is towards solidarity and participation."[55] *The Plague* presupposes that humans are necessarily social beings. More significantly, perhaps, the main characters in the novel do not capitulate to the present as might the absurd person. While faith in the future might be idiotic, it will be suggested below that it is not at all clear that any

---

[51] Camus is remarkably perceptive about the everyday management of a plague (see especially *The Plague*, 118f, for Tarrou's description of everyday life in Oran). His one key oversight in keeping the theaters and cinemas open may have its justification in artistic license. If the theaters were closed, the scene in which an opera singer, playing Orpheus, collapses on stage, could not be included (200–201). Perhaps there is an allusion here to image of the collapsing stage set from *The Myth of Sisyphus*.

[52] Camus, *The Plague*, 72.

[53] Camus, *The Plague*, 68.

[54] Camus, *The Plague*, 120.

[55] Cited in Foley, *Albert Camus*, 199–200.

THE MEANING OF A PANDEMIC   89

of the novel's principal characters abandon the future. They continually strive to recover their (Heideggerian) temporality. Entwined with this is the problem of representing the plague and its progress. While it may be most readily grasped statistically—as pure quantity—Tarrou, Rieuz, and even Paneloux struggle to represent, narrate, and explain it. Ultimately, this entails that the plague, as absurdity, more closely approaches the account given by Heidegger—the plague is "unmeaning," a present-at-hand that disrupts the fore-structure of their worlds. These themes may be pursued by suggesting that the problem of representation lies at the heart of *The Plague*.

Repeatedly the narrator of *The Plague* comments on the difficulty that people have in communicating during their isolation.[56] The plague makes language and representation problematic. In the light of this, it is significant that five of the six principal characters in the novel may be considered to be writers. Rambert is a journalist, although the reader is given no example of his work. We know only that he was researching an article on the condition of the Arab population of the town.[57] Rieux is the novel's narrator. Tarrou keeps a chronicle of the plague. The Jesuit Paneloux is conducting research on Saint Augustine and the African Church, has contributed to the bulletin of the Geographical Society of Oran, and given lectures on Christianity and modern individualism.[58] Significant extracts from two of his sermons are given in the novel.

Grand, a civil servant, obsessively works on the opening sentence of a projected novel, describing a woman riding in the Bois de Boulogne. Superficially, Grand's struggle with his novel appears to be little more than a comic aside, at best illustrative of the absurd—akin to the happy Sisyphus, that Camus invites his reader to imagine at the end of *The Myth of Sisyphus*,[59] accepting his endless

---

[56] See Camus, *The Plague*, 76.
[57] Camus, *The Plague*, 12.
[58] Camus, *The Plague*, 92f.
[59] Camus, *The Myth of Sisyphus*, 111.

90 CAMUS'S *THE PLAGUE*

task. At a deeper level, Grand's struggle, to write a perfect sentence, exemplifies the problem of representation and the hermeneutic circle that lies at the heart of *The Plague*.[60] Grand assumes that a sentence, through the careful choice of words—their reference, sound, and rhythm—can evoke its subject matter precisely: "he set to looking for an epithet that would promptly and clearly 'photograph' the superb animal."[61] In this, he echoes Camus's assumption, in *The Myth of Sisyphus*, that particular experiences can be objectively described. Yet the comic effect of Grand's struggle comes from its hermeneutic failing. The perfect sentence, which must ultimately be a particular within the whole of the novel, is assumed to make sense in isolation from that whole. Grand does not see that the opening line of a novel can only be revised, adequately, in the light of the novel as a whole. Grand never strays beyond his first sentence. He thus contracts the hermeneutic circle to the sentence—each word is a particular; the sentence the only whole.

The obsession with the opening sentence, and its curtailing of the hermeneutic circle, may be seen to reflect a broader quality of Grand's life, and its relationship to temporality and time. Grand looks to a future when publishers will salute his novel ("Hats off").[62] Yet he lacks the capacity to bring about this future. Throughout the plague he works diligently at his bureaucratic duties, not least in keeping a statistical record of the plague, heroically committing himself to the plague as quantity, not narrative quality. Just as he is unable to look to the whole of his novel, so, too, he expresses the inability of the absurd person to look beyond their immediate experience. This leaves his future, as a writer, as an illusion (and one that he perhaps accepts, as he orders that his manuscript should be burned after his death, albeit that, saved from death, and perhaps with life endlessly stretching before him once more, he begins

---

[60] Camus, *The Plague*, 101f.
[61] Camus, *The Plague*, 135.
[62] Camus, *The Plague*, 105.

THE MEANING OF A PANDEMIC   91

again his unfinishable task of revising the sentence).[63] Here he is not simply absurd, but exemplary of the person caught up in the habit and illusion of everyday life. His novel thus reflects his lack of temporality, for just as he cannot anticipate the whole of the novel, neither can he understand his present in terms of an authentically projected future and recollected past. Representation and temporality thus, in Grand, become one, and the absurd or unmeaning quality of the plague fails to touch him. Lost in habit, Grand lacks the play of fore-structure and as-structure that would allow him to give concrete meaning to his life.

Tarrou may be seen to develop this theme. As noted above, when he is introduced in the novel, he appears to be an exemplary absurd person, severed from his past and burying himself in an ethic of quantity. He writes a "chronicle" of the plague—making himself an historian of that which has no history.[64] In this chronicle the plague itself remains silent. Tarrou seemingly makes no attempt to explain it or to make it intelligible. The chronicle is merely the gathering together of descriptions of particular experiences that had caught his attention. It is thus composed of representations of a series of "nows." While set against the general background of the plague, each "now" is self-contained. One imagines that the chronicle could be read in any order. Again, the hermeneutic circle is foreshortened—for Tarrou there is no fore-structure through which the particularity of the plague can be grasped *as* something. The plague is not even present-to-hand. The chronicle thus confirms Tarrou as the absurd person.

This initial impression is dispelled in an intimate conversation that Tarrou has with Rieux. Tarrou confesses that he understands himself as already infected by the plague. For him, the plague is (metaphorically) the place that the death penalty—and thus injustice—has in the social system, and his implication in that

---

[63] Camus, *The Plague*, 263–264.
[64] Camus, *The Plague*, 24.

92   CAMUS'S *THE PLAGUE*

system. Here, Camus focuses on humans as social beings, and explicitly as constituted by their cultural environments. For Tarrou, most significantly, this lies in his experience of watching his father, a prosecuting counsel, demand the death penalty for a convicted criminal,[65] and later witnessing a firing squad. He regards himself as having indirectly supported the deaths of thousands of men by approving the actions and judicial principles that facilitated those deaths.[66] Tarrou nonetheless retains hope ("for some peace or . . . a decent death"),[67] although his "exile" is due to his awareness of the injustice of the social system, and thus his refusal to take the side of the pestilence.[68]

Tarrou's temporality is thereby revealed. He is not an absurd person. He has a strong sense of himself as a unity of past, present, and future. The awareness of injustice is the fore-structure through which the particular experience of the plague can be interpreted— the plague *as* metaphor of injustice. The chronicle is then not obviously coherent with Tarrou's conversation with Rieux, but disturbingly in tension with it. With Tarrou, the absurd has been reinterpreted as injustice, and humans who are complicit with this injustice, either knowingly or passively absorbed into the habits of everyday life, have no history. The chronicle is structured, in its deliberate curtailing of the hermeneutic circle, as a document of injustice—hence his growing obsession with the criminal activities of Cottard.[69] The plague, it turns out, is not the splintering of life into separate events, but rather must be reinterpreted as an awareness of injustice and criminality.

Rieux reveals himself as the author of the narrative that is *The Plague*. He takes it upon himself to bear witness to the experiences and suffering of the people of Oran. He attributes objectivity to his

---

[65] Camus, *The Plague*, 249f.
[66] Camus, *The Plague*, 251.
[67] Camus, *The Plague*, 252.
[68] Camus, *The Plague*, 254.
[69] Camus, *The Plague*, 195.

THE MEANING OF A PANDEMIC   93

narrative—albeit that he is aware, following his conversation with Tarrou, that no narrative representation can be a purely neutral description. He strives to suppress his own voice and feelings, in order to speak for all the victims of the plague.[70] His narrative is unlike Tarrou's chronicle. It has a structure, following, in its five parts, the rise and fall of the plague itself, and thereby expresses a sense of a whole. As narrator, he has made decisions as to when to begin and when to end his account: as to what is to be included and what left out. Its parts cannot be read in any order. There is thus a hermeneutic circle between part and whole, as the reader gradually comes to understand the text (typically through repeated readings, each respecting the circle as parts and whole are reinterpreted in the light of each other).

If Rieux therefore brings the events of the plague into a coherent whole, then, following the link between representation and temporality found in Grand, it may be suggested that Rieux is not, as some commentators suggest, living without hope,[71] and because of this, the plague is neither truly absurd nor meaningless. While "faith" in hope may be idiotic, Rieux, like Tarrou, suggests something more subtle: that is the difference between Heidegger's anticipation and expectation. Faith in the future would be passive expectation, and precisely what Camus condemns as an illusion. In contrast, Rieux struggles against the plague, actively striving for a projected future in which the plague is defeated. The present moment of the plague is understood through anticipation of this future but also through Rieux's own grasp of his past as a doctor and healer. There is thus a fore-structure—a sense of the temporal whole—that allows the plague to be interpreted *as* an opponent (and hence the military metaphors Rieux uses—the plague "was in retreat all along the line.")[72]

---

[70] Camus, *The Plague*, 301–302.
[71] See Masters, *Camus*, 46.
[72] Camus, *The Plague*, 271.

94   CAMUS'S *THE PLAGUE*

Tarrou and Rieux, it is being argued, have the resources—the fore-structure and sense of their lives as a meaningful whole—to give meaning to the plague, and fruitfully so insofar as they thereby come to struggle against it. The non-writer, Cottard, can similarly make sense of the plague, but to very different ends. The reader first encounters Cottard as an unsuccessful suicide.[73] Surprisingly, Cottard appears to flourish during the plague. It suits him well, he says,[74] for it severs him from his criminal past, and the authorities will be too busy to pursue him while it lasts. Further, Cottard, through association with black marketeers, makes money. Paradoxically, fully aware of his past, and thus his temporality, he nonetheless forestalls any projection into the future (which can, after all, only entail his arrest). He lives knowingly in the present, giving meaning to the plague *as* opportunity for personal liberty and enrichment. It is only when the plague is defeated that the absurdity of his situation once more overwhelms him, and he involves himself in an inevitably fatal confrontation with the police.[75]

Paneloux's response to the plague can be contrasted with Rambert's. Both struggle to give meaning to it, yet unlike Tarrou, Rieux, and Cottard, they can only do so by engaging fully in the hermeneutic circle, in that any experience of plague as absurd or unmeaning requires, for both of them, a fundamental reinterpretation of their lifeworlds—the fore-structure that makes a meaningful interpretation of the plague possible. Paneloux's initial position is to incorporate the plague into his seemingly unshakable religious faith, and so interpret the plague *as* God's will. Paneloux has a rich store of imagery to draw upon, characterizing the plague—"the angel of the pestilence . . . Lucifer"[76]—as bringing a moral judgement on the people of Oran, who should see the plague as a demand to reflect, but not to give up hope. Paneloux's hope

[73] Camus, *The Plague*, 19.
[74] Camus, *The Plague*, 158.
[75] Camus, *The Plague*, 302f.
[76] Camus, *The Plague*, 96.

THE MEANING OF A PANDEMIC   95

is precisely that which Camus condemns in *Myth*. Subsequently, Paneloux witnesses the death of a child—"that child, anyhow, was innocent"[77]—and it is this, rather than the plague itself, that becomes the moment of unmeaning that disrupts his sense of an intelligible whole. A second sermon adopts a position oddly close to that of Camus's absurd person, except for its insistence on the existence of God (and thus its "philosophical suicide"). Paneloux argues that one should not attempt to explain the plague, but merely to accept it. "[W]e must believe everything or deny everything."[78] In demanding that the Christian should consent to the plague, and the humiliation that it entails, Paneloux comes close to Camus's image of the happy Sisyphus, and Paneloux's God—"the love of God is a hard love"[79]—close to Sisyphus's pagan gods.

If Paneloux approximates the absurd person, he does not thereby vindicate Camus's arguments from *Myth*. Paneloux cannot live according to this reinterpretation of the plague (and indeed, more deeply, his understanding of God). He refuses medical treatment, as "it's illogical if a priest consults a doctor,"[80] and dies, but without any of the symptoms of the plague.[81] Paneloux obscurely sees that the plague has fundamentally challenged his beliefs—the fore-structure—and that the absurdity of the child's death and the plague itself must be addressed. Yet he is left between blind faith in a difficult, if not cruel, love of God, and a capitulation to the absurd. Unable to engage in a genuine and constructive hermeneutic—and thus unable to understand himself temporally—he dies.

Rambert is perhaps the one character who not only needs to reinterpret himself but does so successfully. Initially, Rambert, who came to the town only to fulfil a journalistic commission, struggles to escape and to return to his lover. He insists that he is a stranger

---

[77] Camus, *The Plague*, 218.
[78] Camus, *The Plague*, 224.
[79] Camus, *The Plague*, 228.
[80] Camus, *The Plague*, 229.
[81] Camus, *The Plague*, 233.

96   CAMUS'S *THE PLAGUE*

in the town.[82] Yet, while organizing his escape he works alongside Rieux and Tarrou. Seemingly, this experience changes him. He decides not to escape, explaining only that "[u]ntil now I always felt a stranger in this town . . . But now . . . I belong here whether I want it or not. This business is everybody's business."[83] Rieux then asks, significantly, if he has given up on happiness. This marks, again, a key step away from Camus's position in *The Myth of Sisyphus*. Rambert has not, as Paneloux strove to do, capitulated to the condition of a happy Sisyphus, shouldering his burden, from moment to moment, of work in the hospitals. Rather, he has reinterpreted his life. His decision rests upon a question of identity and meaning—not primarily happiness.[84] The initially unmeaning experience of the plague— which was at best an inconvenience keeping him from his previously happy life—becomes the present-at-hand that must be given meaning in the fore-structure. But this can be achieved only at the cost of reconsidering what that fore-structure itself means—which is to say, a reconsideration of the temporal unity of his future, past, and present that is Rambert's self-understanding. Hence, his move from "stranger" to recognizing the contingency or "thrownness" of being in Oran, whether he likes it or not, and thus taking this as the authentic ground for projecting and anticipating his future.

In this section, it has been suggested that the plague thrusts the citizens of Oran into an awareness of absurdity. Time itself is distorted. Yet Camus shows each of his principal characters continuing to struggle against, rather than to capitulate to, the absurdity of their condition. Each strives to make sense of, and to represent, the plague, thereby restoring their temporality—their sense of identity—anticipating a future and acting meaningfully in the present.

---

[82] Camus, *The Plague*, 106.

[83] Camus, *The Plague*, 209–210.

[84] Even though he might, by good fortune, achieve happiness at the end of the novel, through being reunited with his wife, by staying in Oran he risks that very happiness, thereby seeming to give priority to a meaningful life over a happy one.

Camus's Absurd in the 2020 Pandemic

The Covid-19 pandemic is, in certain respects, more absurd than Camus's plague (if there can be degrees of absurdity). There exists a history of plagues (to which Paneloux refers in his sermons[85]), and thus the plague is not wholly silent. Camus models his fictional plague on those that afflicted Europe throughout the Middle Ages, and indeed into the seventeenth century (and hence the epigraph to *The Plague* cites Daniel Defoe, and his account of the 1665 plague in the United Kingdom). There already exists a serum for the plague that Oran awaits from Paris.[86] In contrast, there was little precedent for Covid-19. The SARS (2002–2004) and MERS (2012) epidemics had been faced by a number of countries, but the populations of the global north were left with the illusion that modern technology, in its seemingly complete domination of nature, protected them from pandemic (despite numerous government advisory bodies arguing otherwise).[87]

Covid-19 is thus unmeaning. It seems at first stubbornly silent when interrogated by medical science, so that when it emerged little was known of how to treat it (there was no "serum"), how it spread, whether there was natural immunity, or that it had after-effects such as "long Covid." Further, responses to the pandemic led to an unparalleled disruption of everyday life. Social interaction was curtailed and citizens were isolated and confined, as in Oran; businesses closed; administrative workers were encouraged to work from home, leaving city centers deserted. The quietness of the cityscape, in the northern spring, allowed birdsong to be heard clearly. Governments took on new financial responsibilities, giving the lie to the narrative of economic

---

[85] Camus, *The Plague*, 92f and 220f.
[86] Camus, *The Plague*, 47.
[87] HM Cabinet Office, *National Risk Register of Civil Emergencies*, September 14, 2017, 33–38.

98   CAMUS'S *THE PLAGUE*

austerity that had characterized the previous decade. In sum, both personally and at the level of the community and nation, people were cut off from their pasts and futures. Covid-19 confined people into a present, of which they typically no longer had the resources to make sense.

Further, while Camus's plague was generally amenable to being counted, Covid-19 was more elusive. The statistical description of disease is more complex and nuanced than Camus allows. Deaths, in particular—which for Camus are generally attributed with little difficulty to the plague—are more problematically linked to Covid-19. The attribution of Covid-19 as the immediate cause of death is often contested. Covid-19 deaths are more typically like Paneloux's than Tarrous's. In England, patients who die, having been diagnosed with Covid-19 within the previous twenty-eight days, are classified as Covid-19 deaths. This methodology leaves open the possibility that Covid-19 may not have been the immediate cause of death. Comparisons between international statistics are problematic, as different criteria are employed across the globe to classify and record Covid-19 deaths. While nature may not be as silent as Camus suggests, it is typically ambiguous as to what it is saying.

This very ambiguity leaves Covid-19 open to the interpretations of conspiracy theorists and pandemic deniers. Some people, the secular kin of Paneloux, have turned to conspiracy theories (thereby sparking a moral panic on the part of Western media, concerning in particular QAnon). Through conspiracy theory one could at once deny the importance (or even existence) of the pandemic, and readily incorporate it in an already given fore-structure: the plague *as* Chinese biological warfare, for example, or the plague *as* plot to undermine Donald Trump's presidency. Paneloux's own explanation, of the plague *as* divine judgement, was articulated by some. More problematic is the appropriation of the pandemic by authoritarian rulers in order to clamp down further on their political opponents: the plague *as* political opportunity, and as such

THE MEANING OF A PANDEMIC 99

somewhat akin to Cottard's interpretation of the plague *as* a criminal opportunity.[88]

Tarrou remarks: "What is natural is the microbe. All the rest—health, integrity, purity (if you like)—is a product of human will, of a vigilance that must never falter."[89] This suggests precisely the need to go, interpretatively, beyond a meaningless nature to the social conditions that mediate the pandemic and its appropriation. Any given person's experience of Covid-19 is as much shaped by their government's response to the pandemic as by the disease itself. It is the closing of Oran that is significant, and it is lockdown and social distancing (and indeed, latterly, the organization of vaccinations) that mediates experience of the pandemic. Camus thus acknowledges that in experiencing the plague the potential victim is forced to reflect on broader social and political issues. If, as the example of Rambert makes explicit, one makes sense of the plague—overcoming its unmeaning—only by reflecting upon one's own sense of identity, then Covid-19 has done much to challenge many people's existing, habitual sense of identity. As Covid-19 was seen to infect poor and minority groups disproportionately, and to do so not due to any natural or biological reason, but due to issues of housing conditions, nutrition, and great risk of exposure to the virus in the workplace (not least hospitals), the political structures of society came into question, and thus, as for Tarrou, each person's complicity with them (as victim or collaborator). Tarrou's concern with injustice is echoed in the demands of the Black Lives Matter movement, which, while its renewal may have been sparked by events unrelated to Covid-19, may nonetheless be suggested to have drawn strength and significance from the pandemic's framing and highlighting of the racial and class injustice of contemporary societies.

---

[88] Anon, "Would-Be Autocrats," April, 23, 2020.
[89] Camus, *The Plague*, 253.

100 CAMUS'S *THE PLAGUE*

At the conclusion of *The Plague*, Rieux can only reflect on the temporary nature of Oran's victory over the disease.[90] Little, it seems, has changed. Time threatens to reassert itself over temporality. At its best and most constructive, the hermeneutic challenge to make sense of Covid-19 has led, if one is allowed some faith, to the anticipation of new futures—both for individuals and societies. Such futures begin to articulate a society that is more just (and in which black lives genuinely do matter) and ecologically sustainable. The initial absurdity and unmeaning of Covid-19, seemingly stripping us from past and future lives, can thus, through hermeneutic reflection and the resultant reimagining fore-structures and as-structures, lead to a new sense of identity and a new temporality for the individual, and a new history for society.

Works Cited

Anon. "Would-Be Autocrats Are Using Covid-19 as an Excuse to Grab More Power." *The Economist*, April 23, 2020. https://www.economist.com/intern ational/2020/04/23/would-be-autocrats-are-using-covid-19-as-an-exc use-to-grab-more-power.

Camus, Albert. *The Myth of Sisyphus*. Translated by Justin O'Brien. Harmondsworth, UK: Penguin, 1955.

Camus, Albert. *The Plague*. Translated by Stuart Gilbert. New York: Vintage, 1991.

Foley, John. *Albert Camus: From the Absurd to Revolt*. London: Routledge, 2008.

Gray, Margaret. "Layers of Meaning in *La Peste*." In *The Cambridge Companion to Camus*, edited by Edward J. Hughes, 165–177. Cambridge: Cambridge University Press, 2007.

Heidegger, Martin. *Being and Time*. Translated by John Macquarrie and Edward Robinson. Oxford: Blackwell, 1962.

HM Cabinet Office. *National Risk Register of Civil Emergencies*. London: Cabinet Office, September 14, 2017, 1–71. https://www.gov.uk/governm ent/publications/national-risk-register-of-civil-emergencies-2017-edition.

Husserl, Edmund. *Logical Investigations* Vol. 1. Translated by J. N. Findlay and D. Moran. London: Routledge, 2001.

---

[90] Camus, *The Plague*, 308.

THE MEANING OF A PANDEMIC   101

Masters, Brian. *Camus*. London: Heinemann, 1974.
Sartre, Jean-Paul. *Nausea*. Translated by Robert Baldick. Harmondsworth, UK: Penguin, 1965.
Sherman, David. "Absurdity." In *A Companion to Phenomenology and Existentialism*, edited by Hubert L. Dreyfus and Mark A. Wrathall, 271–279. Oxford: Blackwell, 2006.
Sherman, David. *Camus*. Oxford: Wiley-Blackwell, 2009.

5. Käthe Kollwitz (1867–1945). *Woman with Dead Child*. 1903. Print. 42 x 48 cm. 1949.0411.3926. British Museum/London/Great Britain. © 2022 Artists Rights Society (ARS), New York.

4

Grief and Human Connection in *The Plague*

Kathleen Higgins

Camus's *Plague* and Our Plague

Human connection has been strained by the Covid-19 pandemic. The virus has rendered in-person social interaction risky and abnormal. Lockdowns have resulted in isolation from friends and family and/or the constant presence of household members. Those who are hospitalized fear death in the absence of loved ones. In the United States, it has also widened social divisions, making visible disparities in health care among racial and ethnic subgroups within the population and inflaming ideological disagreements, with some seeing the observance of health measures as a badge of partisan affiliation. Social media amplify dubious theories about the pandemic and the political motives of those who are fighting it. The arrival of available vaccines has not eased political divisions, and many are disinclined to get vaccinated, some persuaded by conspiracy theories or skeptical of anything advocated by government officials.

In this context Albert Camus's novel *The Plague* (1948) has become extremely popular, with many readers noting striking parallels with the current situation. Although the novel is set during a fictional plague in the Algerian city of Oran, Camus had aimed to write a book that would speak to those confronting real calamities. *The Plague* has often been read as designed to represent the German occupation of France and the struggle of the

Camus's The Plague. Peg Brand Weiser, Oxford University Press. © Oxford University Press 2023.
DOI: 10.1093/oso/9780197599327.003.0005

104   CAMUS'S *THE PLAGUE*

Allies to overcome Nazi fascism, and Camus seems to confirm that he wanted readers to see the connection, but he also asserts that he wanted it to be interpreted on multiple levels.[1] While the epidemic in the novel is open to various metaphorical interpretations,[2] Camus sought to reflect the circumstances of actual plagues, having extensively researched accounts of historical outbreaks. The novel's relevance for organizing thoughts about our own situation seems to be in keeping with the author's aims, even though it does not exhaust them. I will be focusing on the complicated affective burden that situations like epidemics provoke and the symptoms of grief that are involved. These symptoms are visible in the novel, and they are evident in our experience, too. Camus suggests that joining with others in efforts to improve the situation is not only essential to limiting the harmful impact of a plague (literal or metaphorical); it is also the best way to overcome the psychological damage that results when people face massive disruptions in their lives.

Psychological Reactions in the Novel

Though identified only near the end of the novel, the narrator of *The Plague* is a physician, and we may have guessed his identity on the basis of his detailed description of the stages of the epidemic's progress.[3] Dr. Bernard Rieux chronicles both the spread of the disease and its toll on both physical and psychological health. The reported effects of the epidemic on the mental health of Rieux's city bear comparison with the psychological impact of Covid-19.

Rieux reports that the initial reaction is the tendency to downplay evidence of an epidemic. When rumors circulate about a

---

[1] See Kellman, *The Plague: Fiction and Resistance*, 3; and Camus, "Letter to Roland Barthes," 339.

[2] One of the novel's characters, for instance, describes the acceptance of capital punishment as a plague. See Camus, *The Plague*, 251.

[3] Because the identity of the narrator remains a puzzle through most of the book, Kellman describes Camus's *The Plague* as "a mystery novel." See Kellman, *The Plague*, 23.

GRIEF AND HUMAN CONNECTION IN *THE PLAGUE* 105

fever, people dismiss this as nothing unusual. This is true even of physicians, including Rieux himself. Only when goaded by a physician who has seen plague cases before is he willing to follow the evidence that points to the diagnosis, and even then he comments, "It's hardly credible."[4] Even realizing that it is plague, Rieux concludes simply that "serious precautions" should be taken.[5] When the medical community meets to consider the situation, they agree only to "take the responsibility of acting as though the epidemic were plague."[6] The authorities, too, at first make only half-hearted efforts to alert the community. These efforts to minimize the threat of the disease will sound familiar to those who resided in the United States during the Covid-19 outbreak.

Once quarantine is declared, incredulity gives way to dwelling on what has been lost. Many of the townspeople are preoccupied with being separated from loved ones outside the city. Obsessing on what they cannot do, the townspeople tend to focus on "the host of small details that, while meaning absolutely nothing to others, meant so much to them personally."[7] Rieux describes their state as a "feeling of exile—that sensation of a void within which never" leaves,[8] an apt characterization also for the current nostalgia for features of ordinary life that were barely noticed before they were disrupted.

This period of exile is marked by a strange alteration in the perception of time, another resemblance to the experience of many during the Covid-19 pandemic. The present is unfulfilling, and many initially feel an "irrational longing to hark back to the past or else to speed up the march of time, and those keen shafts of memory that [sting] like fire."[9] Any solace sought in memories is

[4] Camus, *The Plague*, 36.
[5] Camus, *The Plague*, 39.
[6] Camus, *The Plague*, 50.
[7] Camus, *The Plague*, 183.
[8] Camus, *The Plague*, 71.
[9] Camus, *The Plague*, 71.

106 CAMUS'S *THE PLAGUE*

"illusive," for they draw attention back to those who are absent and often provoke regret.[10] Memory also becomes gradually less reliable, making distant or lost loved ones harder to picture. Having no sense of when their purgatorial state will be over, people eventually stop thinking about the end of their situation and anything else in the future. With present options for activity severely reduced, the townspeople drift through life, with time reduced to "a series of present moments" that are consistently monotonous.[11] Every aspect of time is unsatisfying; the townspeople feel "hostile to the past, impatient of the present, and cheated of the future."[12]

In the second phase of the epidemic as the narrator reports it, the typical frame of mind is one of habitual despair, apathy, and lethargy. Interpersonal interactions are superficial. In this new phase, people have stopped dwelling on what has been taken from them. Everything with personal meaning has been abandoned, and the city's residents sleepwalk through their days, taking only a shallow interest in things. "Even their tenderest affections" have come to seem "abstract," more notional than heartfelt.[13]

In the midst of a quarantine, Oran's townspeople feel a general sense of social isolation.[14] Funerals are restricted and eventually eliminated, and the bereaved are forced to mourn privately. Concerns for one's own health make other people seem threatening, as is evident when a hotel manager describes a family with a relative who died of plague as being "under suspicion." Even when Jean Tarrou, a hotel guest, responds that everyone is under suspicion, this only underscores the danger of associating with

---

[10] Camus, *The Plague*, 71.

[11] Camus, *The Plague*, 182.

[12] Camus, *The Plague*, 73. The narrative itself reflects the transformed temporal focus by gradually shifting from calendrical dating to vaguer temporal references that are yoked specifically to the quarantine period.

[13] Camus, *The Plague*, 183.

[14] Kellman, *The Plague*, 80. Kellman observes that "Camus projects a world of solitary men," and this underscores the isolation that typifies life during the plague. This may account for the virtual absence of women in the novel, though not for the other absences that Kellman points out, those of Arabs and Jews. See Kellman, *The Plague*, 76–79.

GRIEF AND HUMAN CONNECTION IN *THE PLAGUE*   107

anyone.[15] Although the fictional Oran does not adopt some of the policies that have been established in some places to ensure social distancing during the Covid-19 pandemic (such as the shutdown of inside dining in restaurants and the cancellation of musical performances), the awareness that anyone could be infected, separation from loved ones, and restrictions on funerals are all aspects of the current situation.

In Camus's Oran, communication is severely curtailed. Letters are banned and contact with the outside world reduced to telegrams. This is unlike the situation during the Covid-19 pandemic, and this difference reflects the fact that the fictional plague is contained within the city, while the Covid-19 is ubiquitous. More comparable to recent experience, however, is the fact that so many restrictions on ordinary life leave Oran's people with little to talk about. Conversation is reduced mostly to comments about general topics in trite, conventional terms.[16] We might compare our experience during the Covid-19 pandemic, when despite technology that allows us to chat with distant loved ones, many of us find ourselves at a loss when conversing, feeling that we have little of interest to say.

In the novel, protest against the standardization and depersonalization of life in plague conditions flares up from time to time. Raymond Rambert, a visiting journalist, argues that he is inappropriately trapped in the city walls because he is an outsider, and he ineffectually insists that he should be allowed to leave. Family members often resist when plague victims are removed to isolation units. Their objections are similarly fruitless, but they demonstrate that people become angry when they perceive that a beloved person is treated anonymously, as just another biohazard. The restrictions

---

[15] Camus, *The Plague*, 115.

[16] Some of the central characters in the novel, it should be noted, do not limit their conversation so extremely, and many engage in personal conversations of some length, a fact that will be further noted. But such conversations often take the participants by surprise; they sometimes "find themselves" confiding in someone without planning to do so. Even then, the necessities of the time are always pressing, and such conversations are temporary respites from the routine, no longer regular occurrences in daily life.

108 CAMUS'S *THE PLAGUE*

on funerals are also met with widespread outrage, although policies do not change as a result.

The resistance to health measures among the people in the novel differs in many respects from that which has arisen in the Covid-19 period. In addition to opposition to policies that separate people from their loved ones, subject patients to standardized policies, and limit funerals, hostility has also been directed at perceived restrictions on personal liberties, particularly in the United States. Even requirements to wear face masks have been interpreted as infringements on civil rights. Some of those in office have also resisted establishing policies recommended by health experts. The issue of whether to close or restrict the operation of certain businesses has been contentious, not only because of the constraints mandated closings impose on personal freedoms but because of the economic harms that result.

Camus's novel does not provide much of a mirror for either the economic hardships of our pandemic or the racial inequality it has exposed. Although Rieux reports some business closures and notes the establishment of rationing policies, the economic fallout of the city's quarantine is not a major focus. Nor does the novel take up the theme of differential impact of the epidemic on various subgroups within the population. *The Plague* has often been criticized for concentrating on male, Christian characters of French ethnicity, ignoring the Arabic, Amazigh (or Berber), and Jewish populations of Oran and giving only cameo appearances to women.[17] The book also does not depict organized efforts to challenge the imposition of quarantine restrictions (albeit a criminal syndicate of smugglers is organized in circumventing them).

Perhaps we find the closest similarity to recent resistance to health measures in the attitude of Rambert, who for much of the novel considers himself an exception to whom the general policies should not apply. He seems quite willing to flout the law, and he

[17] See, for example, Kellman, *The Plague*, 76–79.

GRIEF AND HUMAN CONNECTION IN *THE PLAGUE*   109

exerts considerable effort to find an illegal means to exit the city after he fails to persuade authorities to allow him to leave. Camus presents him as having a change of heart, however, of a sort that is probably unlikely among those who feel that to wear a facemask would be to renounce an important part of their political identity. If Camus's novel speaks to this outlook, it does so by presenting an alternative attitude toward personal freedom, one in which a sense of personal efficacy is sustained through a pandemic by enlisting in collective efforts to fight the plague. But before considering this alternative, let us further analyze the symptoms evident in the fictional Oran and in the actual world in the context of Covid-19.

Oran's Experience and Grief

The psychological response that typifies plague-ridden Oran, in summary, involves incredulity, feelings of exile that encourage dwelling on what has been lost, an abnormal sense of temporality, apathy and despair, the loss of personal meaning, outrage at the anonymity of the official world's procedures, a sense of isolation, and an incapacity to communicate. This profile corresponds to the symptomatology associated with grief. Taking bereavement as the paradigmatic case for grief, we find a similar pattern of symptoms: incredulity, brooding over the loss, temporal disorientation, apathy and despair, feelings of emptiness, outrage at the world's carrying on as usual, an acute sense of disconnection with other people, and a felt inability to communicate.

Disbelief of sorts is typical in bereavement, though perhaps we should describe this as an incapacity to assimilate the loss. Elisabeth Kübler-Ross and David Kessler interpret the comment "I can't believe it" in this context to mean that the fact of the death is "too much" for the psyche of the speaker.[18] Matthew Ratcliffe proposes

---

[18] Kübler-Ross and Kessler, *On Grief and Grieving*, 8.

110   CAMUS'S *THE PLAGUE*

that even though one is cognitively aware of the death, one is still relying on a framework of habits and expectations that depend to some extent on the lost loved one.[19] Saying "I can't believe it!" is to confess an inability to internalize the actuality.

The state of stunned incredulity gives way to an overwhelming tendency to brood on one's separation from the loved one. Memories of the deceased arise spontaneously, much as memories of those absent accost those who are suddenly sequestered in *The Plague*. The felt importance of being connected with the person makes one reluctant to undertake activities that might distract one's attention.

Temporality is also transformed by bereavement. Poet Denise Riley describes her condition after the death of her son as that of "living in suddenly arrested time: that acute sensation of being cut off from any temporal flow."[20] Philosopher and psychiatrist Thomas Fuchs analyzes such feelings of temporal stasis as stemming from the dissociation of the time of the social world, which flows on, and the "dyadic time" that was shared with the deceased. Speaking of circumstances in which the external world seems to operate normally, Fuchs points out that the bereaved person recognizes the contrast between social temporality, which flows into the future, and the "dyadic" temporality of time shared in relationship with the lost loved one, a temporality that continues to be experienced and preserves a sense of the deceased person's presence. A sense of motionless time results. Although this arises spontaneously, the bereaved willingly linger in it, resisting any activity that is future-oriented or involves "taking part in the ongoing life of others."[21]

In this situation apathy takes hold. "With the standstill of time," observes Fuchs, "the future is no longer experienced as an open field of possibilities and projects."[22] The sorts of concerns that previously seemed meaningful no longer yield a sense of purpose,

---

[19] See Ratcliffe, "Relating to the Dead," 207.
[20] Riley, *Time Lived*, 13.
[21] Fuchs, "Presence in Absence," 49–51.
[22] Fuchs, "Presence in Absence," 51.

GRIEF AND HUMAN CONNECTION IN *THE PLAGUE* 111

for the meaning one hitherto took them to have was premised on projecting oneself toward an anticipated future that importantly included the loved one. Nothing seems worth caring about, and one's life seems empty and aimless.[23]

Outrage at the social world's obliviousness with respect to one's loss is commonplace in bereavement.[24] Anthropologist Renato Rosaldo describes the intensity of his own rage after the accidental death of his wife, sometimes directed at the disinterested people he dealt with, such as "a life insurance agent who refused to recognize Michelle's death as job-related."[25] The impression that others are behaving routinely, without consideration of one's personal loss, is perceived as intolerable.[26]

Dissociation from the shared, flowing time of the social world, indifference toward any prospect of participating in "the ongoing life of others," and experiences of rage directed outward all contribute to a sense of isolation. This is exacerbated by a felt communicative gap between oneself and other people. One can't really convey what one is feeling, a point Riley makes in connection with the experience of temporal stasis: "Your very *will to tell* your violently novel state of timelessness is sapped, because you sense that your most determined efforts can't reach others."[27] One's experience is simply too abnormal to seem verbalizable.

Initial incredulity, absorption with the loss, disconnection from temporal flow, apathy and despair, loss of any sense of meaning, fury at anonymizing routines, communicative incapacity, and a general disconnection from other people—these tendencies of grief abound in Camus's novel. And this should not surprise us, for the people of Oran are grieving. Many are literally bereaved and

---

[23] Cf. Auden, "Stop All the Clocks," 141.
[24] See Kübler-Ross and Kessler, *On Grief and Grieving*, 12–13, 16.
[25] Rosaldo, "Grief and a Headhunter's Rage," 10.
[26] My thanks to Steven Feld (personal communication) for suggesting this interpretation of anger in grief.
[27] Riley, *Time Lived*, 65.

112 CAMUS'S *THE PLAGUE*

grieve family members. Many also mourn in connection with distant loved ones, fearing their relationships may not survive the separation. In general, people are grieving the loss of their previous lives, uncertain as to when and if they will ever resume. Unlike the bereaved in usual times, they do not experience their temporally static condition as in contrast with the flow of social time for those around them, but they are alienated from social time as they previously knew it, and the town's common condition of temporal dislocation does not bring people together.

Besides grieving such evident losses, the townspeople also suffer from anticipatory grief over losses yet to come. Family members know that they and their loved ones could fall ill at any moment, and in light of the isolation policies, diagnosis alone might mean they will never see their relatives again. Each death portends the possibility of others. Thus, Rieux responds to the death of his friend Tarrou by reflecting on the prospect of death parting him and his mother. Each death also preempts envisioned futures, inspiring further grief, as we see when Rieux mourns both his friend and the loss of a future in which their friendship would have "time to enter fully into the life of either."[28]

Widespread grief has been noted in connection with the Covid-19 pandemic. Many have lost loved ones, and the pandemic has taken a toll on relationships and material well-being for many more. Therapist Lori Gottlieb draws attention also to "the smaller losses that also affect our emotional health," such as "missed graduations and proms, canceled sports seasons and performances, postponed weddings and vacations, separation from family and friends when we need them most," as well as "the predictability that we take for granted in daily life."[29]

Like Gottlieb, Kessler does not hesitate to employ the term "collective grief." He claims, "We are grieving on a micro and a macro

---

[28] Camus, *The Plague*, 291.
[29] Gottlieb, "Grieving the Losses of the Coronavirus."

GRIEF AND HUMAN CONNECTION IN *THE PLAGUE*   113

level" in relation to "the loss of normalcy; the fear of economic toll; the loss of connection." Kessler also points out that anticipatory grief contributes enormously to the stress of the pandemic: "With a virus, . . . our primitive mind knows something bad is happening, but you can't see it. This breaks our sense of safety."[30]

Louise Richardson and colleagues analyze responses to the pandemic in terms of grief, noting that lockdown has resulted for many in the loss of their "assumptive world," much as does the loss of a loved one. "One's system of core assumptions about how the world is" has taken a blow, and one's habits do not match the world as it currently presents itself. "Unlike the case of bereavement, there is not a loss of a single concrete thing around which their assumptions about the future coalesce. But the upshot might be the same: a future that has become unimaginable and 'dark.' "[31]

The Impasse of Grief and Its Resolution

To heal psychologically, Oran's citizens need to overcome an impasse, one that typifies grief. We have noted how it typically manifests in bereavement: one feels isolated and adrift but resists taking steps toward reconnecting with the social world and engaging in purposeful action. Although Oran's grief is only partially focused on the death of loved ones, by and large, its citizens are stuck, if not in this, then in a comparable impasse. Their desire to preserve a modicum of personal life and meaning has led them to retreat into psychological isolation. Their impasse is a form of the inertial entrapment that is characteristic of grief in general, the abandonment of future-oriented activity. Often this impasse derives, at least partially, from a sense that this would amount to

---

[30] Kessler, interviewed in Berinato, "That Discomfort You're Feeling Is Grief."

[31] Richardson et al., "The Covid-19 Pandemic and the Bounds of Grief." They attribute the use of the term "assumptive world" in this connection to Colin Parkes. See Parkes, "Bereavement as a Psychosocial Transition," 53–65.

114   CAMUS'S *THE PLAGUE*

giving up what remains of personal life and acquiescing to the terms of the alien world in which one now finds oneself.

Notably, one minor character within *The Plague* finds a way to overcome this impasse. M. Othon, a conservative magistrate, is taken to a quarantine camp when his son Jacques falls ill. This has the merciful consequence that he does not witness his son's prolonged and heart-rending death struggle, but he is inadvertently kept in the camp much longer than policy dictates. He writes to Rieux, who facilitates his release, and afterward Othon calls on the doctor. Rieux is amazed when the magistrate informs him that he is returning to the camp, this time as a volunteer worker. "It would keep me busy, you see," Othon explains. "And also—I know it may sound absurd, but I'd feel less separated from my little boy."[32]

Othon's response is in keeping with what phenomenologists and psychologists see as the optimal way of resolving the impasse bereavement involves. If one develops an internalized impression of the deceased, this can serve as a basis for maintaining the relationship while one moves forward in one's life. Psychologist Nigel Field observes that adjusting to the death of a loved one can be expedited through "awareness of the continuing positive influence of the deceased on the individual's current life through an internalization of what has been gained in the past relationship, including identification with the deceased person's values and ideals." Such awareness can accompany the bereaved in the course of their activities going forward, as happens when one refers to the deceased as "an important reference point when making important autonomy-promoting decisions."[33] More broadly, suggests psychologist Nico Frijda, one can assimilate "one's recollections or recreations of the lost person's mode of being and way of viewing things," adding them to one's own repertoire, and this "may enrich . . . one's fund of modes of experiencing."[34]

---

[32] Camus, *The Plague*, 259.
[33] Field, "Whether to Relinquish," 118. Field draws on the work of Therese A. Rando in *Treatment of Complicated Grief.*
[34] Frijda, *The Laws of Emotion*, 299.

GRIEF AND HUMAN CONNECTION IN *THE PLAGUE* 115

Of course, the construction of such an internalized representation involves a process that is neither quick nor entirely voluntary, and resolution of the impasse of grief will take a somewhat different form in cases of loss not involving bereavement. Nevertheless, Othon's behavior suggests a way of approaching forward-directed action in these other cases as well. The magistrate assumes a role in helping to ameliorate the harmful effects of the plague, and this connects him with the larger world and future-directed projects while preserving and honoring his relationship with his son. In cases not involving bereavement, we can analogously carry what was of value in our previous life forward into unfamiliar circumstances in which loss is palpable. Drawing on the repertoire learned in relation to people one is missing and repurposing aspects of one's activities in more normal times might be comparable to ways of making absent loved ones present and giving present activity both meaning and continuity with what one takes to be one's life.

Camus's Existentialist Perspective

The way Othon finds to act in solidarity with others in fighting the plague grows directly out of his personal attachments and offers him a basis for finding meaning in his continuing life. While the novel acknowledges the potential for conflict between the motivations of personal happiness and felt obligation, it also suggests that happiness and obligation are not in essential conflict.[35] Doing "what needs to be done," it suggests, can be the best way to nurture the personal and to find meaning in challenging circumstances. This is in keeping with Camus's broader existentialist vision and its emphasis on personal meaning through solidarity.

---

[35] Indeed, happiness is one of Camus's basic ethical values. Cf. Solomon, *Dark Feelings*, 127–128. Kellman observes, however, that happiness, though praised as a goal, is largely absent from Camus's *The Plague*. See Kellman, *The Plague*, 84–85.

116 CAMUS'S *THE PLAGUE*

Although he rejected the label, Camus is commonly considered an existentialist, for he joins others so identified in emphasizing concrete human circumstances and in denying that reality is rationally penetrable or cosmically just. Camus contends that as human beings we inevitably want to make sense of the world and to be convinced that it is governed by a moral order, but these desires are inevitably frustrated. The world is "absurd," meaning that it is devoid of intrinsic meaning and does not operate in accordance with our demands for rational order and justice. We should recognize this fact, yet we should also resist the temptation to capitulate to absurdity. We can create meaning in our lives by being as conscious as possible and by struggling against what is inhumane, senseless, and unjust within our world. To embrace this struggle is an act of individual will, but once we have made it, we will be led to the recognition that one shares one's situation with all other human beings. If one rebels against the inhuman and inhumane aspects of our world, one sees "that human reality, in its entirety, suffers from the distance which separates it from the rest of the universe. The malady experienced by a single man becomes a mass plague. In our daily trials, rebellion plays the same role as does the *"cogito"* in the realm of thought . . . I rebel—therefore we exist."[36] To rebel against the inhuman and inhumane is to recognize our common plight, and to make any headway in one's struggles, one must seek solidarity with other people. Solidarity is our best hope for finding meaning and having any impact in fighting whatever assaults our humanity.[37]

Camus's vision of reality acknowledges grief as intrinsic to the human condition. Even in the unlikely circumstance that one never experiences the loss of a loved one, one's desire to make sense of

---

[36] Camus, *The Rebel*, 22.

[37] Strictly speaking, an emphasis on solidarity is not evident in Camus's earliest work, but by the time he writes *The Plague*, it has become central to his outlook. For a discussion of this theme in Camus's later work, see Sherman, *Camus*, 106–135. Sherman draws attention to a pertinent line from Camus's *Letters to a German Friend*, "Fourth Letter," 28: "I merely wanted men to rediscover solidarity in order to wage war against their revolting fate."

GRIEF AND HUMAN CONNECTION IN *THE PLAGUE* 117

the world and to see the complete triumph of goodness will never be achieved, and one has cause to grieve over one's incapacity to make things otherwise. Nevertheless, Camus's vision is affirmative. Enlisting with others in efforts to make the world more humane is a way of finding meaning in life, and this is so even when one adopts the dispassionate realism Camus encourages.

The Plague concretizes Camus's proposed way of approaching our lives, not only illustrating the form solidarity might take when combatting a situation in which people unfairly suffer, but showing the way it might emerge through experiential trajectories of a deeply personal nature. The characters who recognize the need for solidarity do not reach this conclusion because they are persuaded by reasoning. Instead, their realization emerges from experiences (including grief) that galvanize their sense of concern and love for real human beings.[38]

Routes to Solidarity

As a physician, Rieux's working to combat the disease is not the result of a new decision. Although he is reluctant to acknowledge the disturbing diagnosis, once he does, he recognizes that he is one of those on the front line of providing medical care to those who need it. His medical vocation is directed at relieving suffering, and he knows that with such a dangerous, infectious disease, collective efforts are essential if the city is not to be decimated. He admires

---

[38] The novel's emphasis on caring response over abstract theorizing is in keeping with a sense of priorities that is also evident in Camus's criticism of some of his fellow leftists whom he saw as more impressed by ideological commitments than by particular human beings. This may be a fair characterization of one of the grounds for his conflict with Sartre. Sartre was more optimistic than Camus about the promise of revolution to deliver a world that is more just, and he saw violence in pursuit of this end as sometimes justified. Camus contended that even if a just social order were attainable, it could not be built on a fundamental injustice, and any ideology or system claiming the right to kill human beings is unjust, no matter the nobility of its aims. The reader of *The Plague* will recognize Tarrou as a spokesperson for this position.

118   CAMUS'S *THE PLAGUE*

those who come together to assist in fighting the disease, but he sees them as having recognized that this is "the only thing to do" under the circumstances.

Tarrou, a visitor to Oran who has been marooned by the epidemic, joins the fight against the disease when he sees that officials are overwhelmed, and that the situation is nearly out of control. He has talent as an organizer, which he uses to form "sanitary squads" of volunteers who do what needs to be done to support physicians' efforts. Tarrou also joins in this supportive work himself. When Rieux asks him why he got involved, Tarrou refers to his "code of morals," which he says is simply "comprehension,"[39] the same kind that he experienced when he realized that the whole social order condoned and committed the murder of human beings through capital punishment.[40] Having committed himself to working to end the death penalty, he was dedicated to fighting what would bring death to anyone, and for this reason, he knew that he had to work at Rieux's side.

Very different reasoning inspires Rambert to join efforts to fight the plague. A romantic, his ideal is to live and die for love, and as we have already considered, he seeks to leave the town, for he wants to rejoin his distant love, who is elsewhere. He reconsiders only when Tarrou mentions to him that Dr. Rieux himself has been separated from his wife, who had gone to a distant sanitorium for cancer treatment shortly before the epidemic began. The following day Rambert volunteers to work alongside the doctor temporarily. Later, a realistic escape plan becomes available, but Rambert decides not to leave the city. In explanation he says he would feel ashamed if he escaped and this would poison his relationship with his partner back in Paris. He adds, "Now that I've seen what I have seen, I know that I belong here whether I want it or not. This business is everybody's business."[41] Although he expresses himself in

---

[39] Camus, *The Plague*, 130.
[40] Camus, *The Plague*, 248.
[41] Camus, *The Plague*, 209–210.

GRIEF AND HUMAN CONNECTION IN *THE PLAGUE* 119

general terms, his change of heart seems prompted by his coming to see the doctor in a personal light. The awareness that his separation from a loved one is not unique enables him to see himself as being a part of the same situation as others.

Joseph Grand is an elderly civil servant whose work includes compiling statistics. His work in resisting the plague grows out of his occupational role. At first he regularly delivers the latest statistics to the doctor. Later he becomes "a sort of general secretary to the sanitary squads," amassing, analyzing, and graphing statistics as the epidemic progresses. The narrator sees him as a hero, albeit an "insignificant and obscure" one, because he "embodied the quiet courage that inspired the sanitary groups" and was motivated simply by "goodness of heart."[42]

A far more flamboyant character is Father Paneloux, a Jesuit priest. Although he preaches vehement sermons about the plague as collective punishment and the need to accept God's will, he is tireless in his efforts on behalf of those taken ill. We first meet him offering an arm to help an unwell man, who proves to be the novel's first plague victim. He subsequently joins Rieux and his team in their efforts, and he offers to take over Rambert's work when the latter appears on the brink of leaving town.

Paneloux is the spokesperson in the novel for a view that Camus fiercely opposes—that such maladies as the plague are collective punishment and part of God's beneficent plan. Nevertheless, Camus portrays him sympathetically. Rieux articulates what seems to be Camus's view of this character when he says that whatever the tone of his sermons, Paneloux's real motivation is concern for the suffering. Although he struggles with how to understand the plague in light of his religious worldview, he does not allow his theological worries to interfere with his offering help to those who need him. Rieux articulates what seems to be Camus's view of this character when he says that whatever the tone of his sermons, Paneloux's real

[42] Camus, *The Plague*, 133, 137, and 134.

120 CAMUS'S *THE PLAGUE*

motivation is concern for those who suffer. Paneloux does deny himself medical care when he falls fatally ill himself, on the ground that seeing a doctor's care would be inconsistent with his belief that he should acquiesce to God's will, but his religious views take precedence over his compassion only in the case of the one person whose suffering he does not recognize—himself.

Only one of the central characters in the novel is never moved to fight the plague. This character is Cottard, a secretive profiteer and smuggler, whom we first meet after he has made a suicide attempt. This (perhaps half-hearted) effort to sever his connection from the human community attests to his psychological alienation from others. Throughout the novel, he is unsympathetic to those who are suffering. "The plague suits me quite well," he remarks, "and I see no reason why I should bother about trying to stop it."[43] The plague is good for his smuggling business, and since he is terrified of arrest, he is glad when the authorities become preoccupied with the epidemic. Tarrou is convinced that even this misanthrope longs for human connection, writing in his journal that Cottard feels good during the epidemic because "he's in it *with the others*."[44] Sharing the situation with others may be a comfort to Cottard, yet one that is short-lived. When the epidemic ends and the rest of the town celebrates, he gets a gun and starts shooting randomly, ensuring that he will finally be visited by the fate he so greatly fears, his arrest. The last we see of this man with "an ignorant, that is to say lonely, heart" is his being hauled off by the authorities.[45]

Apart from Cottard, the main characters all devote themselves to working together, and each does so on the basis of his own experiences and considerations. While their collective efforts are insufficient to halt the plague in its tracks, they mitigate its damage, and by doing so help to heal themselves. Exhausting as it is, their work does not compete with their ability to seek personal meaning. Instead, it is only

[43] Camus, *The Plague*, 158.
[44] Camus, *The Plague*, 195.
[45] Camus, *The Plague*, 302.

GRIEF AND HUMAN CONNECTION IN *THE PLAGUE*   121

when they pursue joint efforts that they are again able to function as full persons, countering the plague's injurious effect on their capacity to feel and their ability to sustain relationships of love and friendship.[46]

These characters develop interpersonal bonds in the course of working together, as becomes evident in the scenes where they confide in each other, sometimes to their own surprise. Grand unburdens himself to Tarrou and the doctor; Tarrou tells Rieux about his background and his moment of truth; Rieux feels an impulse to confide in Tarrou, and at one point he finds himself telling Grand about his wife. Even Paneloux and the doctor share their personal outlooks on what is important in their work after the death of Othon's son, each endeavoring to be understood by the other.

The nurturing of personal relationships through the work is most evident in the case of Rieux. Although he reports that the plague damaged everyone's capacity for feeling, we see his capacity for friendship and love becoming more fully actualized as the novel develops. Early on, when the doctor refuses to give Rambert a certificate that states that he does not have the plague, Rambert complains that Rieux is living "in a world of abstractions,"[47] in which he sees only the reasons why such a document would be an absurdity and fails to recognize the needs of the heart. While the doctor resists this accusation, he recognizes that "a bleak indifference" is "steadily gaining on him." He sees it as a means of coping with "the almost unendurable burden of his days," but he recognizes that his abstraction is a symptom.[48] As readers, we are aware that he is also enduring a separation from his wife, and his failure to bring this into focus is perhaps evidence of his being emotionally numb.

Even at that point, Rieux's abstraction is not total. Although he numbs himself when he arranges for sick people to be isolated against

---

[46] Cf. Kellman, *The Plague*, 29. Kellman argues that Rieux (along with Rambert, Tarrou, and Paneloux) all "develop as social beings during the plague."

[47] Camus, *The Plague*, 87. Cf. Kellman, *The Plague*, 101–106. Kellman suggests that the book is aimed at resisting the kind of abstraction that typifies allegorical reading: "If the book is indeed an allegory, it is in a sense an allegory against allegorization."

[48] Camus, *The Plague*, 91.

122   CAMUS'S *THE PLAGUE*

the protests of their families, he allows himself "the faint thrill of pity" afterwards.[49] Despite exhaustion, he invests time in friendly interaction, as when he joins Tarrou and Rambert for a drink. He takes an interest in Rambert's progress in trying to circumvent policy, never trying to stop him. The doctor's camaraderie with Tarrou evolves into a friendship for which he takes time, despite the relentless demands of his caseload, even (despite the quarantine) joining him in an illicit late-night swim.[50] And when Tarrou is stricken with the plague, the doctor brings him into his own house to be able to tend to him. Tarrou's death prompts the previously mentioned sorrow that their friendship cannot develop further. In addition, it makes him aware of his great love for his mother (who has joined him in watching over his dying friend) and of his sadness when he realizes that they will never attempt to put their love into words.

Rieux also stands as a representative of those facing personal loss, for he learns of his wife's death shortly before the quarantine is ended. Because the chronicle is written in retrospect, Rieux is already bereaved when he begins his account. Kellman suggests that the disguising of Rieux's identity ensures a "movement from lonely widower to chronicler and back to lonely widower within each separate reading of the novel," a movement which "reenacts the metamorphosis from *solitaire* to *solidaire* so important to Camus."[51] If, as Kellman suggests, each reading reenacts the shift from the solitary to the socially affiliated, this reflects the healing shift in grief from isolation to reconnection with the social world. Kellman describes the end of the novel as offering "the poignant image of a bereaved widower futilely trying to lose himself in the rejoicing mob."[52] While this image draws our attention back to the isolation of bereavement, the novel itself serves as a gesture of reconnection with the social world. Rieux may not easily partake in the joyous

[49] Camus, *The Plague*, 193.
[50] Camus, *The Plague*, 256–257.
[51] Kellman, *The Plague*, 29.
[52] Kellman, *The Plague*, 27.

GRIEF AND HUMAN CONNECTION IN *THE PLAGUE* 123

celebrations of those reunited with their loved ones, but he views their happiness with approval and engages with the larger world in a manner he finds possible—he writes.[53] Writing for him is also a means of memorializing in the wake of loss, and we might see it as his means of healing from grief over the many plague victims treated and the loss of his wife and of Tarrou. His chronicle may also be a means through which Rieux grows through grief, confronting the regrets that are part of his grief over these personal losses.[54]

Rieux concludes his narrative with the reminder that the happiness he sees around him will not be the last word, and plagues will continue to recur. Healers will always be necessary, and so will collective efforts. But to be a healer involves being responsive to actual people, and this requires appreciation of the personal side of life. Rieux's account suggests that when solidarity is combined with cultivation of this personal dimension, the physician can begin to heal him or herself.

Conclusion

Despite the differences between Camus's plague and ours, his novel is helpful for us in our struggles to cope with the Covid-19 pandemic. The historically grounded account of the psychological impact of the fictional plague in Oran offers encouragement

---

[53] See Camus, *The Plague*, 300–301, 308. Rieux claims that he wrote the account to bear witness on behalf of all the plague-stricken, recognizing that his personal sufferings were not unique to him. He observes "that in a world where sorrow is often so lonely, this was an advantage" (302). For discussion of the many characters devoted to some form of writing, see Smith, "What Dies in the Street," 199. See also Solomon, *Dark Feelings*, 123.

[54] In keeping with Kellman's observation that Rieux has grown as a social being during the epidemic, we might see the doctor's regretful reflections in his grief on his own failures in his relationships as testimony to his having developed a fuller emotional capacity than was evident earlier in the novel. Even his sorrow at having counted "overmuch on time" to build the solid bond with his wife that had not yet materialized demonstrates an emotional awareness that presumably had been lacking earlier in their marriage, given that at their parting, both had promised "a new start" when they were reunited (Camus, *The Plague*, 300 and 310).

124   CAMUS'S *THE PLAGUE*

by suggesting that our current experiences are not entirely unprecedented. It may also help us to understand our current emotional condition by pinpointing some of its features, which taken together suggest the profile of grief. In depicting characters who each find a measure of personal meaning during an epidemic, Camus recommends solidarity in endeavoring to improve things as a means for overcoming the sense of purposelessness and isolation that afflict the grief-stricken, whether they are reeling from the loss of loved ones, their former way of living, or both. His portrayal of collective efforts as beneficial to those who are overwhelmed by adverse circumstances may even help us to understand one of the appeals of partisanship during the pandemic, in that it involves joining with others in efforts one considers worthwhile, even if they may not be beneficial for controlling the pandemic and its harmful effects. Finally, Camus's novel encourages a charitable view of other people at a time when our nerves are frayed and our patience overtaxed. At the end of the novel, Dr. Rieux says that he has written his chronicle both as a memorial to those who died "and to state quite simply what we learn in time of pestilence: that there are more things to admire in men than to despise."[55] Camus's novel primes us to see with greater compassion, and if it accomplishes only that, it has given us a lot.

Works Cited

Auden, W. H. "Stop All the Clocks" ["Funeral Blues"] (1936). In *Collected Poems*, edited by Edward Mendelson, 141. New York: Random House, 1991.
Berinato, Scott. "That Discomfort You're Feeling Is Grief." *Harvard Business Review*, March 23, 2020. https://hbr.org/2020/03/that-discomfort-youre-feeling-is-grief.

---

[55] Camus, *The Plague*, 308.

GRIEF AND HUMAN CONNECTION IN *THE PLAGUE* 125

Camus, Albert. "Letter to Roland Barthes on *The Plague*." In *Lyrical and Critical Essays*, translated by Ellen Conroy Kennedy, 338–341. New York: Vintage Books, 1970.

Camus, Albert. *Letters to a German Friend, in Resistance, Rebellion, and Death.* Translated by Justin O'Brien. New York: Vintage Books, 1989.

Camus, Albert. *The Plague.* Translated by Stuart Gilbert. New York: Vintage, 1991.

Camus, Albert. *The Rebel: An Essay on Man in Revolt.* Translated by Anthony Bower. Revised edition. New York: Alfred A. Knopf, 1956.

Field, Nigel P. "Whether to Relinquish or Maintain a Bond with the Deceased." In *Handbook of Bereavement Research and Practice: Advances in Theory and Intervention*, edited by M. S. Stroebe, R. O. Hansson, H. Schut, and W. Stroebe, 113–132. Washington, DC: American Psychological Association, 2008.

Frijda, Nico H. *The Laws of Emotion.* Mahwah, NJ: Lawrence Erlbaum, 2007.

Fuchs, Thomas. "Presence in Absence: The Ambiguous Phenomenology of Grief." *Phenomenology and the Cognitive Sciences* 17, no. 1 (2018): 43–63.

Gottlieb, Lori. "Grieving the Losses of the Coronavirus." *The New York Times*, March 23, 2020. https://www.nytimes.com/2020/03/23/well/family/coronavirus-grief-loss.html.

Kellman, Steven G. *The Plague: Fiction and Resistance.* New York: Twayne, 1993.

Kübler-Ross, Elisabeth, and David Kessler. *On Grief and Grieving: Finding the Meaning of Grief through the Five Stages of Loss.* New York: Scribner, 2005.

Parkes, Colin. "Bereavement as a Psychosocial Transition: Processes of Adaptation to Change." *Journal of Social Issues* 44, no. 3 (1988): 53–65.

Rando, Therese A. *Treatment of Complicated Grief.* Champaign, IL: Research Press, 1993.

Ratcliffe, Matthew. "Relating to the Dead: Social Cognition and the Phenomenology of Grief." In *Phenomenology of Sociality: Discovering the "We,"* edited by Thomas Szanto and Dermot Moran, 202–215. London: Routledge, 2016.

Richardson, Louise, Matthew Ratcliffe, Becky Millar, and Eleanor Byrne. "The Covid-19 Pandemic and the Bounds of Grief." *Think* 20, no. 57 (Spring 2021): 89–101.

Riley, Denise. *Time Lived, Without Its Flow.* Revised edition. London: Picador, 2019.

Rosaldo, Renato. "Grief and a Headhunter's Rage." In *Culture and Truth: The Remaking of Social Analysis*, 1–21. Boston: Beacon Press, 1993.

Sherman, David. *Camus.* Malden, MA: Wiley-Blackwell, 2009.

Smith, Marc. "What Dies in the Street." *French Forum* 41, no. 3 (2016): 193–208.

Solomon, Robert C. *Dark Feelings, Grim Thoughts: Experience and Reflection in Camus and Sartre.* New York: Oxford University Press, 2006.

6. Paul Fürst, Copper Engraving of Doctor Schnabel / Dr. Beak, a plague doctor in seventeenth century. Rome, circa 1656, print. Alamy Stock Photo.

5

Examining the Narrative Devolution of the Physician in Camus's *The Plague*

Edward B. Weiser

Albert Camus's Nobel Prize–winning novel, *The Plague*, inserts the reader into the life of residents in the small city of Oran in northern Algeria sometime in the mid-1940s. While many notions for analyzing Camus's work exist, *The Plague* highlights medicine more than any other topic and is a story told, as we learn late in the work, through the eyes of the central character, Dr. Bernard Rieux, a local general practice physician.[1] Unlike many medical narratives which incorporate the thoughts and emotions of patients (in this case, citizens stricken by *Yersinia pestis*, the causative bacteria of the historically infamous bubonic, septicemic, and pneumonic transmitted plague), this narrative is told completely through the eyes of a physician. To compare the fictional events Camus has created with contemporary factual occurrences during the Covid-19 pandemic, reference is best made to observations and descriptions that come from the physicians battling the twenty-first-century virally mediated Covid-19 public health crisis. The similarities are substantial and equally frightening—the commonality is the presence of widespread illness and death that grips a society. In Camus's case this was a single city: now we face worldwide misery that will not likely

---

[1] Camus, *The Plague*, 301.

Camus's The Plague. Peg Brand Weiser, Oxford University Press. © Oxford University Press 2023.
DOI: 10.1093/oso/9780197599327.003.0006

128 CAMUS'S *THE PLAGUE*

fade spontaneously but require intervention in the form of prevention and mitigation by vaccines, antiviral agents, and advanced public health policies. My comparison is mainly an examination of the effect on the health care providers of the rise and progression of both pandemics and less on how the pandemics ultimately did or will be controlled and (hopefully) conquered. An understanding of the mind of the physicians of both worlds is helpful to the serious student of human pandemic and how changes in modern medicine do little to modify the reaction of a physician faced with overwhelming and seemingly uncontrollable communicable disease.

I will argue that any physician, when faced with the responsibility of the care of dying patients for whom he can do little, will react in much the same way regardless of whether it is "194-" or 2020.[2] Their emotions and despair will seem almost universal by historical comparisons. Bizarre and unrealistic therapies will appear and flourish until truly effective mitigations are invented. The solution to Covid-19 will come from the enormously powerful research that can understand the genetics and epidemiology of this infectious agent. This will provide the relief that came to Oran as plaque regressed into the shadows of human cities and their rat cohabitants. But until these truly effective paths to control Covid-19 emerge, physicians now will react and ultimately devolve as medical personnel have always done until real therapies are found.

Patients of the twenty-first century have become accustomed to efficacious therapies for an entire host of conditions that might affect a human being. What of those conditions for which we have no immediate answers? If those illnesses are sporadic and isolated, physicians are generally not reasonably expected to be forthright with effective answers. When the illnesses are common, easily communicated, and often deadly, the absence of worthwhile treatments turns physicians from a source of relief and comfort to helpless documentarians of the extent of human misery. Counting

---

[2] Camus, *The Plague*, 3.

THE NARRATIVE DEVOLUTION OF THE PHYSICIAN   129

the dead and dying is not a role that physicians easily accept as their primary duty. While providing comfort to relieve respiratory distress and other related symptoms is an important function in care of the Covid-19 patient, it is a poor substitute for other aspects of the role of the contemporary physician who has grown accustomed to not only relief of symptoms but also of long-term control of disease, if not outright cure. This alteration to the physician role is a counterintuitive progression of medical capabilities—it is an unwelcome evolution in medicine—a *de*-volution of major proportions. The proportion of medical resources devoted to the care of Covid-19 patients is enormous and without precedent in the developed world. The effect of this change in how physicians self-describe is profound and disturbing. How the mind of the physician is changed by recent events and who, in the future, elects for a career in medicine may well never return to the pre-Covid-19 "normal."

Did Camus understand this change inflicted by his plague on the mind and spirit of Dr. Rieux? Are Camus's observations an accurate insight into what happens to the caregiver who can do little but count and document the deaths that accumulate? Is there a difference between simply reacting as any human might to the overwhelming numbers of deaths when confronted with a disease for which historically little can be done (like pre-antibiotic plague) and confronting a new disease which seems to run rampant in a way that entire generations of physicians have never experienced but only read about in histories of past pandemic flu-like illnesses?

Doctor Rieux's humanity is well developed in the Camus narrative. His reactions are those of a compassionate caregiver as well as a detached clinician. His despair is mainly for the misery of his patients. Physicians dealing with Covid-19 are overwhelmed not only by the sheer workload that the disease creates but also by what they *cannot* do and to what they have grown accustomed: to control and cure an infectious illness. Of course, Camus could not have predicted these events, but parallels exist in *The Plague* that are a universal lesson for the physician and her seemingly unlimited

130 CAMUS'S *THE PLAGUE*

potential for the cure of *any* human illness. Rather than driving physicians to abandon their life's work, perhaps discarding the developing notion of medical infallibility will be that which the medical profession learns best from Covid-19.

To understand any comparison with the story told by Camus, we need to understand the nature of his plague. Few modern physicians have ever treated a case of plague. As described by the Centers for Disease Control and Prevention:

> Plague is a disease that affects humans and other mammals. It is caused by the bacterium, *Yersinia pestis*. Humans usually get plague after being bitten by a rodent flea that is carrying the plague bacterium or by handling an animal infected with plague. Plague is infamous for killing millions of people in Europe during the Middle Ages. Today, modern antibiotics are effective in treating plague. Without prompt treatment, the disease can cause serious illness or death. Presently, human plague infections continue to occur in rural areas in the western United States, but significantly more cases occur in parts of Africa and Asia.[3]

Most laypersons, as a result of modern communications, are familiar with at least rudimentary facts about Covid-19. Like plague, it is highly contagious. Unlike plague, it does not require an intervening vector like the rodent flea. Covid-19 is caused by a virus, not a bacterium. Consistently effective antivirals currently are only in the development stages. The most likely long-term control will be via prevention of transmission and inoculation. Plague regressed because of reduction in vectors (rats carrying the fleas die from the illness as well as humans) and reduced human-to-human transmission. Inoculation and isolation appear to produce the same effect for Covid-19. Death rates for pandemic plague are higher than that of Covid-19, at least 50 to 60 percent in untreated

---

[3] Centers for Disease Control and Prevention, "Plague," August 6, 2021.

THE NARRATIVE DEVOLUTION OF THE PHYSICIAN 131

populations,[4] at least ten times that of Covid-19, for which the death rate varies from 1 to 9 percent seemingly dependent upon the medical resources of the location where it occurs.[5] Nonetheless, because Covid-19 hospitalization rates are about 14 percent for symptomatic individuals, in the United States almost 500 persons were hospitalized in 2020 per 100,000 population, so that there were a total of about 1,650,000 inpatients with symptomatic Covid-19 infections in 2020.[6] These hospitalizations often last weeks, with many deaths occurring after extreme medical interventions have been expended. This has created an enormous strain on medical resources, including on physicians, nurses, and allied health professions. When a patient dies under these circumstances, in countries around the world, the emotional and professional impact on health care personnel is profound.[7]

Physicians during Covid-19 describe depression leading to suicidal ideation, professional frustration with diminished resources such as personal protective equipment and absent effective therapeutic interventions, and "burnout" leading to premature retirements.[8] Camus's Dr. Rieux, despite similar frustrations, was relieved by the end of the plague epidemic but never expressed leaving the profession or suicide. He hoped for effective therapy but never surrendered to its absence. Perhaps this was related to sample size, but I maintain it was more closely associated with the medical attitudes of the time, that epidemics of this magnitude were widely fatal especially when plague was involved. Rieux, by Camus's account, was resigned during the plague to often be simply a documentarian and dispenser of information but not a therapist.[9]

---

[4] World Health Organization, "WHO Report on Global Surveillance of Epidemic-prone Infectious Diseases," March 23, 2021.

[5] Johns Hopkins Coronavirus Resource Center, "Mortality Analysis," March 24, 2021.

[6] Centers for Disease Control and Prevention, "COVID-NET-Associated Hospitalization Surveillance Network," August 4, 2022.

[7] Suryavanshi et al., "Mental Health and Quality of Life," 12; Subasi et al., "Healthcare Workers' Anxieties," 3; Bettinsoli et al., "Mental Health Conditions," 1063.

[8] Anzaldua and Halperin, "Can Clinical Empathy Survive?" 23.

[9] Camus, *The Plague*, 192–193.

132   CAMUS'S *THE PLAGUE*

Recently, German psychiatrist Moritz Wigand and his coauthors examined the population response to pandemic by comparing three events in history.[10] Their analysis of the descriptions of plague in Athens in 430 BCE described by Thucydides in *The History of the Peloponnesian War*,[11] Giovanni Boccaccio's description of the plague in Florence in 1348 in *The Decameron*,[12] and Camus's *The Plague* is noteworthy for the range of psychosocial reactions typical of such events. Despite these events occurring over nearly two-and-one-half millennia of human history, the consistency of responses is striking. They describe a pattern of phased responses using Camus's work as a template:

> [Responses in *The Plague* included] *denial and disbelief*, "they believed in pestilences" (p. 37); *fear and panic*, "the perplexity of the early days gradually gave place to panic" (p. 23); *acceptance paired with resignation*, "they had adapted themselves to the very condition of the plague" (p. 181); *hope mixed with uncertainty*, "Though this sudden setback of the plague was as welcome as it was unlooked-for, our townsfolk were in no hurry to jubilate" (p. 269); *elation mixed with grief*, "as he listened to the cries of joy rising from the town, Rieux remembered that such joy is always imperiled" (p. 308).[13]

Do Dr. Rieux's observations of the townspeople provide further insight into his own professional adaptations, given his helplessness in providing more than simple psychological support? If we are to believe the interpretation of Camus's portrayal of the practice of medicine in colonial Algeria fostered by Giuliana Lund in her monograph, Rieux is an "ideal witness and diagnostician of social ills."[14]

---

[10] Wigand, Becker and Steger, "Psychosocial Reactions to Plagues," 443.
[11] Thucydides, *History of the Peloponnesian War*, 48.
[12] Usher, "Boccaccio's Ars Moriendi in *The Decameron*," 624.
[13] Wigand, Becker and Steger, "Psychosocial Reactions to Plagues," 443.
[14] Lund, "A Plague of Silence," 135.

THE NARRATIVE DEVOLUTION OF THE PHYSICIAN   133

The implication is that Rieux behaves not as a physician might but simply as an observer. Lund would have us believe that Rieux is not an authentic physician but a literary foil for Camus's narrative to describe the social and political ills of postwar Algeria. Are not physicians caring for patients in a pandemic both clinicians and part of the afflicted population as a whole? The ability of Camus's Dr. Rieux to describe his town populated by persons with reactions and adaptations that Wigand et al. have found elsewhere argues against Rieux as a "non-physician."

There are other authors who have argued that Camus made sufficient clinical mistakes in *The Plague* that the book has limited value for the teaching of, for example, medical ethics, and also brings into question Rieux's identity as an authentic physician. Eric H. Deudon, a professor of French literature with prior medical training in Paris, describes in his monograph, "A Case for Literary Malpractice: The Use of Camus's *The Plague* in American Medical Schools,"[15] a number of clinical errors in *The Plague*, four of which are the "most obvious." Deudon argues that the diagnosis of plague should have been immediately apparent to even the "most careless practitioner." The use of a "serum" described by Camus was unlikely to have been widely successful, but nowhere does Camus suggest that the use of antibiotics could have been effective. Sulfonamide antibiotics, first developed in 1938, had, by the time Camus completed his novel, reduced the mortality of bubonic plague to 9 percent. This would have dramatically reduced mortality and made Camus's characterization of Oran unrealistic as a Black Death city in the Middle Ages. Deudon describes Rieux's reaction to Rambert's decision to escape the quarantine as irresponsible, in that Rieux was obligated to "turn him in to the authorities." Lastly, Deudon criticizes the absence of intervention by Rieux in the agony of the young boy's death as unrealistic and unjustified, given the contemporary agents that could have relieved the pain that the plague had visited on the child.

[15] Deudon, "A Case for Literary Malpractice," 73–79.

134 CAMUS'S *THE PLAGUE*

While Deudon's analysis is clinically correct, the issue becomes not whether Rieux and his contemporaries made medical errors of (mainly) omission but, given Camus's set of medical circumstances (poor understanding of the early manifestations of plague, absent antibiotics, etc.) consistently observed in the novel, were Rieux's reactions and emotions those which were both believable and reasonable for a legitimate clinician to manifest? If so, then whether Camus made glaring clinical errors is not consequential to the literary impact of the narrative. The argument that Deudon advances, that *The Plague* has no place in a medical school curriculum, is not pertinent to the analysis of Rieux as a human reacting to plague in the environment, however artificial and false, that Camus has created. As such, it may still have value for the teaching of the student of pandemics in general.

An overriding theme that multiple medical authors have described from analysis of *The Plague* is that of isolation and suffering. Tuffuor and Payne, in their recent essay, emphasize the importance of social connections in "affirming the patient's identity."[16] These social connections, they further assert, are also of importance to the treating physician. When physicians demonstrate "compassionate fatigue," a form of "emotional burnout," they often react by withdrawal and, as Camus describes,

> It was by such lapses that Rieux could gauge his exhaustion. His sensibility was getting out of hand. Kept under all the time, it had grown hard and brittle and seemed to snap completely now and then, leaving him the prey of his emotions. No resource was left him but to tighten the stranglehold on his feelings and harden his heart protectively. For he knew this was the only way of carrying on.[17]

---

[16] Tuffuor and Payne, "Isolation and Suffering Related to Serious and Terminal Illness," 401.

[17] Camus, *The Plague*, 192.

THE NARRATIVE DEVOLUTION OF THE PHYSICIAN   135

Camus goes on to realign physician Rieux's priorities and capacities for action from a treating clinician to a documentarian.

> In any case he had few illusions left, and fatigue was robbing him of even these remaining few. He knew that, over a period whose end he could not glimpse, his task was no longer to cure but to diagnose. To detect, to see, to describe, to register, and then condemn—that was his present function.[18]

Even religion and appeals to the deity offered Rieux little comfort or strength.

> "After all," the doctor repeated, then hesitated again, fixing his eyes on Tarrou, "it's something that a man of your sort can understand most likely, but, since the order of the world is shaped by death, mightn't it be better for God if we refuse to believe in Him and struggle with all our might against death, without raising our eyes toward the heaven where he sits in silence?"[19]

To Rieux, death was "A never ending defeat."[20]

When Rieux withdraws, argues Abram, he finds relief in diverting his emotional attention to "abstractions."[21] Accused by the journalist Rambert, "You can't understand. You're using the language of reason, not of the heart; you live in a world of abstractions."[22] Rieux's reliance on notions of facts, without emotion, is a transition that Camus chronicles throughout the early phases of the plague. This devolution is no less real for current health care providers in the era of Covid-19. Camus's portrayal of the following scene gives us a sense of the ultimate "indifference" that Rieux used to cope with the avalanche of misery and death.

[18] Camus, *The Plague*, 192.
[19] Camus, *The Plague*, 128.
[20] Camus, *The Plague*, 128.
[21] Abram, "Death and Dying in Camus' *The Plague*," 189.
[22] Camus, *The Plague*, 87.

136 CAMUS'S *THE PLAGUE*

Lifting the coverlet and chemise, he gazed in silence at the red blotches on the girl's thighs and stomach, the swollen ganglia. After one glance the mother broke into shrill, uncontrollable cries of grief. And every evening mothers wailed thus, with a distraught abstraction, as their eyes fell on those fatal stigmata on limbs and bellies; every evening hands gripped Rieux's arm, there as a rush of useless words, promises, and tears; every evening the nearing tocsin of the ambulance provoked scenes as vain as every form of grief. Rieux had nothing to look forward to but a long sequence of such scenes, renewed again and again. Yes, plague, like an abstraction, was monotonous; perhaps only one factor changed, and that was Rieux himself. Standing at the foot of the statue of the Republic that evening, he felt it; all he was conscious of was a bleak indifference steadily gaining on him as he gazed at the door of the hotel Rambert had just entered.[23]

Clearly, this change that comes over Rieux is, one could assert, most familiar to those dealing with an entire ward filled with dying patients afflicted by Covid-19.

The link between isolation and suffering is envisioned by Camus as part of the absurdity of death. While both the *Yersinia* plague and Covid-19 are natural occurrences, the absurdity is manifest, concludes theologian Bentley, in the "effect it has on our experience of life."[24] Both events are associated with narratives that would not be apparent in "normal" times, including prolonged and isolating lockdowns and devastated witness descriptions of the afflicted suffering and dying. Bentley goes on to argue that, despite Rieux's dismissal of God and religion, Rieux's notions of the absurd, ostensibly reflecting those of Camus himself, create a world appreciating the gift of life that "can be exercised responsibly, existentially and in participation with the divine."[25] Despite Bentley's yearning for

---

[23] Camus, *The Plague*, 87.
[24] Bentley, "Reflections on the Characters of Dr Rieux and Fr Paneloux," 6.
[25] Bentley, "Reflections on the Characters of Dr Rieux and Fr Paneloux," 6.

THE NARRATIVE DEVOLUTION OF THE PHYSICIAN   137

an interpretation of Rieux's embracing absurdity as a justification for the existence of a controlling deity, Camus clearly characterizes Rieux as objective and atheistic. Rieux will have no part of notions that rely on God for explanation. Rieux has nowhere to escape but his indifference.

Where is the reader left to understand Dr. Rieux and the ethical and emotional journey that is his plague? Rieux begins his narrative as a combination of humanist and scientist that we envision of any idealized modern physician. By the time that Camus is nearly done, Rieux has become withdrawn, fatigued, cynical, and emotionless. These traits, though negative, have allowed him to persist and function, albeit at a level he laments. At the end of the narrative, however, Rieux emerges with newfound strength and purpose.

> Nonetheless, he knew that the tale he had to tell could not be one of a final victory. It could be only the record of what had had to be done, and what assuredly would have to be done again in the never ending fight against terror and its relentless onslaughts, despite their personal afflictions, by all who, while unable to be saints but refusing to bow down to pestilences, strive their utmost to be healers.[26]

We find ourselves now in the twenty-first century dealing with a new pandemic, Covid-19. What lessons might we see that Camus envisioned and can we expand our understanding of the human patient population now afflicted that includes the contemporary physician?

Adrian Anzaldua and Jodi Halperin examined the notion of "clinical empathy" among health care workers.[27] The concept they describe is based upon their thesis that "burnout begets burnout." Because of the poor clinical conditions seen with the Covid-19

---

[26] Camus, *The Plague*, 308.
[27] Anzaldua and Halperin, "Can Clinical Empathy Survive?" 24.

138 CAMUS'S *THE PLAGUE*

pandemic (reduced patient contact, unavailable personal protective equipment, limited therapeutic modalities, huge case rates, etc.), the behaviors commonly available to prevent burnout often, they assert, cannot be deployed. Clinical empathy depends upon genuine emotional engagement, requiring "the mental freedom to process difficult emotions." The loss of mental freedom forces, they believe, health care personnel to substitute duties not requiring emotional input to substitute for clinical empathy. As empathy wanes, the vicious cycle continues, spiraling down to worsening burnout and eventual withdrawal. Health care workers remain engaged to an injurious workplace as long as they possibly can because, the authors posit, they "tend to identify personally with their professional roles." Further, medical personnel often suffer in virtual silence:

> The virtuous nature of medical professionalism becomes a force that traps workers in clinical environments that undermine their ethical goals, exposes them to psychological injury, and precludes them from striking or protesting.[28]

Camus's Rieux seemed to understand the progressively declining emotional engagement, despite performing those tasks he could still do.

> "Doctor, you'll save him, won't you?" But he wasn't there for saving life; he was there to order a sick man's evacuation. How futile the hatred he saw on faces then! "You haven't a heart!" a woman told him on one occasion. She was wrong; he had one. It saw him through his twenty-hour day, when he hourly watched men dying, who were meant to live. It enabled him to start anew each morning. He had just enough heart for that, as things were now. How could that heart have sufficed for saving life?[29]

---

[28] Anzaldua and Halperin, "Can Clinical Empathy Survive?" 25.
[29] Camus, *The Plague*, 192.

THE NARRATIVE DEVOLUTION OF THE PHYSICIAN   139

Lastly, Anzaldua and Halperin introduce the concept of "malignant virtue." They argue that the basis for medical professional adherence to duty is an internalized sense of virtue ethics.

A virtue-based medical professional ethics can be beneficial save for one notable weakness: internalized virtue cannot be silenced or shed at the end of the day. This means that clinical conditions that violate medical ethical principles directly threaten the health care worker's sense of self. When this happens, virtue ethics morphs into a malignant force.[30]

Malignant virtue, conversely, is the increasing pressure brought to bear by increasing caseloads, reduced staffing, public criticisms, and absent outlets for complaint and resolution. The authors conclude by suggesting that a new professionalism is required to demand concessions from the system as a whole to build upon the need for clinical empathy in a setting of provider well-being. Camus summarizes the role of Rieux at the end of the plague, perhaps predicting the need for such change:

Dr. Rieux resolved to compile this chronicle, so that he should not be one of those who hold their peace but should bear witness in favor of those plague-stricken people; so that some memorial of the injustice and outrage done them might endure; and to state quite simply what we learn in time of pestilence: that there are more things to admire in men than to despise.[31]

While it is valuable to understand the ethical pressures faced by modern health workers in the era of Covid-19, it is unlikely all providers have the internal strength and courage (that Camus's Rieux most certainly manifests) to withstand the professional and

[30] Anzaldua and Halperin, "Can Clinical Empathy Survive?" 25.
[31] Camus, *The Plague*, 308.

140 CAMUS'S *THE PLAGUE*

personal onslaught that overwork and overstress can produce. Many studies have documented health care providers suffering from the same mental health maladies as does the population as a whole. For example, a report from Turkey reports the rise of sexual dysfunction among health care workers.[32] Another report from Pakistan speaks of the level of fear and anxiety among health care workers resembling that of the general population.[33] A collaborative study in the United States among physicians in otolaryngology (ENT) shows burnout levels, anxiety, mental distress, and depression at levels seen at many other levels of society.[34] What all these and other multiple reports would strongly suggest is that health care providers' response to the pandemic is similar to that seen among nonproviders. While there are certain qualitative differences, the conclusions are clear. As editorialized by Dr. Jin Jun and colleagues, mitigating the personal and professional threat posed by Covid-19 will mean providing adequate personal protective equipment (PPE), assuring that staffing levels allow adequate sleep, nutrition, and hydration, and providing access to adequate short- and long-term mental health services.[35] Further, they write, fostering collaboration and team building helps to reduce the isolation and withdrawal that Covid-19 has produced.

Camus's portrayal of Dr. Rieux is admittedly only a limited view of the life of a physician engaged in the frustration of caring for a dying population in a pandemic. Camus does not suggest what could have been handled differently or better; only that Rieux simply survived to tell his story. The allegorical nature of the work may have limited the degree to which Camus wanted to examine the specific challenges faced by health care providers in Algeria. Camus portrays the physician as an unintentionally heroic and

---

[32] Bulut et al., "The Effect of COVID-19 Epidemic," 6–7.
[33] Hassan et al., "The Impact of Covid-19 Pandemic on Mental Well-Being," 1319–1320.
[34] Civantos et al., "Mental Health among Otolaryngology Resident," 1606–1607.
[35] Jun, Tucker, and Melnyk, "Clinician Mental Health and Well-Being," 182–183.

THE NARRATIVE DEVOLUTION OF THE PHYSICIAN   141

noble figure. In a conversation with his friend Tarrou, Rieux listens as he hears of his own role through another's eyes. After describing the two categories of persons as either afflicted or carriers of the plague, Tarrou adds, "I grant we should add a third category: that of the true healers. But it's a fact one doesn't come across many of them, and anyhow it must be a hard vocation."[36] After listening to Tarrou's long analysis of this plague and his aspirations to sainthood and predictions for continued plagues, Rieux responds.

> "Perhaps," the doctor answered. "But, you know, I feel more fellowship with the defeated than with saints. Heroism and sanctity don't really appeal to me, I imagine. What interests me is being a man."[37]

What may be Rieux's most useful observation comes in the last paragraph of the work, where Camus offers caution in the celebration of human victory over deadly disease.

> And, indeed, as he listened to the cries of joy rising from the town, Rieux remembered that such joy is always imperiled. He knew what those jubilant crowds did not know but could have learned from books: that the plague bacillus never dies or disappears for good; that it can lie dormant for years and years in furniture and linen-chests; that it bides its time in bedrooms, cellars, trunks, and bookshelves; and that perhaps the day would come when, for the bane and the enlightening of men, it would rouse up its rats again and send them forth to die in a happy city.[38]

The parallels that can be made from an examination of *The Plague* in the context of the current Covid-19 pandemic are significant and instructive. While furthering a realistic understanding of

---

[36] Camus, *The Plague*, 254.
[37] Camus, *The Plague*, 255.
[38] Camus, *The Plague*, 308.

142 CAMUS'S THE PLAGUE

the nature of pandemics in general, Camus also offers the lessons of resilience and persistence and solidarity. When viewed from a care provider perspective, these demonstrably positive human qualities promote optimism and hope for a future postpandemic world where Covid-19 is but another historical bookmark. Perhaps by understanding this and other "histories" of enveloping and destructive epidemics we will be able to move beyond a microcosmic view of each person's infection and appreciate the global survival of the human species seen after each such event. Pandemics foster fear and sometimes justifiably selfish behavior that we can understand when persons we love perish. Nonetheless, medical care providers have always stood at the forefront to combat the next waiting pandemic. As Camus reminds us, despite their courage, they are human and have human frailties.

Works Cited

Abram, Harry S. "Death and Dying in Camus' *The Plague*." *Life-Threatening Behavior* 3, no. 3 (Fall 1973): 184–190.

Anzaldua, Adrian, and Jodi Halperin. "Can Clinical Empathy Survive? Distress, Burnout, and Malignant Duty in the Age of Covid-19." *Hastings Center Report* 51, no. 1 (January–February 2021): 22–27.

Bentley, Wessel. "Reflections on the Characters of Dr Rieux and Fr Paneloux in Camus' *The Plague* in a Consideration of Human Suffering during the COVID-19 Pandemic." *HTS Teologies Studies/Theological Studies* 76, no. 4 (2020): 1–7.

Bettinsoli, Maria Laura, Jaime L. Napier, Daniela Di Riso, Lorenzo Moretti, Michaelangelo Delmedico, Andrea Piazzolla, Biagio Moretti, and Pierfrancesco Bettinsoli. "Mental Health Conditions of Italian Healthcare Professionals during the COVID-19 Disease Outbreak." *Applied Psychology: Health and Well-Being* 12, no. 4 (2020): 1054–1073.

Boccaccio, Giovanni. *The Decameron*. Translated with an Introduction and Notes by G. H. McWilliam. New York: Penguin Books. 1972.

Bulut, Ender Cem, Kasim Ertas, Dilek Bulut, Murat Yavuz Koparal and Serhat Cetin. "The Effect of COVID-19 Epidemic on the Sexual Function of Healthcare Professionals." *Andrologia* 53 (2021): e13971. doi:10.1111/and.13971.

THE NARRATIVE DEVOLUTION OF THE PHYSICIAN 143

Camus, Albert. *The Plague*. Translated by Stuart Gilbert. New York: Vintage Books. 1991.

Centers for Disease Control and Prevention. "COVID-NET: COVID-19-Associated Hospitalization Surveillance Network Website." Last modified August 4, 2022. https://www.cdc.gov/coronavirus/2019-ncov/covid-data/covid-net/purpose-methods.html.

Centers for Disease Control and Prevention. "Plague." Page last reviewed August 6, 2021. https://www.cdc.gov/plague/index.html.

Civantos, Alyssa, Yasmeen Byrnes, Changgee Chang, Aman Presad, Kevin Chorath, Seerat K. Poonia, Carolyn M. Jenks, *et al.* "Mental Health among Otolaryngology Resident and Attending Physicians during the COVID-19 Pandemic: National Study." *Head & Neck* 42 (2020): 1597–1609. https://doi.org/10.1002/hed.26292.

Deudon, Eric H. "A Case for Literary Malpractice: The Use of Camus's *The Plague* in American Medical Schools." *Linacre Quarterly* (May 1988): 73–80.

Hassan, Nabila, Hina Akmal Memon, Noreen Hassan, Shobaha Luxmi, and Farhat Sultana. "The Impact of Covid-19 Pandemic on Mental Well-Being of Health Care Workers: A Multi-Centre Study." *Journal of Business and Social Review in Emerging Economies* 6, no. 4 (December 2020): 1313–1322.

Johns Hopkins Coronavirus Resource Center. "Mortality Analysis." Last updated September 8, 2022. Baltimore, MD: Johns Hopkins University. https://coronavirus.jhu.edu/data/mortality..

Jun, Jin, Sharon Tucker, and Bernadette Mazurek Melnyk. "Clinician Mental Health and Well-Being During Global Healthcare Crises: Evidence Learned from Prior Epidemics for COVID-19 Pandemic." *Worldview on Evidence-Based Nursing* 17, no. 3 (2020) 182–184.

Lund, Giuliana. "A Plague of Silence: Social Hygiene and the Purification of the Nation in Camus's *La Peste*." *Symposium: A Quarterly Journal in Modern Literatures* 65, no. 2 (2011): 134–157.

Subasi, Damla Ozcevik, Aylin Akca Sumengen, Enes Simsek, and Ayse Ferda Ocakci. "Healthcare Workers Anxieties and Coping Strategies during the COVID-19 Pandemic in Turkey." *Perspectives in Psychiatric Care* 57, no. 4 (2021): 1–9. https://doi.org/10.1111/ppc.12755.

Suryavanshi, Nishi, Abhay Kadam, Gauri Dhumal, Smita Nimkar, Vidya Mave, Amita Gupta, Samyra R. Cox, and Nikhil Gupte. "Mental Health and Quality of Life among Healthcare Professionals during the COVID-19 Pandemic in India." *Brain and Behavior* 10, no. 11 (2020): 1–12. https://doi.org/10.1002/brb3.1837.

Thucydides. *History of the Peloponnesian War*. Translated by Rex Warner. London: Penguin Books, 1972.

Tuffuor, Akosua, and Richard Payne. "Isolation and Suffering Related to Serious and Terminal Illness: Metaphors and Lessons from Albert Camus' Novel, *The Plague*." *Journal of Pain and Symptom Management* 54, no. 3 (September 2017): 400–403.

144 CAMUS'S *THE PLAGUE*

Usher, Jonathan "Boccaccio's Ars Moriendi in *The Decameron*." *The Modern Language Review* 81, no. 3 (1986): 621–632.

Wigand, Moritz E., Thomas Becker, and Florian Steger. "Psychosocial Reactions to Plagues in the Cultural History of Medicine." *The Journal of Nervous and Mental Disease* 208, no. 6 (June 2020): 443–444.

World Health Organization, Department of Communicable Disease Surveillance and Response. "WHO Report on Global Surveillance of Epidemic-prone Infectious Diseases," January 2000, pp. 25–31. https://www.who.int/publications/i/item/WHO-CDS-CSR-ISR-2000.1.

7. *Scientific American* illustration: Richard Borge (richardborge.com).

6

Horror and Natural Evil in *The Plague*

Cynthia A. Freeland

Introduction

The Plague opens by emphasizing the ordinariness of a town in which extraordinary events will occur. The town, Oran, is gray and ugly, bereft of pigeons and flowers, and miserable in all seasons except winter. Its landscape is uninspiring, "treeless, glamourless, soulless."[1] As the plague bears down on this hapless city, events of nature conspire against its residents, blasting them with wind, rain, heat, and mud. Horrors accumulate: bloated rats, parents losing children, fevers and black buboes, pneumonia and clumps of blood, dead bodies dumped into a burial pit, and putrid cremation smoke cloaking the city.

The horror of any plague, whether in ancient Athens, Camus's Oran, or our own Covid-19 pandemic, is not like the horror of famous books and films. Fictive horrors typically take the form of freakish monsters, psychotic killers, alien lizards, and so on. Horror plots engage us with the fate of protagonists who try to understand and confront a monster. But a virus is not a monster. In a plague, pain and suffering are dispensed randomly by an indifferent nature. In doing so, to use Camus's words, an epidemic operates with "hideous and ridiculous justice."[2]

---

[1] Camus, *The Plague*, 6.

[2] Camus, *The Plague*, 193. Camus writes, "la hideuse et dérisoire justice" (Camus, *La Peste*, 211); I do not think Gilbert's translation of "hideous, witless justice" captures the meaning of "dérisoire" here.

Camus's The Plague. Peg Brand Weiser, Oxford University Press. © Oxford University Press 2023.
DOI: 10.1093/oso/9780197599327.003.0007

148   CAMUS'S *THE PLAGUE*

In this chapter I will describe how Camus foregrounds the horror arising from natural phenomena in plagues and pandemics. I refer to these events as cases of natural evil, a term to be explained below. I will also consider implications of *The Plague* for understanding the current Covid-19 epidemic. We, too, are struggling to cope with evils brought by a killer virus: separations, suffering, horrible deaths. People have resorted to denials, religious justifications, heroic actions, or diversions that place blame on some nefarious agents—animals, nations, scientists, politicians, or individuals. Could it possibly be that nature itself is evil?

I will argue that natural evil does exist in the sense that natural processes inevitably produce pain, suffering, and death. We usually ascribe evil to agents with intentions, but sometimes nature becomes the adversary. The virus or plague bacillus is not a monster, and yet our human world is suffused with horror. Camus's novel addresses old questions perhaps most famously raised by Ivan's imagined dialogue with God in the "Grand Inquisitor" chapter of *The Brothers Karamazov* by Fyodor Dostoevsky. Why does suffering exist? Why do innocent people, especially children, have to die in agony? Is there any possible justification for a world in which such things happen? If not, what should be our response?

Rats and Bats

The first glimmering of what is about to descend upon Oran comes when Dr. Rieux accidentally steps on the soft body of a rat. Later that day he encounters a large rat that is clearly ill. While "trying to get its balance," the rat falls over on its side with a little squeal. "Its mouth was slightly open and blood was spurting from it."[3] Camus mentions rats on eighteen pages of his book. The rodents emerge in

---

[3] Camus, *The Plague*, 8.

HORROR AND NATURAL EVIL IN *THE PLAGUE*   149

ever-greater numbers, and finally, after the city has collected 8,000 dead rats, the first wave of panic hits the town.

Rats have died in other plagues, too, of course—Rieux even refers back to one in Canton. Rats are frequent harbingers of disease and are commonly featured in scary movie scenes. But Camus, via his novel's narrator Dr. Rieux, keeps observations about the rats oddly low-key despite the implicit horror of what he is describing. Stepping on a squishy rat body or witnessing a rat spurt blood and fall over dead would be quite disturbing, yet Rieux describes these events in a neutral or clinical voice. He even initially dismisses the rats: "The rats?" he said. "It's nothing."[4]

Perhaps Rieux is seeking to avert panic, but his attitude toward the dead rats foreshadows his general approach to death and disease throughout the novel. Even when he grasps the grave seriousness of situations, he just buckles down to the work at hand. Rieux's mother adopts a similarly detached tone: "The garbage cans of all the houses in the street were full of rats. The doctor's mother took it quite calmly. 'It's like that sometimes,' she said vaguely."[5]

In *Dracula*, Bram Stoker conjured up the horror of rats using much more lurid language than Rieux. In this passage, Jonathan Harker is helping to find the coffin that is Dracula's hiding place, but he has a frightening encounter:

> [U]ndoubtedly some nervousness was growing on us, and we saw a whole mass of phosphorescence, which twinkled like stars. We all instinctively drew back. The whole place was becoming alive with rats.... [T]he lamplight, shining on their moving dark bodies and glittering, baleful eyes, made the place look like a bank of earth set with fireflies. The dogs dashed on, but at the threshold suddenly

---

[4] Camus, *The Plague*, 11.
[5] Camus *The Plague*, 14.

150   CAMUS'S *THE PLAGUE*

stopped and snarled, and then, simultaneously lifting their noses, began to howl in most lugubrious fashion. The rats were multiplying in thousands.[6]

Notice how emotively loaded Stoker's description is. These rats are so baleful that they even frighten the dogs.

As rat deaths multiply in Oran, their agonies are described with more poignancy. Perhaps the doctor now foresees the pitiful deaths that humans, too, will soon experience.

On the fourth day the rats began to come out and die in batches. From basements, cellars, and sewers they emerged in long wavering files into the light of day, swayed helplessly, then did a sort of pirouette and fell dead at the feet of the horrified onlookers.[7]

During the current Covid-19 pandemic, the focus has been not on rats but bats. Various epidemics ranging from syphilis and typhus to Spanish flu have been associated with either rats or bats. Indeed, bats are often linked with rats in horror stories. And so, when the source of our new pandemic was first identified as one of many bat coronaviruses, generations of horror stories leapt into play to haunt our fearful imaginations, the flames fanned by numerous illustrations. Dracula may be signaled by rats, but he is also commonly accompanied by bats. Actually he *is* a sort of bat, biting victims and sucking their blood with his sharp incisors. As with rats, when we encounter bats in nature, the experience can be creepy and threatening (despite recent attempts to rehabilitate bats by showing how much they contribute to the environment). Numerous illustrations have depicted the coronavirus itself, either in molecular form or as DNA, as a molecule strung from the wings or claws of shady-looking, vampire-style bats.

[6] Stoker, *Dracula*, 235.
[7] Camus, *The Plague*, 15.

Rats and bats feature as emblems in horror for several reasons. They look menacing with their sharp teeth, especially when shuffling and massed together in dark smelly locations like sewers or caves. The famous W. S. Murnau silent film *Nosferatu* (1922) depicted its villain not as the suave count later to be portrayed by Bela Lugosi in Tod Browning's 1931 *Dracula*, but as a freakishly skeletal man with narrow, rat-like features. Murnau used numerous live rats to make scenes in the film. In his 1979 remake, *Nosferatu the Vampyre*, Werner Herzog topped him by releasing *thousands* of rats into the city where he was filming in Holland.[8]

Bats, like rats, have long narrow faces, bright eyes, sharp incisor teeth, and claw-tipped "hands." An attack by one can cause a person serious harm. Just as rats startle you by scuttling underfoot, so bats scare you by flapping about in unpredictable zigzags. Both animals are common transmitters of disease. We all soon learned in 2020 that bats are the source of *numerous* viruses that can be transferred to other animals and through them, to humans. One scientific article went so far as to use an ominous label, "This puts bats right up alongside mosquitoes—that spread malaria, chikungunya, dengue, Zika and West Nile virus—at the top of the *zoonotic villains list*" (my emphasis).[9] The idea of bats as "zoonotic villains" was easily purveyed even in scientific articles that showed a bat as if "shedding" the coronavirus itself.

Often rats, bats, or other creatures of the night arrive on ships to "civilized" places like England from "exotic" spots like Transylvania. Horror tales and plague stories often identify the source of monstrous evil as a foreign and thereby suspicious source. When a plague arrives, people blame outsiders for their disaster. The malignant, mosquito-borne cholera was borne from the swamps of Venice in Thomas Mann's 1912 novella *Death in Venice*, in which a noble European author succumbs to his seamy desires while strolling the

---

[8] Koplinski, "Isolation the True Horror," August 7, 2014.
[9] *Economic Times*, April 15, 2020.

152   CAMUS'S *THE PLAGUE*

hot beaches of the city. Similarly, in Philip Roth's *Nemesis*, a tight-knit Jewish suburban community in New Jersey blames a gang of Italian boys for spreading the polio epidemic to their neighborhood.

That plagues come from "somewhere else" has always been so; we can look back to Thucydides for another case.

> It began, by report, first in that part of Ethiopia that lieth upon Egypt, and thence fell down into Egypt and Africa and into the greatest part of the territories of the king. It invaded Athens on a sudden and touched first upon those that dwelt in Piraeus, insomuch as they reported that the Peloponnesians had cast poison into their wells (for springs there were not any in that place). But afterwards it came up into the high city, and then they died a great deal faster.[10]

And similarly, the current Covid-19 virus originated "elsewhere"—in Wuhan, China. Early stories in the Western media associated this emerging virus with "foreign" practices of people in Asia.[11] An image was widely circulated purporting to show a woman eating a bat in some soup in a restaurant in China—a picture shocking enough that it is hard to forget, even though it was discredited early on.[12] Criticisms were voiced in the West about suspicious Chinese "wet markets" selling live wild animals to be consumed for "traditional" (i.e., "primitive") purposes, such as boosting sexual potency.[13] Such animals were hypothesized to be the intermediaries that had transmitted the virus from bats to humans.

---

[10] Thucydides, *The Peloponnesian War*, 115.

[11] For the image and early coverage, see Randall, "Coronavirus: Woman Eats Whole Bat," January 24, 2020.

[12] "The woman in the video, who news outlets have identified as Wang Mengyun, is a host of an online travel show who was actually eating a dish in Palau, an island country located in the western Pacific Ocean. The video was also reportedly filmed in 2016." Miller, "No, Coronavirus Was Not Caused by 'Bat Soup,'" January 29, 2020.

[13] See Fickling, "China Is Reopening Its Wet Markets," April 5, 2020.

The Weather and the Wind

Another staple of plague literature, as in horror films, is that bad omens occur in nature just before a city experiences a plague. In *Alien* (1979), for example, members of a spaceship receive urgent SOS signals and land on a planet where they discover strange giant orbs inside a cave. Superstitions abound in time of plague, and people seek help from prophets and rituals. For example, here is how Daniel Defoe describes people seeking protection at the start of the great plague of London:

> . . . the astrologers added stories of the conjunctions of planets in a malignant manner and with a mischievous influence, one of which conjunctions was to happen, and did happen, in October, and the other in November; and they filled the people's heads with predictions on these signs of the heavens, intimating that those conjunctions foretold drought, famine, and pestilence.[14]

Camus describes the early stage of the plague in Oran as a period "of bewildering portents."[15] By late in the same year, citizens become so superstitious that they rush around seeking all kinds of religious paraphernalia to help save them. *The Plague* features many portents of evil that take the form of ominous and eerie weather events. This is similar to Peter Weir's spooky film *The Last Wave* (1977), which opens with an eerie scene in which violent hail suddenly arrives on a clear sunny day to batter children at an outback school. This bizarre weather immediately creates an atmosphere of dread. Bad weather is, like rats and bats, another staple of the horror genre. "It was a dark and stormy night" is always an indicator that something bad is about to happen. Dr. Frankenstein, for example, must wait until a thunderstorm in order to harness

---

[14] Defoe, *A Plague in London*, 21.
[15] Camus, *The Plague*, 23.

154   CAMUS'S *THE PLAGUE*

the lightning strike that will shock his horrible creature into life. Horror films often rely for atmosphere on extreme weather in settings from the Arctic to steamy jungles. Many films feature harsh desert landscapes or foggy scenes where a monster may be lurking.

Camus makes an especially striking use of wind as an ongoing symbol of horror in *The Plague*. Wind recurs ominously throughout the novel and is the most nebulous and disturbing weather phenomenon in the book. It is frightening when it blasts and sinister when it hisses. (One can well imagine it being dramatized in a film.) There are many mentions of wind in the book. On only rare occasions is it a light or refreshing breeze. More typically, gusts rush into the city's homes like feverish breath. Hot wind is often associated with death scenes and even, as we shall see, with Lucifer himself.

After the first victim, M. Michel, has died of the plague, the weather becomes especially oppressive:

> [T]he sky clouded up and there were brief torrential downpours, each of which was followed by some hours of muggy heat. The aspect of the sea, too, changed; its dark-blue translucency had gone and, under the lowering sky, it had steely or silvery glints that hurt the eyes to look at. . . . you felt, as it were, trapped by the climate. . . . Indeed, the whole town was running a temperature; such anyhow was the impression Dr. Rieux could not shake off.[16]

To try to reassure citizens after a month of the plague, the Catholic Church plans a "Week of Prayer" during which the scholarly Father Paneloux will deliver a sermon. Dr. Rieux attends and reports on it in detail. Nature haunts this event from the very start. The church is crowded with an ominous atmosphere; it is literally dark.

> The sky had clouded up on the previous day, and now it was raining heavily. Those in the open unfurled umbrellas. The air

---

[16] Camus, *The Plague*, 30–31.

HORROR AND NATURAL EVIL IN *THE PLAGUE*   155

inside the Cathedral was heavy with fumes of incense and the smell of wet clothes when Father Paneloux stepped into the pulpit.[17]

The priest tells the crowd that the plague is something they "deserve," comparing them to the ancient Egyptians punished for their heresies and oppression of the Jews by horrific plagues sent by God. As if driving home this threat of punishment, outside "the downpour had increased in violence"; and at the very same time, the priest is lamenting, "God's light withdrawn, we walk in darkness, in the thick darkness of this plague."[18]

The priest's sermon becomes even more apocalyptic as he invokes the staff of Lucifer. The people of Oran will be tossed aside like chaff since the devil is "spreading carnage and suffering on earth."[19] The devil's horrific flail will spill drops of blood, crushing houses and entering them to bring the plague. Once more, Camus provides a weather chord of concurrence as the narrator notes, "A wet wind was sweeping up the nave, making the candle-flames bend and flicker."[20]

After the sermon, the town's weather worsens, and deaths increase. Spring never really arrives because it is "crushed out by the twofold onslaught of heat and plague."[21] Reinforcing the priest's threats, "the hot weather set in with a vengeance."[22]

First a strong, scorching wind blew steadily for a whole day, drying up the walls. And then the sun took charge, incessant waves of heat and light swept the town daylong, and but for arcaded streets and the interiors of houses, everything lay naked to the dazzling

---

[17] Camus, *The Plague*, 94.
[18] Camus, *The Plague*, 96.
[19] Camus, *The Plague*, 97.
[20] Camus, *The Plague*, 98.
[21] Camus, *The Plague*, 113.
[22] Camus, *The Plague*, 111.

156 CAMUS'S *THE PLAGUE*

impact of the light. The sun stalked our townsfolk along every byway, into every nook; and when they paused, it struck.[23]

Rieux, who now fears that "the whole town will be a madhouse,"[24] seeks temporary respite by having a drink with the writer Grand. While sitting at the café he hears the peculiar sound of wind overhead. "[T]here was a low soughing that brought to his mind that unseen flail threshing incessantly the languid air of which Paneloux had spoken."[25] Like the virus, the wind is everywhere and will not let up. The general oppression of the plague is being funneled by the heat and wind into the town through windows and doors—exactly as threatened by Paneloux.

The danger of this hot wind is especially marked in the narrator's account of the agonized death of Othon's son. The boy's little body is tossed about as "the fierce breath of the plague" attacks him with "gusts of fever."[26] Again in Part Three when Rieux reports on the city in mid-August, he notes that people had been "swallowed up" at the "climax of the summer heat and disease."[27] He devotes an entire paragraph to describing the horrible winds which disperse a "gray crust [that] had formed on everything."[28] Camus concludes this tour-de-force paragraph by saying that the town, "loud with the shrilling of the wind, seemed a lost island of the damned."[29]

Suffering and Death

As I noted earlier, Rieux uses a detached, clinical style to describe the disease of plague and its effect on sick people. This contrasts

---

[23] Camus, *The Plague*, 111.
[24] Camus, *The Plague*, 101.
[25] Camus, *The Plague*, 101.
[26] Camus, *The Plague*, 214.
[27] Camus, *The Plague*, 167.
[28] Camus, *The Plague*, 168.
[29] Camus, *The Plague*, 168.

HORROR AND NATURAL EVIL IN *THE PLAGUE*   157

with descriptions given by other plague authors, for example, Thucydides and Defoe. They highlight the intense suffering of people who have the plague, as well as their sometimes-bizarre behavior, giving descriptions that are often dire and disgusting. Here, first, is a passage from Thucydides:

> Their bodies outwardly to the touch were neither very hot nor pale but reddish, livid, and beflowered with little pimples and whelks, but so burned inwardly as not to endure any the lightest clothes or linen garment to be upon them nor anything but mere nakedness, but rather most willingly to have cast themselves into the cold water. . . . For this was a kind of sickness which far surmounted all expression of words and . . . exceeded human nature in the cruelty wherewith it handled each one.[30]

And here is Defoe:

> The swellings, which were generally in the neck or groin, when they grew hard and would not break, grew so painful that it was equal to the most exquisite torture; and some, not able to bear the torment, threw themselves out at windows or shot themselves . . . Others, unable to contain themselves, vented their pain by incessant roarings, and such loud and lamentable cries were to be heard as we walked along the streets that would pierce the very heart to think of.[31]

These two authors each close their narrative by describing social changes wrought by the disaster in their cities. Thucydides casts his entire story as the tragic fall of Athens, as the city's moral behavior disappears in the desperation of the people. Defoe concludes his book with a stern rebuke of people who now offer insincere thankfulness to God: "It might too justly be said of them as was said of

---

[30] Thucydides, *The Peloponnesian War*, 116.
[31] Defoe, *A Plague in London*, 43.

158   CAMUS'S *THE PLAGUE*

the children of Israel after their being delivered from the host of Pharaoh, when they passed the Red Sea, and looked back and saw the Egyptians overwhelmed in the water: viz., that they sang His praise, but they soon forgot His works."[32]

Camus will also end his tale with moral reflections, but this is not so evident early on. Even when Rieux notices the telltale lumps in the body of Michel, the first victim, he says only, "Go to bed at once, and take your temperature. I'll come to see you this afternoon."[33] The doctor strives to remain calm:

> True, the word "plague" had been uttered; true, at this very moment one or two victims were being seized and laid low by the disease. Still, that could stop, or be stopped. It was only a matter of lucidly recognizing what had to be recognized; of dispelling extraneous shadows and doing what needed to be done.[34]

Rieux copes with mass suffering by adopting the attitude and actions of the doctor and scientist he is. He requests quarantining and tries "to get his nerves into some sort of order."[35] He works as well as he can, exhausted and sleeping only four hours a day, much like frontline workers in the current Covid-19 pandemic.

Not until three-fourths of the way through the book does Camus finally present at close-up a scene that conveys the horror of a victim's agonized death. Significantly, it is a small boy. His death is a prolonged ordeal, and the account of it extends for nearly three full pages. Paneloux prays, Castel collapses, Rieux clenches his jaw, Tarrou looks away. Then Camus writes, "A gust of sobs swept through the room, drowning Paneloux's prayer, and Rieux, who was still tightly gripping the rail of the bed, shut his eyes, dazed with exhaustion and disgust."[36]

---

[32] Defoe, *A Plague in London*, 109.
[33] Camus, *The Plague*, 18.
[34] Camus, *The Plague*, 40.
[35] Camus, *The Plague*, 31.
[36] Camus, *The Plague*, 217.

HORROR AND NATURAL EVIL IN *THE PLAGUE* 159

Paneloux's Second Sermon

The Othon boy's death marks a turning point for the three central characters, Rieux, Paneloux, and Tarrou, as each confronts Ivan's question from *The Brothers Karamazov*: can one endorse a world premised upon the suffering of an innocent child? Rieux snaps angrily at the priest, " 'Ah! That child, anyhow, was innocent, and you know it as well as I do!' "[37] Once more, the weather echoes the doctor's feelings of exhaustion and despair:

> He felt like shouting imprecations—anything to loosen the stranglehold lashing his heart with steel. Heat was flooding down between the branches of the fig trees. A white haze, spreading rapidly over the blue of the morning sky, made the air yet more stifling.[38]

After this scene the priest prepares to deliver his second sermon, which addresses issues of theodicy. He has also begun to write an essay titled "Is a Priest Justified in Consulting a Doctor?" Father Paneloux's second sermon, like his first, has eerie meteorological accompaniments. As it is about to begin, an ominous wind blows: "That evening, when Rieux arrived, the wind was pouring in great gusts through the swing-doors and filling the aisles with sudden drafts."[39]

In the sermon the priest's new message is that "Appearances notwithstanding, all trials, however cruel, worked together for good to the Christian."[40] From outside, the wind forces the church's heavy door repeatedly to blow open and thud closed. Paneloux says, "We must believe everything or deny everything,"[41] and meanwhile the

---

[37] Camus, *The Plague*, 218.
[38] Camus, *The Plague*, 218.
[39] Camus, *The Plague*, 222.
[40] Camus, *The Plague*, 223.
[41] Camus, *The Plague*, 224.

160   CAMUS'S *THE PLAGUE*

wind remains relentless. "Rieux heard more clearly the whistling of the wind outside; judging by the sounds that came in below the closed doors, it had risen to storm pitch."[42] Paneloux preaches that we must all reconcile ourselves to hard truths by submitting our will to God's. The wind makes a fifth and final appearance as Rieux prepares to leave the church: "a violent gust swept up the nave through the half-open doors and buffeted the faces of the departing congregation."[43] The wind, which has threatened the church from the start, in the end gets inside to invade and buffet people's faces. Its inexorability parallels that of the plague.

Not surprisingly, Father Paneloux's second sermon is followed by an account of the priest's contagion and death. The priest refuses to have a doctor called, conforming to his own manifesto. He becomes feverish and sweaty and keeps retching. "At these moments he seemed to be vainly struggling to force up from his lungs a clot of some semisolid substance that was choking him."[44] He finally coughs up the red clot of matter that had been choking him and is found dead the next morning.

Dr. Rieux is clearly moved by the Othon boy's death, as noted above. Yet despite acknowledging the suffering of victims, he remains distanced because the horrors of the illness are deadened by the monotony of repetition. The medical staff manage to "carry on automatically, so to speak, their all but superhuman task."[45] Suffering becomes deadening when it is very extended—"the habit of despair is worse than despair itself."[46] We have seen something like this now with the phenomenon of "Covid fatigue" and people's yearning for some return to "normalcy."

By January 25, Rieux observes more optimism in the town, but when Tarrou spots one of the reemerging rats, it is surely

---

[42] Camus, *The Plague*, 225.
[43] Camus, *The Plague*, 228.
[44] Camus, *The Plague*, 231.
[45] Camus, *The Plague*, 236.
[46] Camus, *The Plague*, 181.

HORROR AND NATURAL EVIL IN *THE PLAGUE*   161

a bad omen. He goes to bed "feeling very tired."[47] Tarrou's fate is foreshadowed by the brooding weather, "which after being very cold had grown slightly milder, broke in a series of violent hailstorms followed by rain."[48] Tarrou fights valiantly, but despite his robust build and vitality, loses his battle. His painful death scene is set amid more hostile weather: "[A]nother rain-squall was sweeping the town, mingled presently with hailstones that clattered on the sidewalk. Window awnings were flapping wildly."[49] The storm outside mirrors the "turmoil of the unseen battle" in Tarrou's body.[50] Even when things quiet down, the plague still haunts the city, and Rieux hears the wind's malevolent hissing. "[I]t was whistling softly in the stagnant air of the sickroom, and this it was that Rieux had been hearing since the long vigil began.[51]

> The storm, lashing [Tarrou's] body into convulsive movement, lit it up with ever rarer flashes, and in the heart of the tempest he was slowly drifting, derelict. . . . This human form, his friend's, lacerated by the spear-thrusts of the plague, consumed by searing, superhuman fires, buffeted by all the raging winds of heaven, was foundering under his eyes in the dark flood of the pestilence, and he could do nothing to avert the wreck.[52]

After Tarrou dies, the world goes cold, "with frosty stars sparkling in a clear, wintry sky."[53]

At long last, Dr. Castel's serum starts working, so patients begin to have hope. The plague's final retreat coincides with the arrival of extreme cold in January. The city's gates are finally opened and loved ones joyously reunited. Now the weather is benign: "[T]he

---

[47] Camus, *The Plague*, 281.
[48] Camus, *The Plague*, 284.
[49] Camus, *The Plague*, 285–286.
[50] Camus, *The Plague*, 286.
[51] Camus, *The Plague*, 286.
[52] Camus, *The Plague*, 289.
[53] Camus, *The Plague*, 290.

162   CAMUS'S *THE PLAGUE*

sun was pouring on the town a steady flood of tranquil light. . . . Cold, fathomless depths of sky glimmered overhead, and near the hilltops stars shone hard as flint."[54] Notice, though, that this apparently beautiful weather has inhumane aspects, being described as "fathomless" and "hard." Nature retains its power to stir up future terrors to be wrought upon innocent people. The final paragraph warns us of this: "the plague bacillus never dies or disappears for good . . . and . . . perhaps the day would come when, for the bane and the enlightening of men, it would rouse up its rats again and send them forth to die in a happy city."[55]

Natural Evil and Dread

It is easy to envisage *The Plague* being made into a horror movie that features disgusting sights in sickrooms and spooky special effects involving rats, rain, and wind. There actually is a film version made in 1992 by the Argentinian director Luis Puenzo. Although the movie has some interesting aspects, it fails to capture the intense aura of dread conveyed by the novel. Puenzo wrote the screenplay as well as directing, and he clearly interpreted the novel along political lines. This is not surprising given his nationality. He presumably chose to reset the plot in a South American city and in the contemporary world as a protest against military dictatorships he knew only too well. Perhaps the film's most effective recasting of Camus's ominous descriptions are two scenes that feature rats. Early on, the journalist Rambert (a woman in this version) finds that a rat has caught a ride up with her in a hotel elevator. The animal rises to stretch its little paws up her leg in a supplicating posture, but she recoils and rushes out when the elevator doors open. The rat, too, emerges, only to collapse, shiver, and die on the carpet.

---

[54] Camus, *The Plague*, 307.
[55] Camus, *The Plague*, 308.

HORROR AND NATURAL EVIL IN *THE PLAGUE*   163

Complementing this is a scene near the end of the film in which joyous people are celebrating the end of the plague in streets and bars. Some attend a stage show where they watch a stripper who playfully flirts with a pet rat. It climbs up her body and onto her shoulder, where she grabs and kisses it. This is a brilliant variation on Camus's use of rats as symbols of continuing threat.

The horror of natural disasters like plagues does not fit well into one prominent theory of horror: that presented by Noël Carroll in his book *The Philosophy of Horror* (1990). Carroll's account makes horror center on plots about monsters, entities "whose existence is denied by contemporary science."[56] Monsters are threatening, repulsive, and disgusting. A natural creature like a virus cannot be a monster on Carroll's theory, because by definition what is part of nature is not unnatural. If we respond by pointing to stories that appear to feature monsters that *are* parts of nature, Carroll dodges the problem. For example, he says that the shark in *Jaws* is *super*natural because it has powers, intelligence, and aims going beyond those of any real shark.

Carroll acknowledges that there are some artworks that evoke something akin to horror without featuring monsters. Often such stories feature a creepy place or ominous event; they work upon audiences by sustaining a very strong oppressive mood. Carroll says that such works evoke a feeling related to horror, which he labels "art dread." Artworks evoking art dread are more vague and less focused than horror because dread is a mood and not an emotion. Such works can be unsettling when they depict an extended period of undirected anxiety.

Carroll's notion of art dread is useful for understanding Camus's novel. Elsewhere I have written about films that qualify for this category by associating evil with a natural *place* that seems uncanny and threatening.[57] Think, for example, of the frigid Rockies of *The Shining*,

---

[56] Carroll, *Philosophy of Horror*, 40.
[57] Freeland, "Horror and Art-Dread."

164 CAMUS'S *THE PLAGUE*

the parched fields of *The Texas Chainsaw Massacre,* or the gloomy Maryland woods of *Blair Witch Project.* There are also weather-permeated stories or films of art dread. I have mentioned one example, Peter Weir's *The Last Wave.* In it, a rather ordinary attorney (Richard Chamberlain) in Sydney, Australia, is recruited to defend an Aborigine man accused of "spirit murder." He begins to have visions of plagues, such as a horrifying rain of frogs. These lead up to a final scene in which he encounters a terrifyingly huge wave that will wipe out the earth. There are other examples of scary nature in films, such as the haunting Snow Maiden sequence in Masaki Kobayashi's *Kwaidan,* titled *The Woman of the Snow* (1964). Here a beautiful icy lady releases a frightened man with a terrible threat.

Like these and other artworks, *The Plague* evokes art dread by depicting something in Nature that is uncanny or disturbing. Such works hint at a vague externalized source of cosmic evil "out there" in the world. One response to this hypothesis is to dismiss it. Fears about "things that go bump in the night" are childish and reflect a "primitive," animistic kind of thinking. But there are indications in Camus's novel that he is indeed treating the plague in Oran as evil. He sometimes anthropomorphizes the plague. For example, he comments: "It was, above all, a shrewd, unflagging adversary; a skilled organizer, doing his work thoroughly and well."[58]

Just before the close of the book, Rieux explains why he has recorded this story:

> [S]o that he should not be one of those who hold their peace but should bear witness in favor of those plague-stricken people; so that some memorial of *the injustice and outrage done them* might endure; and to state quite simply what we learn in a time

---

[58] Camus, *The Plague,* 180.

HORROR AND NATURAL EVIL IN *THE PLAGUE*   165

of pestilence: that there are more things to admire in men than to despise.[59] (my emphasis)

This is strong language; the plague has dealt with "innocent" people unjustly. I do not think we can interpret the doctor's words to imply that conditions in Oran or bureaucracy or human psychology were the true sources of the plague's "injustice and outrage." Rather, Camus is raising the possibility that Nature or aspects of it can actually count as evil.

Recall that Ivan Karamazov's problem in "The Grand Inquisitor" was whether he could accept God's offer of a world full of happiness given one condition, the suffering of an innocent child. Rieux seems to be directing this question to the cosmos itself: can we accept a universe that routinely deals out dire fates to the innocent? Father Paneloux attempted to preserve his faith that injustice, if willed by God, is still acceptable. Tarrou, oddly enough, sought sainthood, too. Despite his lifelong fight against contamination by the plague, he could not rid himself of a desire to be "pure" in the way he hoped. He endorsed a goal that was impossible by denying the inevitability of the world's horrors. Rieux calls the plague an *injustice* done to humans, and yet at the same time he accepts it. What he calls for instead is a belief in the endurance of innocent humans and their ability to rise above such an unfair fate.

If innocent people are punished by suffering and death, this seems to be a bad thing, an "abomination" in Rieux's wording.[60] But surely Camus was aware that the cosmos as a whole is not a purposive agent. Nature's cold hardness, the sky's indifference, and the plague's shrewdness are just ways we humans describe things we come up against in nature. Even the worst disasters of nature—whether hurricanes, wildfires, volcanic eruptions, or rampaging

---

[59] Camus, *The Plague*, 308. The French wording is "pour laisser du moins un souvenir de *l'injustice et de la violence* qui leur avaient été faites" (again my emphasis, Camus, *La Peste*, 331).

[60] Camus, *The Plague*, 214.

166   CAMUS'S *THE PLAGUE*

diseases—are not truly "evil." The modern paradigms of evil are human-caused events like African slavery or the Holocaust, with their associated nefarious agents.

In contrast to this modern view, as Susan Neiman reports in *Evil in Modern Thought: An Alternative History of Philosophy*, as recently as the 1700s a natural disaster like the Lisbon earthquake of 1755, which killed thousands, *was* taken to be a paradigm of evil. It posed a challenge much discussed by theologians and philosophers, including Voltaire. In the medieval religious framework, natural disasters were explained by saying that God has some reason for them, perhaps punishment or to test people's faith. But with the rise of early modern science, philosophers explained disasters as consequences of natural causes. Evil required some form of malevolent agency.

Neiman argues, however, that this modern conception of evil has itself been undermined by examples of contemporary collective evil in events like the Holocaust. She cites Hannah Arendt's *Eichmann in Jerusalem*, which argued that Adolf Eichmann did not fulfill the conventional requirements for an evildoer.[61] He did not particularly care about results of his deeds, was not an anti-Semite, and did not think of himself as a killer. Instead, he illustrated what Arendt termed "the banality of evil." Much the same applies to later cases like the Hiroshima atomic bomb or drone killings that create so-called collateral damage; the role of intentions and malevolence is diffused. When intentions and responsibility get dissipated, it raises doubts about individual agency.

Some interpretations of *The Plague* construe it as an allegory of Nazism; the plague symbolizes the cruelty humans can do to one another. This appears parallel to how Tarrou views the plague, for example. Similarly, as I noted earlier, Puenzo, the Argentinian filmmaker, rewrote aspects of Camus's novel to deliver a more pointed

---

[61] Arendt, *Eichmann in Jerusalem*.

political message in his movie version. It is true that while Camus was writing this novel he was participating in the French Resistance and that his book contains numerous swipes against the inhumaneness of bureaucracies. While we cannot discount a construal of the novel's characters and actions as alternative ways of responding to the horrors of the Holocaust or other war crimes, this limits the book's broader relevance, for example, to our current pandemic situation.

Most educated people today would deny that Covid-19 is "evil," since a virus is not an intentional agent any more than is the plague bacillus. Even so, just as Camus at times anthropomorphizes the plague, so, too, we have seen accounts of the Covid-19 virus as clever, with a devious ability to hide and to mutate. This occurs along with attempts to force narratives about the current pandemic into the modern definition of evil as malevolence. Such efforts take two forms. First, many descriptions of the Covid-19 virus in popular and even medical literature in effect anthropomorphize it by referring to it as an "enemy" or "adversary," just as Rieux did. Numerous sketches of the virus represent it as evil-looking creature, resembling a small grenade laden with pointed "spikes" ready to "invade" and "attack" the body of an innocent victim. Often it is pictured in bright red, associating it with stop lights and warning signals. A children's coloring book was published by St. Jude's hospital to introduce the virus to kids. Their website explained: "Unlike any cartoon villain of yore, the orb-shaped title character of a new children's coloring book seemingly floats across the pages wearing a menacing sneer, a suit of spikes and, strangely enough, a crown."[62] There were other pictures of the virus as a big red cartoon creature with spindly legs and sharp teeth threatening our tiny green globe, which tries to stand up to it bravely.

The second way of construing the new coronavirus as evil involves shifting blame by pinpointing some *human* agency

---

[62] "Important Lessons from a Coloring Book," March 31, 2020.

168 CAMUS'S *THE PLAGUE*

responsible for its worldwide path of damage and death. This approach argues that injustices have indeed occurred, that there have been too many deaths and an unfair distribution of deaths, because of human factors: poor political leadership, global economic disparities, the frequency of world travel, science denial, poverty, and so on. Much blame has been directed to China, as with the former U.S. President Donald Trump, who is still referring to it as "the Chinese virus." This attributes evil to an entire people, and it unsurprisingly has aroused enormous suspicion along with racially motivated attacks on members (or perceived members) of the allegedly responsible racial groups. Blame has also been directed against a bioweapons lab in Wuhan, the Chinese government, the "crude" practices of wet markets, or the "primitive" behavior of people who eat wild animals in the hope of acquiring magical powers. On a more liberal note, some people put the blame on humans who have hastened climate change by deforestation and habitat destruction, thus forcing people into ever more intimate contact with previously unknown species of animals, including bats.

The problem with this second sort of effort is that it represents wishful thinking: if there is someone to blame for a bad thing happening, then it could have been avoided. If people just stopped eating bats or making bioweapons or destroying natural habitats, all would be well. This is an unrealistic picture that idealizes an imaginary benevolent Nature, not unlike Father Paneloux's desperate faith in a good God. Dr. Rieux's attitude is different, and I infer that so, too, is Camus's. Things like plagues and Nazism will inevitably recur. When they do, one must work against them without giving up hope.

There is an interesting parallel between *The Plague* and a movie I have discussed as an example of natural evil, Alfred Hitchcock's *The Birds* (1963).[63] In this well-known film, a beautiful but scandalous young San Francisco society woman, Melanie (Tippi

---

[63] Freeland, "Natural Evil in the Horror Film."

Hedren) pursues her love interest, Mitch (Rod Taylor), to his weekend home where he lives with his mother and young sister in remote Bodega Bay, California. As she steers a boat across the water, Melanie is suddenly attacked by a seagull for no apparent reason. Other bird attacks occur, some even fatal. In a particularly frightening sequence, blackbirds gradually mass on a playground outside a school and then fiercely pursue the panicked children as they try to leave. These are ordinary small birds, not wild predators. The film ends with Melanie, Mitch, and his family driving slowly away as thousands of birds cover the landscape with their wings restlessly flapping. The movie's literary source, a novella by Daphne du Maurier, was an apocalyptic tale set in Cornwall reflecting the horror of England's invasion by planes in World War II.

What strikes me about *The Birds*, both novella and film, is that no explanation is ever given for why the birds are attacking. Townspeople speculate: is it due to nuclear testing, a virus, strange weather, or what? Some film scholars have attempted to "rationalize" *The Birds* by interpreting it along psychoanalytic lines.[64] It is taken as an allegory of misogyny showing that Melanie, the heroine, gets punished for her overly aggressive form of female sexuality. I have criticized this line of interpretation, just like the Nazi allegory of *The Plague*, for rejecting the possibility that natural phenomena, whether plagues or rampaging birds, might simply not be subject to our human forms of moral reckoning.[65]

Nature does not have to supply us with reasons. It does not really matter if Nature is evil or just indifferent; there is an inevitability that suffering will continue. On one rare occasion early on in *The Plague*, when Camus observes that the weather is beautiful, he does so only to highlight nature's indifference to human suffering:

---

[64] See for example, Halberstam, *Skin Shows*.
[65] Freeland, "Natural Evil in the Horror Film."

170 CAMUS'S *THE PLAGUE*

About this time the weather appeared set fair, and the sun had drawn up the last puddles left by the recent rain. There was a serene blue sky flooded with golden light each morning, with sometimes a drone of planes in the rising heat—all seemed well with the world. And yet within four days the fever had made four startling strides: sixteen deaths, twenty-four, twenty-eight, and thirty-two. On the fourth day the opening of the auxiliary hospital in the premises of a primary school was officially announced.[66]

Furthermore, once the city's gates are closed, Camus writes that everyone was left "alone under the vast indifference of the sky."[67]

Is There a Hero in This Story?

Typically, horror narratives feature some survivor who has figured out how to stop the monster. This hero arouses audience empathy, while other people who died along the way are portrayed as either foolish or tragic. Think of Ripley (Sigourney Weaver) in the original *Alien* movie (1979). She is smart and courageous enough to evade the nasty Creature, and she resists foolhardy efforts to harness it as a potential bioweapon. It is easy to admire survivors who are brave and sympathetic like Ripley. Is Camus directing us to admire the doctor in his story when he survives, while others die? I think so, but not simply because he has survived.

Rieux's attitude is made plain during Tarrou's fight with the plague. Tarrou's extended death scene shows the human cost of the plague for the first time in the book, even more than in the distant occurrence of Rieux's wife or the poor Othon boy's death, which was less terrible since his parents were not present to

---

[66] Camus, *The Plague*, 61–62.
[67] Camus, *The Plague*, 75.

HORROR AND NATURAL EVIL IN *THE PLAGUE* 171

witness his agonies. When Tarrou dies, we finally see Dr. Rieux not as a stoic clinician but as an individual person grieving the loss of his friend, a man with unique strengths and foibles. Sadly reflecting on his loss, the doctor remarks that Tarrou lived with "the bleak sterility of a life without illusions. There can be no peace without hope."[68] The narrative itself thus indicates that the doctor's decision to live as a man, a human being, rather than as the sort of saint that either Tarrou or Paneloux aspired to being, is the right choice. The doctor has faith in human decency as the proper response to natural evil, which is inevitable. He sustains hope that people will again try to help one another when the plague returns, "in the never ending fight against terror and its relentless onslaughts."[69]

Works Cited

Arendt, Hannah. *Eichmann in Jerusalem: A Study in the Banality of Evil.* New York: Viking Press, 1963.

Camus, Albert. *The Plague.* Translated by Stuart Gilbert. New York: Vintage, 1991.

Camus, Albert. *La Peste.* Paris: Gallimard, 1947. https://archive.org/details/lapestecamu00camu/mode/2up.

Carroll, Noël. *The Philosophy of Horror, or Paradoxes of the Heart.* New York: Routledge, 1990.

Defoe, Daniel. *A Plague in London* (originally published as *The Journal of the Plague Year*, 1722). Boston: Maynard, Merrill, & Co., 1895. https://www.google.com/books/edition/The_Plague_in_London/-ewPAAAAYAAJ?hl=en&gbpv=1.

Dostoevsky, Fyodor. *The Brothers Karamazov.* Translated by Constance Garnett. New York: The Modern Library, 1900.

Du Maurier, Daphne. "The Birds." In *The Birds and Other Stories*, 7–44. Harmondsworth: Penguin Books Ltd., 1963. First published 1952 as *The Apple Tree: A Short Novel and Some Stories* by Victor Gollancz (London).

---

[68] Camus, *The Plague*, 292.
[69] Camus, *The Plague*, 308.

172 CAMUS'S THE PLAGUE

Economic Times, India (English Version). "Anti-Bat Views Must Not Take Wing: More Informed People Must Bat for These Much-Maligned Mammals." April 15, 2020. https://economictimes.indiatimes.com/magazi nes/panache/anti-bat-views-must-not-take-wing-more-informed-peo ple-must-bat-for-these-much-maligned-mammals/articleshow/75150918. cms?utm_source=contentofinterest&utm_medium=text&utm_campa ign=cppst.

Fickling, David. "China Is Reopening Its Wet Markets. That's Good." *Bloomberg,* April 3, 2020. https://www.bloomberg.com/opinion/articles/ 2020-04-04/coronavirus-closing-china-s-wet-markets-isn-t-a-solution.

Freeland, Cynthia. "Natural Evil in the Horror Film: Alfred Hitchcock's 'The Birds.'" In *The Changing Face of Evil in Film and Television,* edited by Martin F. Norden, 55–69. Amsterdam: Rodopi, 2007.

Freeland, Cynthia. "Horror and Art-Dread." In *The Horror Film,* edited by Stephen Prince, 189–205. New Brunswick, NJ: Rutgers University Press, 2004.

Halberstam, Judith. *Skin Shows: Gothic Horror and the Technology of Monsters.* Durham, NC: Duke University Press, 1995.

"Important Lessons from a Coloring Book." St. Jude Hospital, March 31, 2020. https://www.stjude.org/inspire/blogs/inspired-by-your-kindness/coronavi rus-coloring-book.html.

Koplinski, Chuck. "Isolation the True Horror in Herzog's 'Nosferatu.'" *The News-Gazette* (Champaign-Urbana, Illinois), August 7, 2014. https://www. news-gazette.com/arts-entertainment/isolation-the-true-horror-in-herz ogs-nosferatu/article_5646492f-35e7-59a7-a47f-251beb425159.html.

Miller, Korin. "No, Coronavirus Was Not Caused by 'Bat Soup'—But Here's What Researchers Think May Be to Blame." *Health.com,* January 29, 2020. https://www.health.com/condition/infectious-diseases/coronavi rus-bat-soup.

Neiman, Susan. *Evil in Modern Thought: An Alternative History of Philosophy.* Princeton, NJ: Princeton University Press, 2002.

Randall, Lila. "Coronavirus: Woman Eats Whole Bat in Disturbing Footage after Outbreak Linked to Soup." *Daily Mirror,* January 24, 2020. https:// www.mirror.co.uk/news/world-news/coronavirus-woman-eats-whole-bat-21349468.

Roth, Philip. *Nemesis.* New York: Houghton Mifflin, 2010.

Stoker, Bram. *Dracula.* London: Archibald Constable and Company, 1897.

Thucydides. *The Peloponnesian War.* Translated by Thomas Hobbes with notes by David Grene. Chicago: University of Chicago Press, 1989.

8. Werner Forman, *Death Strangling a Victim of the Black Death*, 1376. From the Czech codex called the Clementinum Collection of tracts by Thomas of Stitny. National Museum, Prague. HIP/Art Resource, NY.

7

"I Can't Breathe"

Covid-19 and *The Plague*'s Tragedy of Political and Corporeal Suffocation

Margaret E. Gray

Among the final words pronounced by George Floyd in the course of his brutal murder by a Minneapolis policeman on May 25, 2020, "I can't breathe" captures both the experience of physical suffocation and, more abstractly, the sociopolitical stranglehold of brutal oppression. These literal and figurative uses of "breathing" implicitly overlap in Camus's allegory of fascism, *The Plague*, and during the Covid-19 pandemic when protesters masked against the lung-destroying virus defied curfews to demonstrate against racism, police violence, and brutality across the globe. Returning to Camus's depiction of a world he called "unbreathable" from within our contemporary context of pandemic and oppression offers new resonance to the narrator's experience, as well as to our own.[1] Our understanding of *The Plague* as a work of Camus's cycle exploring tragedy and revolt[2] acquires additional density and nuance from within our own experience of loss (loss of breath, loss of life; loss of livelihoods; loss of our bearings, our present lives, and our visions for the future) as well as of revolt against racist and political

---

[1] Camus, *Journaux de Voyage*, 34.

[2] "Second series: the world of tragedy and the spirit of revolt" wrote Camus in his notebook in April 1941 (*Notebook I*, 193). The four works in what Camus considered his second "cycle" include *The Plague* (1947), the essay *The Rebel* (1951), and the plays *State of Siege* (1948) and *The Just* (1949).

Camus's The Plague. Peg Brand Weiser, Oxford University Press. © Oxford University Press 2023.
DOI: 10.1093/oso/9780197599327.003.0008

176 CAMUS'S *THE PLAGUE*

oppression. This chapter will take breathing and suffocation as master tropes of life and death, freedom and oppression, marking our own ordeal with Covid-19 and sociopolitical tyranny even as they define the suffering of Oran's sequestered citizens. Published in 1947, *The Plague* allegorizes, through the experience of omnipresent biological menace and oppression, the Nazi occupation of France during World War II with its restriction of freedoms for French citizens—to the point, for example, of the forced domestic presence of German soldiers lodged in French homes. And yet, returning to Camus's manipulation of breathing and suffocation via two registers, literal and figural, from within the context of our own experiences, transforms each arena of activity—our reading of *The Plague* and our lives under the Covid-19 pandemic—through the extra resonance appended by the other. Finally, in sinister symmetry to breathing and its internalization of the life-giving oxygen that fills our lungs, the ultimate tragedy of Camus's plague and our own, both biological and political, is—as the text's closing lines emphasize—their dangerous capacity *not* to be permanently exhaled from our bodies, permanently flushed from the recesses of our surroundings, but rather, to lurk within us: indefinitely, but ever ready to reemerge, to be sent forth to infect "a happy city."

As George Floyd lay suffocating for nine minutes and twenty-nine seconds, pinned to the pavement under the knee of a Minneapolis policeman for having ostensibly attempted to make a convenience-store purchase with a counterfeit twenty-dollar bill, he repeatedly gasped, "I can't breathe." Yet Floyd was far from being the first to suffocate in such a way; another unarmed Black man, Eric Garner, died in 2014 in a police chokehold in New York City. Indeed, "I can't breathe" has become a terrible, final refrain for over seventy people while in police custody, according to a 2020 report by the *New York Times*.[3] But Floyd's case—in a country where tensions and hostility between Left and Right had become increasingly

---

[3] Baker et al., "Three Words," June 29, 2020.

"I CAN'T BREATHE" 177

acute under the Trump administration, and where loss of jobs and economic uncertainty brought on by the Covid-19 pandemic were already provoking widespread anger, panic, and frustration—was somehow different. Neither Floyd, who died at the scene, nor police officer Derek Chauvin, who would ultimately be convicted of second-degree (with the intention only of significant bodily harm) murder as well as third-degree (unintentional, but committed with a "depraved mind" lacking in consideration for human life) murder and second-degree manslaughter (causing death by culpable negligence),[4] could have foreseen the international impact of that deadly May 25, 2020, encounter; but protests against racial injustice and brutality erupting not only in 1,700 cities across all fifty states[5] were joined by others around the world, from Hong Kong to Sydney to Edinburgh[6] as the "Black Lives Matter" movement acquired global resonance and visibility. George Floyd's final, suffocating gasps had unleashed a global revolt against stifling racial, political, and social oppression.

The weeks of protests—some of them violent[7]—that followed Floyd's murder led to efforts to expunge traces of the racist past. Monuments seen as complicit with racial oppression were removed, toppled, or defaced. Many statues of Christopher Columbus were removed, for his complicity in abuses against Native Americans, as were statues of American slave owners, including those of Presidents George Washington, Thomas Jefferson, and Ulysses S. Grant, and author of "The Star-Spangled Banner" lyrics, Francis Scott Key. Such actions were not only taken in the United States; a statue of seventeenth-century slave trader Edward Colston was

---

[4] Chauvin was sentenced to 22.5 years in prison, the longest sentence ever received by a Minnesota police officer, on June 25, 2021; he may, however, potentially be released on parole after 15 years.

[5] Gyldén, "Procès de Derek Chauvin," March 8, 2021.

[6] CNN, Saturday, June 13, 2020.

[7] In response to the violence, the governor of Oregon ultimately sent fifty National Guardsmen on July 30, 2020, to the city of Portland, where protests had been held every night since May.

178   CAMUS'S *THE PLAGUE*

dumped into the United Kingdom's Bristol Harbor. Sweeping, self-searching reviews by administrations of varying levels, public and private, were undertaken to identify traces of racial injustice in the histories of their institutions. Within two weeks of Floyd's murder, the words "Black Lives Matter" had been painted on a Washington, DC, street near Lafayette Square in thirty-five-foot yellow letters by order of Mayor Muriel Bowser; a nearby inter-section was named "Black Lives Matter Plaza." New York, Dallas, Los Angeles, Berkeley, and many other American cities sponsored their own versions of such murals. The movement would galvanize Black voters in the United States, ultimately contributing to the November defeat by nearly 8 million votes of incumbent president Donald Trump by former vice-president Joseph Biden, as well as the election not only of the first woman vice-president, but the first vice-president of color. Ayesha Wilson was in a Boston-area Target store when her mother called with the news that Biden and Harris had won the election. "It just felt like our community, our country, can finally breathe again," was her reaction.[8] Being able "finally to breathe" was a friend's assessment of Duchess of Sussex Meghan Markle's situation upon her decision in January 2020, with her husband Prince Harry, to relinquish royal duties and leave Britain for North America[9]; her friend's claim anticipates the revelation in March 2021 that Meghan had found the racist bias and lack of sympathy for mental-health challenges at Buckingham Palace and among the British tabloid press to be, implicitly, "unbreathable."[10] Allusion to suffocating sociopolitical and cultural conditions continues to animate the Black Lives Matter movement; on the eve of Officer Derek Chauvin's trial in March 2021, a protest entitled " 'I Can't Breathe': Silent March for Justice" brought hundreds to the streets in Minneapolis.[11]

---

[8] Thompson, "With Biden-Harris Victory," December 14, 2020.
[9] Coyle, "Meghan Markle Can 'Finally Breathe,' " January 20, 2020.
[10] Markle, "Interview with Oprah Winfrey," CBS, March 7, 2021.
[11] Flores, "Hundreds Take to the Streets," March 7, 2021.

"I CAN'T BREATHE" 179

Oran as a community literally and figuratively unable to breathe is the material for narrator Rieux's chronicle in *The Plague*, published just two years after Germany's surrender to Allied powers in May 1945 ended World War II. As the original French edition's epigraph from Daniel Defoe's *Robinson Crusoe* pointedly informs us, it is "reasonable" to represent one form of imprisonment with another form; and it is equally reasonable to represent something that exists by means of representing something that doesn't. Representing extant things otherwise, differently—through other forms, or through inexistent things—is precisely the project of allegory: "a story, poem or picture which can be interpreted to reveal a hidden meaning, typically a moral or political one."[12] Crucial to *The Plague*'s function as political allegory of the German occupation of France is the trope of asphyxiation, as Camus himself specified in his notebooks: "I want to express by means of the plague the suffocation we all suffered, and the atmosphere of menace and exile in which we lived."[13] He provides a different source of the plague's experience of suffocation in another notebook scribble: "Plague: a world without women and therefore, unbreathable."[14] We remember that for Camus, who began suffering from tuberculosis as a teenager, difficulty breathing was not only a deeply personal issue, but an ongoing, intensely corporeal experience. Indeed, for a period of time during the early composition of *The Plague*, Camus was obliged to leave his wife, Francine, in Algeria and retreat to the Cévennes mountains near then-unoccupied St. Etienne in an effort to recover his health after a relapse of his tuberculosis; the German army subsequently occupied all of France, essentially cutting off contact between France and its North African territory, Algeria. Camus's own experience of forced separation from Francine thus anticipates those of his

[12] Oxford Dictionary of English (Oxford: Oxford University Press, 2005), 2nd ed., revised.
[13] Camus, *Notebooks II*, 53.
[14] Camus, *Journaux de Voyage*, 34.

180 CAMUS'S *THE PLAGUE*

characters: Rambert, the journalist who finds himself stranded in the closed city of Oran, unable to rejoin his far-away wife in France; and Rieux, whose wife's poor health obliges her to leave Oran for a sanatorium in the novel's first few pages.[15]

In Camus's text, the inability to breathe becomes a regular symptom of the plague that strikes the city. Its first victim, the concierge of narrator Rieux's building (staunchly maintaining that there are no rats in his building even as he dies, and thus poignantly anticipating Covid-19 victims who die in hospital intensive-care units even while claiming the virus is a hoax) succumbs in the novel's opening pages, his breath coming "in sudden gasps" as though "stifling" under an invisible weight.[16] During the long agony of Judge Othon's small son, "the fever seemed to recede, leaving him gasping for breath on a dank, pestilential shore."[17] The outsider Tarrou falls ill in the final days of the plague; as the disease progresses, he "was breathing with more difficulty," and his fearful question, "The fever'll come back, won't it, Rieux?"[18] comes with a gasp. Indeed, as the plague evolves, it is defined no fewer than six times in the novel as the "pneumonic plague," from both the Latin *pneumaticus* and Greek *pneumatikos*, meaning "breath."[19] As of Part II, "the plague was becoming pneumonic"[20]; allusion is made to "sufferers of pneumonic plague."[21] Examining the ailing Paneloux in Part IV, Rieux is surprised to find a strange variant with "none of the characteristic symptoms of bubonic or pneumonic plague, except congestion and obstruction of the lungs."[22] Later, as Rieux tells us, "the pneumonic type of infection, cases of which had already been detected, was now spreading all over the town; one

[15] In his letter to Francine Camus of August 31, 1944, Camus indicates that he has been without news of her for months. Quoted in Todd, *Albert Camus, Une Vie*, 501.

[16] Camus, *The Plague*, 22.

[17] Camus, *The Plague*, 193.

[18] Camus, *The Plague*, 287.

[19] Robert et al, *Le Nouveau Petit Robert*, 1465.

[20] Camus, *The Plague*, 123.

[21] Camus, *The Plague*, 194.

[22] Camus, *The Plague*, 233.

"I CAN'T BREATHE" 181

could almost believe that the high winds were kindling and fanning its flames in people's chests"[23]; as it spreads, the illness assumes "more and more the pneumonic form."[24] The apparently "hopeless" case of a young girl in the closing lines of Part IV presents "all the symptoms of pneumonic plague."[25]

As we know, asphyxiation is also an effect of Covid-19, with difficulty breathing as one of its early symptoms. Videos of stricken patients and medical professionals alike, gasping for air as they struggled to speak, went viral as horrified citizens contemplated their own potential fate, or that of friends and relatives fallen ill with the virus. As cases of the virus exploded in spring 2020, American cities and states competed against one another in a desperate scramble to procure life-saving ventilators:[26] essentially, mechanical lungs that take over the patient's breathing function, yet potentially cause lasting damage (meanwhile, it was subsequently discovered that the simple tactic of turning Covid-19 patients onto their stomachs helped ease their breathing). The ventilating procedure of intubating endless waves of intensive-care Covid-19 patients became yet another challenge for medical workers; sometimes, so as to release a bed for the next desperately ill patient, the deceased would be so hastily zipped into body bags as to leave the ventilator tube protruding from their throats: a grim and final emblem of the disease's attack on the lungs, its ruthless asphyxiation of its victims. Yet even the healthy—particularly medical professionals who serve for long hours at a time—are obliged to suffer feelings of restricted breathing under suffocating personal protective equipment (PPE), including tight-fitting face mask, face shield, and goggles; indeed, a lawsuit filed against the

---

[23] Camus, *The Plague*, 236.
[24] Camus, *The Plague*, 258.
[25] Camus, *The Plague*, 264.
[26] New York governor Andrew Cuomo compared the scramble among governors with competing on Ebay against fifty other ruthless and resolute customers. Mervosh and Rogers, "Governors Fight Back," March 31, 2020.

182   CAMUS'S *THE PLAGUE*

mask ordinance of a Florida county deplored the "stifling burden" of face masks.[27]

The suffocation experienced by Covid-19 victims expands in Camus's text to become not only a physical symptom of that plague but also a metaphor for life under its stifling weight. Emerging from the deathbed of Judge Othon's young son, Rieux observes that a "white haze [. . .] made the air yet more stifling" as, lying on a bench after the ordeal of helplessly witnessing the child's agony, he "slowly got back his breath."[28] Being able to breathe signals both a literal and figurative lessening of the plague's grip. Noticing in Part V that a smile is now occasionally seen in public, Rieux is reminded that "[f]or many months the town had been stifling under an airless shroud," but that soon Oran's citizens "would be allowed to breathe freely."[29] Subsequently walking among crowds in Part V, Rieux realizes that throughout the calamity, there had always been a voice "calling them back to the land of their desire, a homeland. It lay outside the walls of the stifled, strangled town."[30] Beyond the "walls" of the disease's stranglehold on Oran, as beyond the physical, social, and economic confines imposed by Covid-19, lies the alluring, nostalgic homeland we once knew, that of being able to breathe freely.

As such a "homeland" in which citizens are "allowed to breathe freely," Oran is laid to ruin at the end of Part I of *The Plague*, upon the telegraphed order from the Algerian capital, Alger: "Declare the state of plague. Close the city."[31] During the Covid-19 pandemic, such abrupt closures of countries, as well as cities, became common, beginning with the lockdown in February 2020, of a dozen towns in the Lombardy region of northern Italy. On March 11, 2020, the World Health Organization declared a state of pandemic; the White House announced that it would close U.S. borders

---

[27] Smith, "The Battle between the Masks," May 29, 2020.
[28] Camus, *The Plague*, 218.
[29] Camus, *The Plague*, 271.
[30] Camus, *The Plague*, 299.
[31] Camus, *The Plague*, 63.

to most of Europe, effective two days later, in a garbled communication that didn't immediately clarify whether American citizens themselves would be allowed to return to their own "homeland." A frenzy to grab seats to return to the United States was unleashed, bringing crushing numbers of Americans from abroad to airports unprepared for the influx, and massive super-spreader events as travelers trapped in crowded, unmasked, shoulder-to-shoulder lines for hours fanned out across the country, spreading infection with them. European countries would ultimately attempt to limit contagion with similar barrier measures, France closing its border early on to travelers from the United States and specific other countries; on January 29, 2021, in response to the circulation of new variants of the virus, it closed its borders to all non-European countries. As of mid-February 2021, several European states were again, as they had in the early stages of the pandemic, closing their borders against each other, in defiance of entreaties by the European Union's governing body to keep the Union's internal borders open. Certain national closures took the form of curfews. In a desperate effort to avoid a third national lockdown, France announced a national curfew of 8:00 pm on December 10, 2020, with an exception allowed for Christmas Eve, but not for New Year's Eve; five weeks later, the curfew was amended to 6:00 pm as it became clear that cocktail gatherings had become sources of infection. In other isolating efforts, quarantines—both for movement within countries and for travelers arriving from beyond—became a major measure in the fight against the virus; in February 2021, the United Kingdom announced that any traveler arriving from a banned country would be required not only to reserve, but to pay, in advance, for a ten-day quarantine in a state-designated quarantine hotel. "Breathing freely," moving freely, whether across borders or outside one's own door, became a lost "homeland" under Covid-19, calling us "back to the land of [our] desire."[32]

[32] Camus, *The Plague*, 299.

184   CAMUS'S *THE PLAGUE*

In an echo of Rieux's efforts to convince the authorities to act in the face of rising numbers of cases, Dr. Anthony Fauci, director of the National Institute for Allergy and Infectious Diseases, worked throughout 2020 to convince the Trump administration that more effective measures were urgently necessary to contain the virus; Fauci was ultimately sidelined by the Trump administration for his zeal. We recall that the young doctor who first raised the alarm with colleagues in Wuhan, China, about a mysterious pneumonia-like illness was harshly reprimanded and silenced by authorities, before succumbing to the virus himself.[33] It is only thanks to an insistence viewed as excessive [déplacée]—since the Prefect views the whole business as a false alarm and wants to avoid provoking anxiety— that Rieux succeeds in forcing the creation of a health commission in Oran in the early days of the plague. When the question is raised of whether or not it is, specifically, a case of the plague that the city is confronting, the behavior of those present betrays their panic at no longer being able to evade the truth; some doctors exclaim, others hesitate, and the Prefect, startled, turns involuntarily toward the door, as though ensuring that he had effectively prevented such a monstrosity from spreading in his corridors.[34] The discussion then erodes into quibbles over the language to be used in representing the situation, with the timid, compromised formulation—"we are to take the responsibility of acting as though the epidemic were plague"—finding general approval as Rieux walks out in frustration.[35] Similarly, the Trump administration, briefed in January 2020, on the dangers of what the president would refer to as the "China virus," considered the warnings excessive. Asked in a January 22, 2020, interview whether there were concerns that the novel coronavirus identified in China could become a pandemic, Trump replied, "No, not at all. It's going to be just fine," he assured

---

[33] Buckley, "Chinese Doctor, Silenced," February 6, 2020.
[34] Camus, *The Plague*, 50.
[35] Camus, *The Plague*, 51.

"I CAN'T BREATHE" 185

the newscaster. "We have it totally under control."[36] Just over a year later, however, in February 2021, the number of U.S. Covid-19 deaths surpassed 500,000. Ironically enough, the first vaccines were administered in the United States on the day another, earlier grim milestone, that of 300,000 deaths, was reached.[37]

Implicit in this staggering figure is the strain on medical resources, including exhausted caregivers who face rising levels of suicide, depression, anxiety, and stress. *The Plague*'s narrator documents the dogged numbness, sapping even the energy to hope, that sets in among Rieux's informal band of fighters of the epidemic: "the stolid indifference that we may imagine the fighting man in a great war, who, worn out by the incessant strain and mindful only of the duties daily assigned to him, has ceased even to hope for the decisive battle or the bugle-call of armistice."[38] Under such relentless, exhausting pressure, Rieux tells us, "[h]is sensibility was getting out of hand. Kept under all the time, it had grown hard and brittle and seemed to snap completely now and then, leaving him the prey of his emotions. No resource was left him but to tighten the strangle-hold on his feelings and harden his heart protectively."[39] America's own version of Rieux, Dr. Anthony Fauci, whose workdays run to nineteen hours, mentioned on August 7, 2020, that he had not had a day off since early January of that year.[40]

To be sure, important differences separate our own experience of the coronavirus from that of *The Plague*'s characters; and yet, curiously, these differences ultimately fade, becoming merely another variation of the same plight. With the closure of Oran, the plague-stricken city is isolated from the larger, unafflicted world. Listening to the radio as far-away, unknown voices helplessly express solidarity and support in discourses either heavy with epic cadences

---

[36] Donald Trump, interview with Joe Kernen, CNBC, January 22, 2020.
[37] Healey et al., "US Starts Vaccine Roll-Out," December 14, 2020.
[38] Camus, *The Plague*, 190.
[39] Camus, *The Plague*, 192.
[40] Spear, "Dr. Anthony Fauci," August 7, 2020.

186   CAMUS'S *THE PLAGUE*

or tritely suggestive of school-prize speeches, Rieux is frustrated at their banal conventionality: their utter inability to render the small, daily, tireless efforts made, for example, by statistician Grand against the plague. The remoteness of such kind, fraternal, encouragement and admiration only demonstrates, as Rieux realizes, the terrible human powerlessness to share in an agony one can't see.[41] In contrast to Oran's ordeal, to be sure, the pandemic of our time leaves no one untouched, as we share the traumas of Covid-19 with those on the other side of the globe in universal suffering. Yet, in a cruel paradox, from within the vast, planetary reaches of our pandemic, we are each trapped within our own confines in so many tiny, monad-like worlds. As Rieux himself puts it, "if it was an exile, it was, for most of us, exile in one's own home"[42]; any protective "bubbles" through which we might enjoy a sense of "safe," if fleeting, human interaction—emblematized in the plastic igloos offered by restaurants for those wishing to dine "safely" outdoors on the sidewalk—only remind us of our isolation.

Similarly, important differences between *The Plague*'s time and our own appear to be at work in communications with others, yet ultimately collapse under comparable pressures. Communication between Oran and the "outside," once letter mail is suspended for fear of transmitting infection, is cruelly reduced and condensed into the "trite formulas" of helplessly clichéd telegrams: "'Am well. Always thinking of you. Love.'"[43] Specificity is obliterated in favor of what poet Mallarmé called "the language of the tribe"; one's most passionate outpourings of love, regret, nostalgia, and longing are boiled down to a common currency of universally bland, stock phrases. Our own communications, to be sure, mushroom and multiply across the high-tech simulacra of media (Zoom, Facetime, Messenger, Facebook); however, these screen faces that

---

[41] Camus, *The Plague*, 138.
[42] Camus, *The Plague*, 73.
[43] Camus, *The Plague*, 69.

are familiar, yet other, risk conveying a strangely uncanny impression of intimacy. Such sessions lose the relaxed ease and spontaneity of bodily proximity; trapped within the rectangles of a screen, one is obliged to maintain focus on one's interlocutor; these personal exchanges take on the implicit agendas of appointments. Virtual cocktail hours, virtual dinners, suffer the same fate. Once the apparatus is turned on and the session initiated, time becomes burdened with purpose, artificially meaning-oriented, as though pressured by some hidden agenda; friendly encounters become implicit business meetings, burdened by an obscure need to advance, somehow, in some way. Just as all intimacy is evacuated by the formulaic telegrams conveying loving yet hollow messages in and out of Oran, so our virtual encounters with loved ones become strangely hollow, emptied of authentic exchange.

Pursuing the psychological impact of disease in Camus's Oran as well as in our own time, *The Plague*'s characters allude only obliquely to their mental anguish; Rieux's tautly controlled chronicle in measured sentences is clearly not given to such discussion, even in his account of receiving—"with composure"—the telegram announcing the death of his wife to tuberculosis. On this occasion, all we are told is what Rieux tells his mother: "he'd been expecting it, but it was hard, all the same," but that "this suffering was nothing new. For many months, and for the last two days [since the death of Tarrou], it was the self-same suffering going on and on."[44] While mental-health challenges such as anxiety and depression accompanying our own experience of Covid-19 are widely discussed by the media and receive explicit administrative attention (from the Centers for Disease Control, for example), the "self-same suffering going on and on" mentioned by Rieux discreetly alludes to psychological distress. Rieux points to the temptation to imagine a time limit to the imprisonment of the plague, such as

---

[44] Camus, *The Plague*, 293.

188   CAMUS'S *THE PLAGUE*

six months, for instance; yet once one has somehow steeled oneself to wait out the ordeal, having "drunk in advance the dregs of bitterness of those six black months,"[45] something—a friend, a news article, a vague inkling, a sudden intuition—"would suggest that, after all, there was no reason why the epidemic shouldn't last more than six months; why not a year, or even more?" Rieux then details the precipitous collapse, in such instants, of his fellow citizens' "courage, willpower and endurance," leaving them mired in "a pit of despond" escaped only at the price of forcing themselves never to think about the future, never to imagine that potential moment of release. But this cautious approach of "feinting with their predicament" left them bereft of any "redeeming" moment of forgetfulness about the plague. "Thus," summarizes Rieux, "in a middle course between these heights and depths, they drifted through life rather than lived, the prey of aimless days and sterile memories, like wandering shadows."[46] Such feelings of numbness and aimlessness, implicitly rendered in Rieux's impression of "drifting," would seem to characterize our own efforts to cope psychologically with the ongoing duration of Covid-19. Even as vaccination programs become widespread, new variants of the coronavirus emerge; other countries announce new lockdowns.[47] The difficulty of identifying an end point to the pandemic, the uprooting of routines, the social isolation, the rising levels of stress, anxiety, and depression, have led to dramatic increases in U.S. emergency rooms of suicidal young patients; the number of such patients needing emergency care in one Oakland, California, hospital was double the figure in fall 2020 that it had been in fall 2019.[48] The number of children and teens treated for suicide attempts at a children's hospital in Indianapolis,

[45] Camus, *The Plague*, 72.
[46] Camus, *The Plague*, 72–73.
[47] A week's lockdown for Auckland, New Zealand, was announced on February 27, 2021, after a local case of unidentified origin was discovered.
[48] Chatterjee, "Child Psychiatrists Warn," February 2, 2021.

Indiana, jumped by 250 percent between October 2019 and October 2020.[49]

Yet a very different reaction to both ordeals—that of Oran's citizens in Camus's novel, and our own during the Covid-19 pandemic—is that of denial: a certain refusal to accept the "suffocation" that so decisively upends our lives. In one episode of *The Plague*, Cottard and Tarrou go the Oran Opera for a performance of Gluck's "Orpheus and Eurydice" by a visiting troupe. Now stranded in the closed city for some months, the troupe performs the same opera every Friday night, as the city's most elegant citizens, bereft of pastimes, continue to attend—intent, as they arrive, not to fail in their own theatrical entrances as they move from one row to another, nodding graciously, and exchanging pleasantries with an assurance they lack in the darkened streets of the stricken city. "Evening dress," observes the narrator in summarizing his fellow citizens' conviction "was a sure charm against the plague."[50] During the performance attended by Cottard and Tarrou, the first act proceeds without incident; during the second, the extra tremolos in Orpheus's aria acquire a slight excess of pathos, while certain jerky gestures appear to be the singer's stylized interpretation of his role. In the third act, however, as Orpheus can't resist looking back and thus losing Eurydice to the underworld in the course of a tragic duet, a murmur of surprise from the audience appears to confirm the singer's own awareness of his malaise; he chooses that instant to advance grotesquely, arms and legs flailing, toward the audience and crashes to the floor, taking the pastoral décor with him in ludicrous irony. The orchestra falls silent as the audience rises and begins to file out, heads down, slowly, and decorously, at first, then with increasing haste, disorder, and panic as Cottard and Tarrou look down from their balcony seats upon the "useless luxury" of abandoned fans and lace trailing on the red velour of

---

[49] Chatterjee, "Child Psychiatrists Warn," February 2, 2021.
[50] Camus, *The Plague*, 200.

190   CAMUS'S *THE PLAGUE*

seats: discarded relics of an obsolete past, absurdly irrelevant to the grim, stifling present imposed by the plague.[51]

This episode is recounted in Tarrou's notebooks, and chosen by the narrating Rieux as worthy of inclusion in his chronicle; its particular weight is further emphasized by Rieux's own paragraph of introduction explicitly underlining the episode's importance as an illustration of the "curious states of mind," the "curiously feverish atmosphere of this period"; "that is why," the account tells us explicitly, "the narrator attaches importance to it."[52] Just how does the opera episode capture so aptly and significantly, in Rieux's view, his fellow citizens' "states of mind"? Just why does he introduce the episode with an entire paragraph emphasizing its significance? We might imagine that Rieux seeks to underscore the audience's denial, its refusal to accept the reality of the plague's danger; its implicit insistence on clinging to the customary distractions and freedoms of the past; its refusal to sacrifice such habitual individual liberties to caution and common sense.

In a chilling echo of *The Plague*'s opera episode, the White House outdoor ceremony on September 26, 2020, to introduce the Trump administration's nominee for the Supreme Court seat vacated by the death of Ruth Bader Ginsburg, Amy Coney Barrett, seemed to unite DC's most powerful social and political actors in a festive gathering where seats were not positioned in accordance with social-distancing measures, and few masks were worn. Photos of the subsequent indoor reception showed no visible effort to protect against infection as guests mingled in closed spaces, still, for the most part, maskless and undistanced. In a variation on *The Plague*'s "evening dress" illusion as "a sure charm against the plague," it seemed, the vestments of power and prestige, the very bastion of the historic White House, warded off the virus. As reported in *The Washington Post*, "Attendees were so confident that the contagion would not invade their seemingly safe

---

[51] Camus, *The Plague*, 200–201.
[52] Camus, *The Plague*, 199.

"I CAN'T BREATHE" 191

space at the White House that [. . .] after guests tested negative that day they were instructed they no longer needed to cover their faces."[53] Yet, in a slow-motion replay of Camus's opera scene, several in attendance at the event—including President Trump and First Lady Melania Trump—began testing positive and falling ill with Covid-19 in the following days; it would subsequently be revealed that doctors had feared needing to administer oxygen to the hospitalized president. As *The Washington Post* put it as early as a mere five days after the event, the "feeling of invincibility was cruelly punctured."[54]

Such denial of the epidemic's deadliness, the illusory feelings of invincibility, and the refusal to renounce customary individual liberties shaping both *The Plague*'s opera episode and the White House event are apparent in wider reactions to the Covid-19 epidemic. These "curious states of mind," as Rieux phrases them,[55] are currently visible in the politicization of protective measures—including enforced business closures and mask-wearing ordinances—viewed as infringements of personal liberties. Republican member of the House of Representatives Marjorie Taylor Green, elected in November 2020, enlisted a familiar feminist slogan—"My body, my choice"—in announcing her refusal to wear a face mask.[56] When the Democratic governor of Virginia announced a state-wide mask mandate in late May 2020, Republicans immediately decried what they viewed as a "coercive" measure, reprising (unknowingly, undoubtedly) *The Plague*'s

---

[53] Rucker et al., "How the Coronavirus Spread," October 2, 2020. *The Post*'s source for this information, the Reverend John I. Jenkins, president of the University of Notre Dame and invited to the event in honor of alumna Amy Barrett Coney's nomination, himself tested positive on October 2.

[54] Rucker et al., "How the Coronavirus Spread," October 2, 2020.

[55] Camus's original French formulation for Stuart Gilbert's translation as "curious states of mind" even more forcefully emphasizes the condition of uniqueness. We might translate the original French more literally as "this singular state of mind" [cette conscience singulière]: an attitude the narrator is at pains to emphasize through the word "singular" as both unusual and monolithic, overriding.

[56] Rabinovitch-Fox, "The Battle over Masks," November 18, 2020.

192   CAMUS'S *THE PLAGUE*

asphyxiation image in calling masks a "stifling burden."[57] Attorney Jeff Childers (despite choosing, himself, to wear a mask) challenged a Florida county's mask mandate, saying that although he doesn't want "to get too flag wavy," he feels that "the foundation of our democracy [is] that we are a country of people who govern ourselves."[58] Such tension between an individual's right of choice and countervailing, public-health measures on behalf of a collective is visible in the evolution of Rieux's role in Oran's epidemic. Before the plague, as a doctor, he was "welcomed as a savior"; in Part IV, however, "he wasn't there for saving life; he was there to order a sick man's evacuation." As isolation is imposed to protect the healthy, Rieux arrives at a family's door "accompanied by soldiers, and they had to hammer on the door with rifle-butts before the family would open it."[59]

In this context of individual rights as opposed to collective, legislative authority, we recall *The Plague's* closing line about the perpetual danger of a resurgence of the epidemic. The narrator reminds us that the plague's bacillus lies dormant in household recesses, until, "perhaps," "it would rouse up its rats again and send them forth to die in a happy city."[60] Interestingly, Camus's choice for *The Plague's* final word is not the obvious French term, "ville," but the more archaic "cité"—bringing a wider, etymological resonance comprising not only a metropolis, but the body politic, the Republic, the State: a federation of autonomous entities such as, for instance, the Greek city-states. Democracy, with its protections of individual rights in the context of collective elected bodies, thus discreetly but decisively inhabits the word "cité." *The Plague* closes upon the danger and risk that epidemic infection brings not only to a city, but implicitly, to wider, vaster political entities under

---

[57] Rabinovitch-Fox, "The Battle over Masks," November 18, 2020.
[58] Rabinovitch-Fox, "The Battle over Masks," November 18, 2020.
[59] Camus, *The Plague*, 193.
[60] Camus, *The Plague*, 308.

democratic forms of government. And indeed, such danger, such risk, is apparent in the debates that pit individual rights against the imposition, by elected officials and elected governing bodies, of collective health measures. Fostered by a political climate of international isolationism and personal authority under the Trump administration, individuals have felt encouraged to make their own voices heard against the public interest; to oppose collective, public protections of the populace so as to assert to the nation and the world, instead, those individual rights enshrined in our Constitution.

As the plague wanes in Oran and the long, suffocating ordeal is gradually lifted, traces of a renewed ability to breathe, both literally and metaphorically, appear in the text. A young patient's case appears hopeless, but by the next morning, "against all the rules," as Rieux tells Tarrou, she "was breathing freely." Tarrou and Rieux climb to a terrace, directed by an old man who assures them, "You'll get a breath of nice fresh air."[61] Indeed, high above the pestilential streets of the plague, their conversation—like their lungs—appears able to open up, as Tarrou enters upon the lengthy confession launched by his claim, "I had plague already, long before I came to this town."[62] The conversation closes, as the moon rises, with Tarrou's suggestion that they go for a swim. Invited by the waters' own "tranquil breathing," Rieux enters the sea ahead of his friend and "drew a deep breath"; as Tarrou swims toward him, Rieux "now could hear his breathing." Marked by the ability to breathe even as the sea's own rising and falling swells in breath-like cadences, this silent episode represents, as Rieux realizes "a respite" (as we might say colloquially, a "breather"), however fleeting—for Tarrou will be one of the epidemic's final victims—from the plague.[63]

---

[61] Camus, *The Plague*, 244.
[62] Camus, *The Plague*, 245.
[63] Camus, *The Plague*, 257.

194 CAMUS'S THE PLAGUE

Yet as *The Plague* closes, Rieux, explaining his decision to bear witness to the ordeal through the account we have just read, warns that his chronicle cannot be that of the "definitive victory"; for the plague bacillus, as we were reminded earlier, doesn't die, but lies dormant—waiting, perhaps, to reemerge. Camus's text ends with an implicit warning about Covid-19; with new variants emerging, such as those identified in Brazil, the United Kingdom, and South Africa, will extant vaccines be effective? The immunity they provide has not been proven to last beyond three months. Will we need a vaccine every year, as we do for the flu? If not, will we need regular booster doses? In Part IV of *The Plague*, the old Dr. Castel feels obliged to temper the optimism of his colleague Dr. Richard; rejoicing at the plague's "high-water mark," Richard is convinced that "thereafter it could but ebb." As Castel points out to him, "the future remained uncertain; history proved that epidemics have a way of recrudescing when least expected."[64] But Richard will not live to see which of the two—himself or his older colleague—is right about the possible retreat of Oran's epidemic; he dies of the plague before the end of the paragraph.

Works Cited

Baker, Mike, Jennifer Valentino-DeVries, Manny Fernandez, and Michael LaForgia. "Three Words. 70 Cases. The Tragic History of 'I Can't Breathe.'" *The New York Times*, June 29, 2020. https://www.nytimes.com/interactive/2020/06/28/us/i-cant.

Buckley, Chris. "Chinese Doctor, Silenced after Warning of Outbreak, Dies from Coronavirus." *The New York Times*, February 6, 2020. https://www.nytimes.com/2020/02/06/world/asia/chinese-doctor-Li-Wenliang-coronavirus.html.

Camus, Albert. *Journaux de Voyage. Oeuvres Complètes d'Albert Camus.* Vol. 7. Edited by Roger Grenier. Paris: Editions du Club de l'Honnête Homme, 1983.

---

[64] Camus, *The Plague*, 235.

"I CAN'T BREATHE" 195

Camus, Albert. *Notebooks I: 1935–1942.* Translated by Philip Thody. New York: Knopf, 1963.

Camus, Albert. *Notebooks II: 1942–1951.* Translated by Justin O'Brien. New York: Knopf, 1966.

Camus, Albert. *The Plague.* Translated by Stuart Gilbert. New York: Vintage Books, 1991.

Chatterjee, Rhitu. "Child Psychiatrists Warn That the Pandemic May Be Driving Up Kids' Suicide Risk." *NPR,* February 2, 2021. https://www.npr.org/sections/health-shots/2021/02/02/962060105/child-psychiatrists-warn-that-the-pandemic-may-be-driving-up-kids-suicide-risk.

Coyle, Matt. "Meghan Markle Can 'Finally Breathe' after Escaping 'Soul Crushing' Life as a Royal, Friend Claims." *The Sun,* January 20, 2020. https://www.thesun.co.uk/news/10756166/meghan-markles-soul-crushing-life-megxit/.

Flores, Adolfo. "Hundreds Take to the Streets on the Eve of Derek Chauvin's Trial for the Killing of George Floyd." *Buzzfeed,* March 7, 2021. https://www.buzzfeednews.com/article/adolfoflores/george-floyd-protest-chauvin-trial.

Gyldén, Axel. "Procès de Derek Chauvin: Ce Que La Mort de George Floyd a Changé (ou Non) aux États-Unis." *L'Express,* March 8, 2021. https://tinyurl.com/dap7b9pp.

Healy, Jack, Amy Harmon, Simon Romero, Noah Weiland, Michael Gold, Roni Caryn Rabin, Karen Zraick, and John Eligon. "US Starts Vaccine Roll-Out as High-Risk Health-Care Workers Go First." *The New York Times,* December 14, 2020. https://www.nytimes.com/live/2020/12/14/world/covid-19-coronavirus.

Markle, Meghan. "Interview with Oprah Winfrey." CBS. March 7, 2021.

Mervosh, Sarah, and Katie Rogers. "Governors Fight Back against Coronavirus Chaos." *The New York Times,* March 31, 2020. https://www.nytimes.com/2020/03/31/us/governors-trump-coronavirus.html.

Rabinovitch-Fox, Elinav. "The Battle over Masks Has Always Been Political." *The Washington Post,* November 18, 2020. https://www.washingtonpost.com/outlook/2020/11/18/battle-over-masks-has-always-been-political/.

Robert, Paul, Josette Rey-Debove, and Alain Rey. *Le Nouveau Petit Robert.* Paris: Dictionnaires Le Robert, 1993.

Rucker, Philip, Josh Dawsey, Ashley Parker, and Robert Costa. "How the Coronavirus Spread in Trump's White House." *The Washington Post,* October 2, 2020. https://www.washingtonpost.com/outlook/2020/11/18/battle-over-masks-has-always-been-political/.

Smith, Tovia. "The Battle between the Masks and the Masked-Nots Unveils Political Rifts." *National Public Radio,* May 29, 2020. https://www.npr.org/2020/05/29/864515630/the-battle-between-the-masked-and-the-masked-nots-unveils-political-rifts.

196 CAMUS'S *THE PLAGUE*

Soanes, Catherine, and Angus Stevenson. *Oxford Dictionary of English*. 2nd ed., revised. Oxford: Oxford University Press, 2005.

Spear, Maggie. "Dr. Anthony Fauci: Maybe This Will Be a Wake-Up Call for Society to Change." *News from Brown*, August 7, 2020. https://www.brown.edu/news/2020-08-07/fauci-sph.

Thompson, Kari. "With Biden-Harris Victory, Some Black Voters Say They Can Finally Breathe Again." *WBUR News*, December 14, 2020. https://www.wbur.org/news/2020/12/14/biden-harris-black-voters-relief.

Todd, Oliver. *Albert Camus, Une Vie*. Paris: Gallimard, 1996.

Trump, Donald. Interview with Joe Kernen. CNBC, January 22, 2020. https://www.cnbc.com/2020/03/17/trump-dissed-coronavirus-pandemic-worry-now-claims-he-warned-about-it.html.

9. Holbein, Hans the Younger (1497–1543). *The Shop-keeper*, from *The Dance of Death*. Ca. 1526, published 1538. Printmaker: Hans Lützelburger (German, died Basel, before 1526). Woodcut. Sheet: 2 5/8 x 1 15/16 in. (6.7 x 5 cm). Rogers Fund, 1919 (19.57.36). Photo: Image copyright © The Metropolitan Museum of Art. Image source: Art Resource, NY.

8

Modern Death, Decent Death, and Heroic Solidarity in *The Plague*

Peg Brand Weiser

The Plague begins on April 16, sometime in the 1940s, in the ordinary but "completely modern" town of Oran: a place where its oddly distinguishing feature is "the difficulty one may experience there in dying," identified by the narrator, Dr. Rieux, as "modern death."[1] By the time a plague is officially proclaimed and quarantine imposed, each person is faced with a new form of "modern" death caused by an antiquated delivery system: fleas upon rats. Tarrou—a newcomer to town—reveals that all he hopes for is "a decent death."[2] In 2008, philosopher Robert Solomon referred to the phenomenon shared by the town's inhabitants as "facing death together."[3] Camus portrayed the residents of Oran, however, in denial, panic, then defeatism, as their original sense of community eroded. Food shortages occurred. Violence erupted in the streets. Residents attempted escape. The loss of freedom was profound.

Threat of death became the ultimate absurdity of a plague bacillus that appeared out of nowhere and grew quickly out of control. Inhabitants struggled to maintain a government-imposed quarantine within the town walls to prevent the spread of disease beyond the gates. Inexplicably—within ten months of its start—the plague

---

[1] Camus, *The Plague*, 5.
[2] Camus, *The Plague*, 252.
[3] Solomon, "Facing Death Together."

Camus's The Plague. Peg Brand Weiser, Oxford University Press. © Oxford University Press 2023.
DOI: 10.1093/oso/9780197599327.003.0009

200   CAMUS'S *THE PLAGUE*

subsided, and the town reopened. "Death"—personified as a foe, an enemy—appeared to be in retreat. Or was it? Dr. Rieux warned that it was merely awaiting its next appearance.

Our own experience of Covid-19 confirms the suspicion that a life-threatening virus can arise at any time. Rereading Camus's narrative provides the opportunity to compare fiction and nonfiction, then and now, and the various responses of current government leaders, the media, medical professionals, and ordinary citizens against the author's intended message of solidarity in resistance. Of philosophical import is whether the population—in Oran or specifically, our own in the United States—acted ethically under pervasive threat of death. Was Camus guilty of "naïve idealism"[4] in having Dr. Rieux voice the claim that even under the most severe conditions of plague, "there are more things to admire in men than to despise?"[5]

For millennia, philosophers have sought to explain human behavior and our tendency to deny death. More recently, social psychologists and neurologists have offered insights that reveal how the mind devises coping mechanisms to avoid "mortality awareness."[6] In facing one's imminent demise, is ethical behavior possible, predictable, and/or can it be learned? *The Plague* offers us insight into the "moral dialogue" that takes place among fictional characters facing possible death and reveals that every major character, except Cottard, cared about helping others.[7] Not only is the choice of the main figure and narrator of the story a physician, but Camus's encouragement to be "true healers"—in contrast to both victims and executioners—reinforces the primacy of caregiving.[8] The concept of care—a basic principle of

---

[4] Kabel and Phillipson, "Structural Violence and Hope in Catastrophic Times," 14.
[5] Camus, *The Plague*, 308.
[6] Solomon, Pyszczynski, and Greenberg, *The Worm at the Core: On the Role of Death in Life*.
[7] Krapp, "Time and Ethics in Albert Camus's *The Plague*," 665–676.
[8] Camus, *The Plague*, 254.

MODERN DEATH, DECENT DEATH, AND HEROIC SOLIDARITY 201

contemporary feminist bioethics that emphasizes relationships and responsibility—explains the work of Dr. Rieux, who does his duty even in the face of seemingly hopeless odds: no cure, no effective serum, and no successful strategy to resist the plague. Care forms the basis of Camus's message of what I call "heroic solidarity" that continues to resonate in our own time as it offers a lesson of concern and hope in our own pandemic era of disease, death, and divisiveness.

Facing "Modern" Death in Oran: Alone or Together?

Robert Solomon offered a provocative interpretation of the inhabitants of Oran. Each person's existence is "collectively threatened" in that each faces not only "personal death"—"the high probability of imminent, horrible death"—but "collective death as well."[9] This observation is meant to capture an extended sense of solidarity and community Camus extols in the narrative. The main character, the physician Dr. Rieux, repeats his exhortation to workers and volunteers to do one's duty, that is, we're all in this together, and to fight the plague, side by side. There is more to Solomon's suggestion, however, in that he aims to extend Camus's meaning of "modern" death beyond merely "the difficulty one may experience there in dying" (to quote Camus's own words) to capture the undeniable fact that the bubonic plague is the specific immediate threat they all face, at the same time, with no end in sight. Like passengers on a plane about to crash, potential victims have no choice but to face the threat, and they do so together, facing "collective death." Such a threat raises questions about how one reacts and indeed, Solomon rightly suggests that it is the moral behavior

[9] Solomon, "Facing Death Together," 163.

202 CAMUS'S *THE PLAGUE*

and not necessarily the happiness of the characters—although the topic is discussed—that occupies Camus's interest. How does one behave when facing the difficult and "modern" collective death of plague in this fictional work set in the 1940s? Likewise, how does one act facing "modern death"—to use the term preferred by physician Haider Warraich in 2017—in an actual, twenty-first-century nonfictional pandemic of our own?[10] Fascinating answers lie in the variations of human behavior: some predictable and praiseworthy, others shocking and appalling. Let us consider first what scholars have meant when discussing facing death together or alone. Second, let us consider the term "modern."

Philosophers have written much about death. Textbooks with introductory readings are meant to acquaint students with such topics as the epistemology, metaphysics, and the "badness" of death as (mere) dying in contrast to the "wrongness" of killing, as might be argued in cases of abortion, euthanasia, and suicide.[11] Epicurus taught his followers in ancient times that death was not to be feared nor even cause for concern: "Get used to believing that death is nothing to us."[12] Montaigne overcame an intense fear of death to offer a stoic approach: "The perpetual work of your life is but to lay the foundation of death."[13] Disavowing the existence of an eternal soul, twentieth-century existentialists offered their own unique thoughts on death as the end point of life but according to Paul Edwards, they often confused common terminology. On the one hand, death was seen as non-being, a "darkness" or a mystery, as captured by Paul Tillich—"[W]e come from the darkness of the 'not yet' and rush ahead towards the darkness of the 'no more.'"[14] On the other hand, death could simply mean the process of dying. For Edwards, confusion of the two "is unquestionably one of the

---

[10] Warraich, *Modern Death: How Medicine Changed the End of Life.*
[11] Brennan and Stainton, "Introduction," xiii–xvii.
[12] Edwards, "Existentialism and Death," 164.
[13] Montaigne, *The Complete Works of Michel de Montaigne,* 205.
[14] Edwards, "Existentialism and Death," 30–31.

MODERN DEATH, DECENT DEATH, AND HEROIC SOLIDARITY   203

factors responsible for the extremely misleading assertions, endlessly repeated by all existentialists, that all of us must die isolated and alone."[15]

Thus, when John Wild states, "death is not something universal. It concerns me as an individual. It is not a replaceable, interchangeable function, but something I must face myself alone,"[16] Edwards argues that the statement makes sense only if "death" really means "dying." He offers only two legitimate senses of "dying alone": (1) physically isolated, for example, an Arctic explorer lost before rescuers arrive; and (2) psychologically or emotionally isolated as in a person "who does not greatly care about anybody else and nobody else cares much about him."[17] Any third, separate sense of "dying alone" proposed by Wild simply does not exist. Rather, "dying alone"—even in the case of a person who is happy and caring and experiencing deep love in his or her final days—simply means "dying" in that it is logically inconceivable for the meaning of "dying alone" to mean anything more, even in this case. The so-called doctrine of the privacy of death, then, which claims that "nobody can get another human being to die for him, to act as his substitute or representative in the matter of death," simply means that "everybody *eventually* dies."[18] According to Edwards, there is no privacy of death because "The dead cannot talk to the living or to their fellow dead or even to themselves" and it is "*senseless* to say about anybody that he is alone in his death" because "To be alone, one has to be alive, and the dead are neither alone nor not alone."[19]

Therefore, death in terms of dying alone is specialized, rare, and not, as Wild suggests, the existential condition of all persons. In this sense, we face death together more often than we admit

---

[15] Edwards, "Existentialism and Death," 28.
[16] Edwards, "Existentialism and Death," 25.
[17] Edwards, "Existentialism and Death," 28–29.
[18] Edwards, "Existentialism and Death," 29.
[19] Edwards, "Existentialism and Death," 31.

204   CAMUS'S *THE PLAGUE*

and Solomon is simply stating something obvious and perhaps reassuring; for example, there is strength in numbers. On this reading, Solomon's suggestion that Oranians are facing death together fails to adequately capture what motivated them to act: ethically or otherwise. The important question is not whether one thinks one faces death together or alone but rather how one acts when confronted with the high probability of an immediate threat of death. We may take comfort in knowing that everyone (eventually) dies, but of concern—for the common good—is each person's set of circumstances: the context in which we make our own decisions to act. Our interest in the characters in *The Plague* belies our desire to know how each fared in facing death.

Facing "Modern" Death in Covid-19 America

Even before the plague struck, Camus stated that "modern death" was often experienced "with difficulty" in the "completely modern town" of Oran. He offered little evidence as to why. "Modern" seemed a feeble linguistic attempt to capture a time, a place, an outlook on life: unspecified within the decade of the 1940s. Why would the narrator, a physician no less, describe his home as such? What makes it modern in the 1940s? In this context, "modern" is merely a placeholder, a trendy post–World War I term of European import. If "modern" is merely a placeholder in Camus's preplague conception of death, then "modern" in our own twenty-first-century world of a pandemic that has claimed victims for over two years has been rendered essentially meaningless. If the 1940s were considered "modern," then the twenty-first century cannot also lay claim to the descriptor. Rather, we might say we face postmodern, or even post-postmodern death, but certainly not death deemed "modern" eighty years prior. The ineptness of the term comes into focus with a publication that offers a closer look.

MODERN DEATH, DECENT DEATH, AND HEROIC SOLIDARITY   205

In 2018, Haider Warraich confidently informed us that "Modern death is nothing like what death was even a few decades ago."[20] In a book titled *Modern Death: How Medicine Changed the End of Life*, we learn about the history of death, the evolution of medical improvements, and the "modern" situation of dying in a hospital, not at home, after nearly every possibly permitted procedure to prolong life has been performed. Warraich writes that modern medicine has "done much to stave off death but little to ameliorate people's fear of dying."[21] In fact, prolonging life, especially for the elderly, has made people even more fearful of death in the twenty-first century; Warraich cites the predictability of a slow, drawn-out process of dying—longer life spans and protracted hospitalizations at the end of life—as the cause. ("Only 12 percent of deaths in the U.S. occur in people younger than fifty."[22]) The increased "sanitization and secularization of medicine" has also added to the "ambiguity and terror at the end of life" in that fewer priests, rabbis, and other caregivers who administer comfort—particularly spiritual comfort—attend a dying person in her final moments.[23] One study showed that 85 percent of Americans profess to hold religious beliefs which augment the feeling that they are never alone, but as patients, they want "the most aggressive care, more invasive procedures, and more time in the intensive-care unit at the end of life and are less likely to want to withhold or withdraw care."[24] Such futile measures can prolong life in harmful ways. Options like hospice, palliative care measures intended to assist terminally ill patients, and do-not-resuscitate orders are routinely rejected.[25] This intense form of death denial—"this flight away from facing

---

[20] Warraich, *Modern Death*, 10.
[21] Warraich, *Modern Death*, 145.
[22] Warraich, *Modern Death*, 146.
[23] Warraich, *Modern Death*, 146–147.
[24] Warraich, *Modern Death*, 149.
[25] In fact, recent studies show patients even more fearful of physician-initiated palliative care consultations; see Warraich, "In Pandemic Era, the Term Palliative Care," September 7, 2020.

206   CAMUS'S *THE PLAGUE*

death calmly" as noted by Elisabeth Kübler-Ross, author of *On Death and Dying* and pioneer of the hospice movement in the United States—is at odds with any acceptance of so-called modern death.[26]

Penned prior to our current pandemic, Warraich's pronouncements have been rendered dubious. During Covid-19, Americans often die alone. "Modern" death has come to revert to conditions operational under Camus's fictional Oran, Daniel Defoe's seventeenth-century London, and Thucydides's ancient Greece. Ventilators do not save lives. Patients are denied visitors. Health care workers covered in personnel protective equipment hold cell phones for the dying to hear loved ones' last words. "Modern death"—as extolled by Warraich citing technological advances—is rendered mute. Sophisticated scientific progress toward eliminating the possibility of dying alone and with difficulty has failed millions afflicted by Covid-19. His claim that "Modern death is nothing like what death was even a few decades ago" rings hollow just two years after publication. However, his claim that people are still fearful of death—perhaps even more so than before—invites more scrutiny, particularly as to whether we come to feel even more terrified because death feels immanent and unavoidable as variants called "Delta" and "Omicron" run rampant worldwide at the start of a third year of Covid-19.

Moral philosopher Shelly Kagan asks whether we—who are busy leading goal-oriented, pleasure-seeking lives in the twenty-first century—should be thinking at all about living in the face of death.[27] Of course, the topic could easily be ignored if not for an

---

[26] Warraich, *Modern Death*, 146. Another palliative care physician, Daniel Rushing, argued for a sixth stage beyond the five proposed by Kübler-Ross of embracing death that "encompasses a spiritual process of regaining the feelings of being universally lovable, which allows one to let go of any fear"; see "Physical, Psychological, and Spiritual Transformation at Life's End," 5.

[27] Kagan, *Death*, 282.

MODERN DEATH, DECENT DEATH, AND HEROIC SOLIDARITY 207

unexpected pandemic that has befallen us beginning late 2019.[28] Kagan notes how natural it is to fear death, but such anticipation may or may not influence future actions. When living in the face of death, he suggests that we follow a possible strategy of carpe diem or, alternately, live a more fulfilling, long-term satisfying life of accomplishments and relationships. A third strategy is a mixture of the two with the possibility that one's deeds "will continue to last after you" such as writing poetry or a novel, making a scientific discovery, or solving a philosophical argument. But these are strategies for individuals *eventually* facing death, not of those facing an immediate threat. Kagan fails to consider the urgency of death during an ongoing pandemic since, of course, he did not write during one and probably could not even imagine the current situation in which we now live. Again, the question is how does one act, how does one *live*—both pre- and post-vaccine—in the face of immediate, pending death from a fast-spreading virus that has no cure and from which there is no certain protection?

As in Camus's fictional town of Oran, death becomes undeniable, ever-present, and threatening, with numbers recorded to track its ebb and flow. Even with "modern" medicine, the United States has suffered the highest death toll in the world during Covid-19. If there was ever a time when average persons could not ignore death and dying—even in their denial of it—it is during a global emergency health crisis. Initially few journalists or essayists broached the topic of individually confronting death, but one author addressed the topic directly in an opinion piece titled "Covid-19 Makes Us Think about Our Mortality. Our Brains Aren't Designed for That." She cited a theory advanced by social psychologists Solomon, Pyszczynski, and Greenberg, known as the terror management theory, that suggests that "existential terror," "existential

---

[28] Achenbach, "NIH Study Suggests Coronavirus May Have Been in U.S. as Early as December 2019," June 15, 2021.

208   CAMUS'S *THE PLAGUE*

anxiety," and "existential shock" account for our feelings of fear, apprehension, and grief, at the thought of immanent death.[29] They were initially motivated by the influential 1973 publication *The Denial of Death* by Ernest Becker, who builds a case that our animalistic (irrational) fear of death tempered by rational thought influences human behavior to fear death and to seek avoidance. The theory suggests that tests show that *making mortality salient*, that is, reminding people of their mortality, can motivate persons to strive for self-esteem and more strongly identify with self-affirming groups. Individuals—especially those with low self-esteem—seek to join others who are like-minded as they defend their shared worldview(s). Reactions can include becoming more humble and grateful, more charitable, more "patriotic" accompanied by aggression toward perceived critics of one's country, or more antagonistic toward other nationalities, religions, and ethnicities. One study done on subjects after the terrorist attacks on September 11, 2001, showed:

> Americans became more pro-US, donated blood, sought out close others, lashed out at any perceived threat to the culture, and memorialized the victims and first-responders to secure their symbolic immortality.[30]

In addition, President George W. Bush's approval rating climbed from 50 to 90 percent in only ten days, verifying followers endorsed a leader with a similar worldview.

In asking ourselves how the situation is different during the current pandemic, we can quickly assess that under former president Donald J. Trump, no memorials were held for victims, families, first

---

[29] Pattee, "Covid-19 Makes Us Think about Our Mortality," October 7, 2020, cites Solomon, Pyszczynski, and Greenberg, authors of *The Worm at the Core: On the Role of Death in Life.*

[30] Greenberg, "This Mortal Coil," 9.

MODERN DEATH, DECENT DEATH, AND HEROIC SOLIDARITY   209

responders, or the public. Moreover, the administration issued no calls for volunteers or increased testing, but rather labeled the pandemic a hoax and cast fellow citizens who wore protective masks as a perceived threat to the great, invincible American way of life. In effect, Americans were divided due to lack of leadership in the White House, which scientists now argue caused tens, if not hundreds of thousands of unnecessary deaths. Only six months into worst-case fatality numbers, observers claimed, "Trump gave up on fighting the virus. Now we're paying for his laziness."[31] Not only did we fail to face death together, but partisan politics wrought destructive divisions among populations, often the most vulnerable among us.

Many other scholars lend credibility to terror management theory that further informs us about growing social divisions we are currently experiencing in America during the pandemic. Political scientist Brendan Nyhan asks in light of true and accurate information seemingly available everywhere, "Why are misperceptions about contentious issues in politics and science seemingly so persistent and difficult to correct?"[32] In other words, why do people persist in believing false claims, resistant to abandoning or correcting them? He states:

Research conducted to date suggests that cognitive and memory limitations, directional motivations to defend or support some group identity or existing belief, and messages from other people and political elites all play critical roles in the spread of misinformation.[33]

The spread of misinformation and disinformation in our current age of pervasive social media has become more important

---

[31] Bassett and Linos, "Trump Gave Up," July 14, 2020.
[32] Nyhan, "Why the Backfire Effect Does Not Explain," 1.
[33] Nyhan, "Why the Backfire Effect Does Not Explain," 2.

210 CAMUS'S *THE PLAGUE*

than truth in insuring inclusion in our chosen groups, confirming worldviews, and bolstering self-esteem; in other words, as one writer summarizes, we are more interested in belonging than in facts.[34]

These behavioral trends help to explain why leaders in the government, from former president Trump on down, including many citizens who followed his lack of leadership in rejecting scientific fact, chose to divide our ranks, rebel against local and state governments, and sabotage Centers for Disease Control (CDC) recommendations to inhibit the spread of a killer virus. Refusal to follow guidelines that were as simple and easy as wearing protective masks, practicing social distancing, and self-quarantining contributed to the rise in "domestic terrorism," as it is now called by the FBI, in the form of the January 6, 2021, storming of the U.S. Capitol and the rise of right-wing hate groups, intolerance, threats, and violence. "Us" versus "them" has inflamed partisan divisions acutely in the face of death when one seeks to increase self-esteem, reduce anxiety, and find comfort in communion with others of similar, even if misguided, thinking. Anti-vaxxers have prevented universal acceptance of vaccines that have been scientifically proven to prevent illness and death. I call this behavior a form of resistance with individuals acting in solidarity, but it is not consistent with the type of resistance Camus advanced in *The Plague*. Rather, he recommended ethical behavior, following the example and exhortations of Dr. Rieux, working together against the plague for the good of all, with care for others. Arguing "it's my body and you can't make me vaccinate" is selfish and maximally *un*caring. Dr. Rieux recruited Tarrou, Grand, even Rambert in his communal efforts *to do something*, even if their efforts fell short of curing plague victims or preventing illness.

---

[34] Fisher, " 'Belonging Is Stronger Than Facts,' " May 7, 2021.

MODERN DEATH, DECENT DEATH, AND HEROIC SOLIDARITY   211

The current behavior of extreme partisanship, the rejection of science, the politicization of wearing a mask and getting a vaccine has engendered a type of solidarity that stands in stark contrast to Camus's intended ethical foundation. Not only has Trump vilified Dr. Anthony Fauci who stands as an analogous figure to Dr. Rieux, he has hypocritically misled his followers after insisting in early 2020 that the virus would quickly disappear. He minimized testing, recommended the ingestion of bleach as a cure for Covid-19 (from which one person died following his advice), and failed to wear a mask at White House events and rallies that functioned as super-spreader events. He received his own vaccine in December 2020, after being hospitalized but did not recommend it to others. (He revealed in December 2021 that he also received his booster shot and finally advocated the vaccine to others.) Evidence shows that in retrospect Trump potentially spread the virus to over five hundred people after testing positive in September 2020, showing he cared little to nothing about his harm to others, including family members, secret service agents, and rally attendees. He cared only about projecting an appearance of health, vigor, and bravado.[35] Within one week of a positive test result (when he debated presidential nominee Joe Biden in person on stage), he was hospitalized with Covid-19 symptoms.

Perhaps the most egregious disservice was his return from Walter Reed Hospital after a serious encounter with the disease. On live national TV, he acted as if he were fine; he ran up a set of stairs and breathlessly announced he felt great and told viewers that whatever cured him would be available to everyone in America. It was a lie, and hundreds of thousands of people would die naively believing his words and actions that day. Here is a hypothetical to ponder: how would the trajectory of the pandemic and our response to it as a nation have changed if in early October 2020 Trump had

---

[35] Parker and Dawsey, "Seven Days: Following Trump's Coronavirus Trail," December 5, 2021.

212 CAMUS'S *THE PLAGUE*

died of Covid-19 at Walter Reed, particularly if he had died alone, with no family at his side, as most of his fellow citizens were then experiencing? Would his death have turned the tide, invalidated the empty but repeated claim of hoax, and motivated ethical cooperation with CDC guidelines by his followers? Would fear of dying like Trump have resulted in more social distancing, mask wearing, subsequent vaccine mandates, and far fewer deaths? Even now the partisan evidence is clear: unvaccinated persons are more likely to test positive, be hospitalized, and die of Covid-19 than those who are vaccinated. In effect, persons in red states and counties die more.[36] Where science, logic, and good sense failed, might terrifying fear have succeeded? With record-breaking demand for vaccines and tests taking hold amid the rise of the Omicron variant in early 2022, we can only lament the number of deaths that could have been avoided in the months since Trump's hospitalization. Fear came too late for far too many, or not at all, as stories from medical workers repeatedly tell of patients—literally on their death beds—denying Covid-19.[37]

A Decent Death: Oran and Now

Trump's behavior was immature, narcissistic, and dangerous, what I call "unheroic," and his followers have joined him in what can only be labeled "unheroic solidarity." His self-centered, uncaring actions were like the actions of Cottard, who sought out like-minded criminals to personally profit during the plague and exploit the weakness of Oran's vulnerable citizens even after he was rescued from an unsuccessful suicide attempt by a neighbor, Grand, who simply says, "one's got to help a neighbor, hasn't one?"[38] Unheroic

[36] Blake, "The Most-Vaccinated Big Counties in America Are Beating the Worst of the Coronavirus," December 4, 2021.

[37] Miranda, "'I Don't Have COVID,'" September 25, 2021.

[38] Camus, *The Plague*, 20.

MODERN DEATH, DECENT DEATH, AND HEROIC SOLIDARITY   213

solidarity shows no care and little concern for others' well-being. Heroic solidarity, in contrast, was exemplified by Dr. Rieux and his fellow physicians and by Tarrou, Rambert, Othon, and Dr. Rieux's mother. Even Grand, who at first is described by Dr. Rieux as someone "who had nothing of the hero about him," was later praised for his work of counting the dead as an "insignificant and obscure hero who had to his credit only a little goodness of heart and a seemingly absurd ideal."[39]

At one point in the narrative, Tarrou—considered a spokesman for Camus himself—expressed a desire for a "decent" death. Is this possible in Oran: a death without difficulty, regardless of whether it's called "modern" or not? Might it be what we now call "death with dignity," a process involving the maximum of (palliative) caregiving, concern, and comfort? The physician Warraich reports that over time he learned to deliver "humane care" to his patients.[40] What Tarrou sought was an experience of death infused with peace. "I have realized that we all have plague, and I have lost my peace," he says when condemning capital punishment, adding:

> And today I am still trying to find it; still trying to understand all those others and not to be the mortal enemy of anyone. I only know that one must do what one can to cease being plague-stricken, and that's the only way in which we can hope for some peace, or failing that, a decent death.[41]

Shortly after his revelation, Tarrou dies a horrifying death of fever, swollen ganglia, and fits of coughing, becoming to Dr. Rieux who was his most immediate friend, "only a masklike face, inert, from which the smile had gone forever."[42] But note that he did not die alone. Both Mme. Rieux and Dr. Rieux were at his side, caring for

---

[39] Camus, *The Plague*, 133 and 137.
[40] Warraich, *Modern Death*, ix.
[41] Camus, *The Plague*, 252.
[42] Camus, *The Plague*, 289.

214   CAMUS'S *THE PLAGUE*

him, and he died in Rieux's own apartment, an exception to quarantine rules. Crying tears of impotence, Dr. Rieux felt helpless to cure or comfort, but his bedside presence provided what can ostensibly be called an attempt at providing a decent death for Tarrou who was surrounded by concerned, caregiving friends. Another, perhaps even more extreme example of an attempt at providing a decent death was that of the long-suffering boy, Jacques Othon, who was surrounded at the end of his life by Dr. Rieux, Father Paneloux, and others. A serum was administered with the hope that it would help alleviate symptoms and progression of the disease, but it proved a disappointment to all. Nonetheless, although his parents were not able to be present, he did not die alone.

As compassionate concern is expected of a physician, perhaps Rambert, then, is Camus's most compelling case because he changed from unheroic behavior in attempting to illegally escape Oran to a member and advocate of the heroic solidarity group. Why he chose to stay and fight the plague tells us much about how one can learn and change behavior over time, at least as portrayed through Camus's optimistic eyes. Recent studies have shown otherwise.

More specifically, one's lack of self-esteem can drive a person toward a leader with shared worldviews of primarily two types, much like the metaphorical view of being stuck between a rock and a hard place. Social psychologist Jeff Greenberg concludes, "Charismatic leaders sell the rock-type world view. Our group is great, there is certain good and evil, right and wrong, and our group is destined to triumph over that evil" thereby ensuring membership in a great nation that fights "evil," often with violence.[43] This approach is often associated with a fundamentalist or conservative worldview that seeks to lessen anxiety through association. The alternative hard place "is a more uncertain world view that

---

[43] Greenberg, "This Mortal Coil," 9.

MODERN DEATH, DECENT DEATH, AND HEROIC SOLIDARITY   215

acknowledges that one person's good could be another person's evil. It stresses tolerance and the validity of different views of the world" and disincentivizes hostility.[44] It captures a more liberal but also more anxious view. Unfortunately for the cause of heroic solidarity, researchers have shown, "The existing evidence supports the position that reminders of death move people toward more rock-type worldviews."[45] A person who feels he is not making a positive contribution to a meaningful world or has low or threatened self-esteem is especially vulnerable to "death anxiety" and can gravitate toward a rock-type leader. Does this explain the "tribal" mentality and antagonistic behavior of members of the Republican Party who continue to valorize Trump even as he denies the reality of his loss in the 2020 presidential election and promises reinstatement in the White House? How far can a desire for shared worldview and group belonging drive self-esteem and groupthink?

We are only beginning to fathom the damaging effects of lack of leadership in 2020, the unnecessary deaths of especially vulnerable populations, and the loss of trust in government and CDC officials. Critics of the Trump presidency will continue to expose the unheroic—and often illegal, most certainly unethical—activity that led to the highest death toll in the world. Lawrence Wright's nonfictional account, *The Plague Year: America in the Time of Covid*, is but the start of revelations of things gone awry. He wrote matter-of-factly in 2021, "The figure that will haunt America is that the U.S. accounts for about 20 percent of all the Covid fatalities in the world, despite having only 4 percent of the population."[46] Even as the number of deaths dramatically declined 90 percent after five months into President Joe Biden's successful vaccine effort, fatalities rose in areas of the country dominated by resistant, unvaccinated populations: whether by choice or because of unavailability

---

[44] Greenberg, "This Mortal Coil," 9.
[45] Greenberg, "This Mortal Coil," 10.
[46] Wright, *The Plague Year*, 241.

216   CAMUS'S *THE PLAGUE*

of vaccines. Low vaccination rates threatened the government's July 4, 2021, goal of herd immunity that would offer protection to others besides oneself.[47] (It should be noted that Red states with Republican governors and/or congressional representatives constitute the least vaccinated populations, e.g., Mississippi, Alabama, Arkansas, Wyoming, Georgia, and Tennessee.)[48] These data further confirm studies that showed that persons thinking *consciously* about death also adopted the attitude "not me, not now" and instead focused on "being safe, being young, being healthy" as they seek to reassure themselves it's not their time so as to relieve anxiety.[49] Resisting medical advice to vaccinate in order to maintain a worldview of unheroic solidarity with other like-minded resistors during an actual pandemic when death is ever-present in the news, social media, and society can strain credulity. Wright notes, "Counties with higher mortality rates from drugs, alcohol, and suicide were more likely to vote for Trump in 2016 than they did for Romney in 2012. It was a shift born of despair."[50] How does one turn such despair into enhanced self-esteem and hope for a future where people care about others in heroic solidarity? Can this behavior be learned during a politically divisive ongoing pandemic?

Finally, consider studies within the "emerging field of existential neuroscience" about a mechanism in the brain that reinforces the "not me, not now" mentality in which "death cues tilt the self-other perceptual system towards the other, shielding the self from existential threat."[51] Unlike Greenberg's studies, this study has little to do with low self-esteem or any desire to belong to a group with a similar worldview. Instead, it describes the human mind's "automatic tendency to avoid awareness of its mortality," thereby

---

[47] Brooks, "Our Pathetic Herd Immunity Failure," May 6, 2021.
[48] Rubin, "Why So Many Republicans Talk about Nonsense," June 20, 2021.
[49] Greenberg, "This Mortal Coil," 7.
[50] Wright, *The Plague Year*, 203.
[51] Dor-Ziderman, Lutz, and Goldstein, "Prediction-Based Neural Mechanisms for Shielding the Self from Existential Threat," 1, 2, and 9.

MODERN DEATH, DECENT DEATH, AND HEROIC SOLIDARITY   217

yielding results that constitute "a plausible neural-based mechanism of death-denial."[52] The authors cite hundreds of experiments conducted under the terror management theory framework over thirty years, but only for the past ten years has neurocognitive research shown how death "cues" or reminders affect the brain.

What the study shows is that "the brain's self-specific system which is constantly and implicitly implementing a functional self/non-self (other) distinction in perception, action, cognition and emotion" is tilted "towards the other, shielding the self from existential threat."[53] In other words, they demonstrate "an automatic tendency to avoid awareness of a person's own mortality and that categorizes death as something unfortunate that happens to other people."[54] Another study has shown that reminders of death or mortality salience within the salience network within the brain can serve to change behavior, or motivate learned behavior, particularly with the inclusion of rewards.[55] Other studies have shown the role that high or low self-esteem plays in processing death-related stimuli, linking the automatic mechanistic response to cognitive capacities.[56] The complexities of these studies show that the interconnections of measured brain function respond to mortality salience, opening avenues of discussion beyond the scope of this chapter. Suffice it to say that for readers of literature and students of philosophy, the invitation to study "existential anxiety" as measured in brain waves, self-esteem, and shared worldviews opens a Pandora's box of cognitive exploration beyond fictional novels, the real world, and philosophical arguments. The goal is to uncover how the *real* threat of death, not just lab-induced suggestion, beckons us toward future research and hypotheses. What seems obvious is that reminders of death operate with stealth and that

---

[52] Dor-Ziderman, Lutz, and Goldstein, "Prediction-Based Neural Mechanisms," 1.
[53] Dor-Ziderman, Lutz, and Goldstein, "Prediction-Based Neural Mechanisms," 2.
[54] Pattee, "Covid-19 Makes Us Think about Our Mortality," October 7, 2020.
[55] Luo et al., "Thoughts of Death Affect Reward Learning," 1.
[56] Luo et al., "Thoughts of Death Affect Reward Learning," 9.

218   CAMUS'S *THE PLAGUE*

Camus intuited the predictability of human behavior in most of his many imaginary characters encountering the plague. Tarrou dies after providing insight into his thoughts in the face of death: the thoughts of a pacifist who aspired to be a secular "saint" but who was a drifter, alone, and befriended only by a caring Dr. Rieux. He sought a decent death by facing the inevitable head-on: not deflecting it onto others.

Noticeable change has taken place in which fear functions to motivate vaccinations.[57] December 2021 marked the deadly variant of Delta and the contagious spread of Omicron with the number of cases on the rise nationwide. But so, too, were vaccines. Persons experienced for the first time in nearly a year of vaccine availability prolonged waits for appointments at local drug stores, as well as some shortages. Fear of a more immediate threat of Omicron appeared to fuel the surge of interest. One philosopher who chronicled what he called the "moral dialogue" among characters wrote in light of Camus's novel, "The vast majority of those who survive the plague do not seem to have learned anything from it" but then subsequently quoted Camus who wrote in his 1941–1952 Notebooks, "Only those who were touched by death directly or in their families learned something."[58] What was happening in the United States in December 2021 is that about 1 in every 420 persons had died of Covid-19; we were "still averaging more than 1,000 deaths per day" and we were seeing the most vulnerable populations, including children and the elderly, succumb.[59] More of us, particularly the unvaccinated, are "touched by death directly," inducing increased fear and action. More are joining the heroic solidarity of care workers, ordinary citizens who are essential workers, and defying party politics. People are realizing that to increase one's chances of continuing to live or even minimize the

---

[57] CDC Covid Data Tracker, December 30, 2021.
[58] Krapp, "Time and Ethics in Albert Camus's *The Plague*," 673.
[59] Blake, "The Most-Vaccinated Big Counties," December 4, 2021.

MODERN DEATH, DECENT DEATH, AND HEROIC SOLIDARITY 219

horror of an unvaccinated "modern" death that is fraught with difficulty—that is, if one wants a decent death—the message is get vaccinated, boostered, self-quarantine when exposed, wear a mask, and socially distance. Ultimately, the freedom to choose one's fate is the answer to what is conveniently termed the "existentialist" threat and fear of death. This crumbling resistance to vaccines offers hope.

Finally, an Ethics of Care

After the plague strikes in Oran, death becomes widespread, extremely painful, and primarily experienced apart from family and home. It was Dr. Rieux's job to extract the sick from their familiar and comfortable surroundings by separating patients from their loved ones. Running makeshift hospitals and performing what he felt were necessary actions, he came to be viewed with resentment. Proscribed policy dictated his procedures; he was no longer revered or respected as the town doctor. He lanced buboes. He administered serum to a boy who nonetheless died an agonizing death. He learns of his wife's death—miles away in a tuberculosis sanitarium: a disease with which Camus was familiar due to his own experience starting at age seventeen. Contrary to Robert Solomon's claim that Dr. Rieux was a "cold fish and a moral prig, . . . an "uncomfortable 'hero,' whose dedication to fighting the plague is compromised by its futility and his own self-righteousness," I would argue that the doctor showed concern, offered comfort, provided care, and inspired meager hope for the town's future through exhortations of solidarity and duty.[60]

Camus was optimistic, arguing "there can be no peace without hope."[61] In separating society into three groups—the victims, the

---

[60] Solomon, "Facing Death Together," 170–172.
[61] Camus, *The Plague*, 221.

220 CAMUS'S *THE PLAGUE*

oppressors, and the healers—Camus was clear to advocate healers as a path toward peace, calling it "the path of sympathy."[62] Like a feminist ethics of care, sympathy is another expression of concern stressing the importance of relationships and responsibility for others, unlike previous traditional principles of bioethics that focus on rights and autonomy.[63] Personal rights may be invoked to justify the refusal of a vaccination and asserting one's autonomy may explain a decision to ignore medical advice and promote disinformation but according to feminists, practical wisdom dictates care and concern for others. An ethics of care will continue to inform ethical decision-making conforming to what I predict will eventually show that heroic solidarity wins out over unheroic solidarity, hope conquers despair. Vaccination rates in the United States are currently more than 66 percent fully vaccinated and 78 percent partially (at least one dose).[64] The inequities of illness and death perpetrated upon vulnerable populations in the United States have been mitigated, at least in part, by President Biden's massive vaccination effort beginning January 20, 2021; its extension worldwide promises to reduce the extensive threat of the modern death of Covid-19 once vaccines are distributed. Camus's recommendation of working together in heroic solidarity to fight the ravages of a town's plague extends to our own case of global pandemic and serves to further the goal of health and justice for more members of the world's population. Americans who have chosen vaccine protection have become the majority, leaving those unprotected at the mercy of their own ignorance. The path of sympathy, after two years' time of facing and fearing death, is emerging, finally offering us the hope of Camus's contentious claim, "what we learn in time of

---

[62] Camus, *The Plague*, 254. See also the Introduction to this volume on Camus on healers.

[63] See, for example, the early work of Nel Noddings, *Caring* (1984), as well as a summary of the field by Anne Donchin and Jackie Scully, "Feminist Bioethics" (2015).

[64] CDC Covid Data Tracker, July 4, 2022. Persons aged sixty-five or older are fully vaccinated at 91.5 percent.

MODERN DEATH, DECENT DEATH, AND HEROIC SOLIDARITY   221

pestilence [is] that there are more things to admire in men than to despise."[65]

Works Cited

Achenbach, Joel. "NIH Study Suggests Coronavirus May Have Been in U.S. as Early as December 2019." *The Washington Post*, June 15, 2021. https://www.washingtonpost.com/health/when-was-coronavirus-first-in-us/2021/06/15/1aaa6b56-cd2d-11eb-8cd2-4e95230cfac2_story.html.

Bassett, Mary T., and Natalia Linos. "Trump Gave Up on Fighting the Virus. Now We're Paying for His Laziness." *The Washington Post*, July 14, 2020. https://www.washingtonpost.com/outlook/2020/07/14/trump-gave-up-coronavirus/.

Becker, Ernest. *The Denial of Death*. New York: The Free Press/Simon & Schuster, 1973.

Blake, Aaron. "The Most-Vaccinated Big Counties in America Are Beating the Worst of the Coronavirus." *The Washington Post*, December 4, 2021. https://www.washingtonpost.com/politics/2021/12/04/big-counties-are-proving-how-vaccination-works/.

Brennan, Samantha, and Robert J. Stainton. "Introduction." In *Philosophy and Death: Introductory Readings*, edited by Samantha Brennan and Robert J. Stanton, xiii–xvii. Ontario, Canada: Broadview Press, 2009.

Brooks, David. "Our Pathetic Herd Immunity Failure." *The New York Times*, May 6, 2021. https://www.nytimes.com/2021/05/06/opinion/herd-immunity-us.html.

Camus, Albert. *The Plague*. Translated by Stuart Gilbert. New York: Vintage, 1991.

CDC Covid Data Tracker. https://covid.cdc.gov. Accessed December 6, 2021, and July 4, 2022.

Donchin, Anne, and Jackie Scully. "Feminist Bioethics." In *The Stanford Encyclopedia of Philosophy*, edited by Edward N. Zalta, 2015. https://plato.stanford.edu/archives/win2015/entries/feminist-bioethics/.

Dor-Ziderman, Y., A. Lutz, and A. Goldstein. "Prediction-Based Neural Mechanisms for Shielding the Self from Existential Threat." *NeuroImage* 202 (November 2019): 1–11. https://pubmed.ncbi.nlm.nih.gov/31401240/.

Edwards, Paul. "Existentialism and Death: A Survey of Some Confusions and Absurdities." In *Philosophy and Death: Introductory Readings*, edited by Samantha Brennan and Robert J. Stainton, 3–37. Ontario, Canada: Broadview Press, 2009.

---

[65] Camus, *The Plague*, 308.

222 CAMUS'S *THE PLAGUE*

Fisher, Max. "'Belonging Is Stronger Than Facts': The Age of Misinformation." *The New York Times*, May 7, 2021. https://www.nytimes.com/2021/05/07/world/asia/misinformation-disinformation-fake-news.html.

Greenberg, Jeff. "This Mortal Coil." *Aeon*, February 20, 2020. https://aeon.co/essays/how-to-apply-terror-management-theory-to-improve-human-lives.

Kabel, Ahmed, and Robert Phillipson. "Structural Violence and Hope in Catastrophic Times: from Camus' *The Plague* to Covid-19." *Race & Class* 62, no. 4 (December 2, 2020): 3–18. https://journals.sagepub.com/doi/full/10.1177/0306396820974180.

Kagan, Shelly. *Death*. New Haven, CT: Yale University Press, 2012.

Krapp, John. "Time and Ethics in Albert Camus's *The Plague*." *University of Toronto Quarterly* 68, no. 2 (Spring 1999): 655–676. https://utpjournals.press/doi/abs/10.3138/utq.68.2.655.

Kübler-Ross, Elisabeth. *On Death and Dying: What the Dying Have to Teach Doctors, Nurses, Clergy and Their Own Families*. New York: Scribner, 1969.

Luo, S., Bing Wu, Xiayue Fan, Yiyi Zhu, Xinhuai Wu, and Shihui Han. "Thoughts of Death Affect Reward Learning by Modulating Salience Network Activity." *NeuroImage* 202 (2019): 1–11. https://www.sciencedirect.com/science/article/abs/pii/S1053811919306561?via%3Dihub.

Miranda, Gabriela. "'I Don't Have COVID': Doctor Says Some COVID Patients Deny Virus, Decry Vaccines from Their Deathbed." *USA Today*, September 25, 2021. https://www.usatoday.com/story/news/nation/2021/09/25/dr-matthew-trunsky-says-some-dying-covid-patients-deny-virus/5866695001/.

Montaigne, Michel de. *The Complete Works of Michel de Montaigne*. Charlottesville, VA: InteLex Corporation, 1993. http://pm.nlx.com.proxy iub.uits.iu.edu/xtf/view?docId=montaigne/montaigne.00.xml;chunk.id=div.montaigne.pmpreface.1;toc.depth=2;toc.id=div.montaigne.pmpref ace.1;hit.rank=0;brand=default.

Noddings, Nel. *A Relational Approach to Ethics and Moral Education, Updated*. 2nd ed. Oakland: University of California Press, 2013. [Originally published in 1984.]

Nyhan, Brendan. "Why the Backfire Effect Does Not Explain the Durability of Political Misperceptions." *Proceedings of the National Academy of Sciences* 118, no. 15 (2021): 1–7. https://www.pnas.org/content/118/15/e191 2440117.

Parker, Ashley, and Josh Dawsey. "Seven Days: Following Trump's Coronavirus Trail." *The Washington Post*, December 5, 2021. https://www.washingtonpost.com/politics/trump-coronavirus-positive/2021/12/05/b1a55fda-544f-11ec-8927-c396fa861a71_story.html.

Pattee, Emma. "Covid-19 Makes Us Think about Our Mortality. Our Brains Aren't Designed for That." *The Washington Post*, October 7, 2020. https://

MODERN DEATH, DECENT DEATH, AND HEROIC SOLIDARITY   223

www.washingtonpost.com/health/covid-thinking-about-death/2020/10/02/1dc0f7e4-c520-11ea-8ffe-372be8d82298_story.html.

Rubin, Jennifer. "Why So Many Republicans Talk about Nonsense." *The Washington Post*, June 20, 2021. https://www.washingtonpost.com/opinions/2021/06/20/why-so-many-republicans-talk-about-nonsense/.

Rushing, Daniel A. "Physical, Psychological, and Spiritual Transformation at Life's End: Toward a Theory of Convergence." *Supportive Oncology* 3, no. 6 (November/December 2005): 439–443.

Solomon, Robert. "Facing Death Together, Camus's *The Plague*." In *Art and Ethical Criticism*, edited by Garry L. Hagberg, 163–183. West Sussex, UK: Blackwell, 2008.

Solomon, Sheldon, Thomas Pyszczynski, and Jeff Greenberg. *The Worm at the Core: On the Role of Death in Life*. New York: Random House, 2015.

Warraich, Haider J. *Modern Death: How Medicine Changed the End of Life*. New York: St. Martin's Press, 2017.

Warraich, Haider J. "In Pandemic Era, the Term Palliative Care Is Even More Scary for Some. So Specialists Want To Rename It." *The Washington Post*, September 7, 2020. https://www.washingtonpost.com/health/palliative-care-supportive-hospice/2020/09/04/07bf5236-e6d8-11ea-97e0-94d2e46e759b_story.html.

Wright, Lawrence. *The Plague Year: America in the Time of Covid*. New York: Alfred A. Knopf, 2021.

Index

For the benefit of digital users, indexed terms that span two pages (e.g., 52–53) may, on occasion, appear on only one of those pages.

Figures are indicated by *f* following the page number

absurd, the (*widersinnig*), 5–7, 12, 22–23, 47–48, 77–82, 84–85, 86–87, 88–91, 92, 93, 94–95, 97–100, 114, 116, 136–37, 212–13
absurdity, 15–16, 22–23, 46–47, 59n.23, 77, 78, 79–81, 82–87, 84nn.35–37, 88–89, 94, 95, 96–97, 100, 116, 121, 136–37, 189–90, 199–200
Algeria, 2–5, 14–15, 16, 16n.44, 17, 18, 19n.56, 32–33, 38, 45–46, 56n.15, 59n.25, 69–70, 127–28, 132–33, 140–41, 179–80
allegory, 1–2, 53–54, 78n.3, 121n.47, 166–67, 169, 175–76, 179–80
Amazigh (or Berber), 108
America, 1–2, 7–8, 9, 44–45, 204–12, 212n.36, 215–16
Anthony Fauci, 40–41, 184–85, 185n.40, 211
antibiotics, 130, 133, 134
anti-vaxxer, 13–14, 210
apathy, 23, 58–59, 106, 109, 110–12
Arab, 2–3, 6–7, 17, 18–19, 80n.14, 89, 108
art dread, 163–64, 163n.57
asphyxiation, 179–80, 181–82

Barthes, Roland, 17, 33–34, 33n.11, 56–57, 104n.1

bats, 23, 148–52, 153–54, 167–68
Beauvoir, Simone de, 3–4, 20–21, 20n.60, 69–70
being-in-the-world (*Dasein*), 84–87, 84n.39
Berber, 2–3, 108
Biden, Joseph, 1–2, 7–8, 12–13, 44–45, 177–78, 178n.8, 211, 215–16, 219–21
bioethics, 21–22, 24–25, 25n.68, 200–1, 219–21, 220n.63
Birds, The, 168–69
Black Death, 14–15, 16, 133, 174*f*
Black Lives Matter, 1–2, 23–24, 45–46, 99, 176–78
bleach, 38–39, 211
Boccaccio, Giovanni, 16, 31, 132, 132n.12
Bolsonaro, Jair, 35, 35nn.19–20
booster, 13–14, 194, 211
Borge, Richard, 146*f*
breathing, 23–24, 175–76, 179–83, 193
Brothers Karamazov, The, 148, 159
buboes, 147, 219
bubonic plague, 5–6, 16, 20–21, 60–61, 133, 201–2

Camus, Albert
    Caligula, 3–4
    Combat, 3–4, 9

226 INDEX

Camus, Albert (*cont.*)
  "La Crise de L'homme"
    ("A Human Crisis"), 81–82
  *Le Premier Homme (The First
    Man)*, 5–6, 80n.11
  "Neither Victims nor
    Executioners," 3–4, 9–10
  Notebooks 1951–1959, 5n.10,
    12n.32
  Notebooks II, 179n.13
  "The Artist at Work," 12n.32
  The Fall, 9
  The Myth of Sisyphus, 3–4, 22–23,
    46–47, 46n.60, 47n.63, 77–78,
    77n.2, 78n.3, 79nn.4–5, 79nn.6–
    9, 80n.11, 80n.15, 81nn.16–17,
    81nn.18–19, 81n.20, 82n.22,
    82n.25, 82–83nn.26–27,
    83nn.28–31, 84n.32, 84n.34,
    85n.43, 88–90, 88n.51, 89n.59,
    95–96
  The Rebel, 4–5, 9, 78n.3, 116n.36,
    175n.2
  The Stranger, 3–4, 9n.24, 17, 78n.3
Camus, Catherine (daughter of
  Albert Camus), 25, 25n.69
capital punishment, 37, 104n.2, 118,
  213
care, ethics of, 24, 219–21
caregiver, 6–7, 22, 59–60, 64–65,
  129–30, 185, 205–6
Carroll, Noël, 163, 163n.56
Castel, (character), 34, 47–48, 58–59,
  158, 161–62, 194
Center for Disease Control (CDC),
  210, 211–12, 215–16, 218n.57,
  220n.64
Chauvin, Derek, 176–78, 177nn.4–5
China, 7–8, 14–15, 34, 38–39, 42–43,
  152, 152n.13, 167–68, 184–85
Christian, 42–43, 45–46, 94–95, 108,
  159–60
Christianity, 89

clinical empathy, 131n.8, 137–38,
  137n.27, 138n.28, 139, 139n.30
collective, 8, 23, 56–57, 56n.16, 62–
  63, 83, 112–13, 117–18, 119–21,
  123–24, 166, 191–93, 201–2
colonial, 17, 18–19, 54–55, 54n.5,
  69–70, 70n.63, 133
colonialism, 54n.4, 69–70
common good, 9–10, 11, 203–4
compassion, 61–62, 98, 123–24
compassionate fatigue, 134
Cottard (character), 13, 36–38, 39–
  40, 58–59, 92, 94–95, 120–21,
  189–90, 200–1, 212–13
Covid fatigue, 160
Covid time, 7–8
Crusoe, Robinson, 21n.63, 32–33,
  179–80

Dasein (being-in-the-world), 84–87,
  84n.39
death
  collective, 201–2
  death toll, 7–8, 13–14, 37, 207–8,
    215–16
  decent, 24, 91–92, 199, 212–19
  with dignity, 213
  modern, 24, 24n.65, 199, 201–12,
    202n.10, 205nn.20–24, 206n.26,
    213n.40, 218–21
  penalty, 91–92, 118
Defoe, Daniel, 16, 16n.43, 20–21,
  32–33, 60–61, 97, 153, 153n.14,
  156–58, 157n.31, 158n.32
devolution, 23, 135
Dracula, 23, 149, 150–51, 150n.6
dread, 23, 153–54, 162–70

Edgar, Andrew, 22–23
effacement, 22, 63–64, 72–73
empathy, 15–16, 131n.8, 137–38,
  137n.27, 138n.28, 139, 139n.30,
  170

INDEX 227

epidemic, 14–15, 16, 31–33, 36–37, 40, 42–43, 58–60, 63–64, 97, 103–5, 106, 108, 118–19, 120, 123–24, 123n.54, 131, 131n.4, 140n.32, 141–42, 147–48, 150, 184–85, 187–89, 191–94
estrangement, 82–83
ethics, 4n.9, 5–6, 17n.45, 21–22, 24, 25n.68, 133, 139, 200n.7, 218n.58, 219–21
ethics of care, 24, 219–21
executioner, 3–4, 9, 12, 18, 200–1
existential, 7n.16, 24, 48n.68, 203–4, 207–8, 216–18, 216n.51
existentialism, 55n.12, 202n.12, 202–3nn.14–15, 203n.19
existentialist, 4–5, 20–21, 115–17

face masks, 35, 45–46, 48, 181–82
fact, 6–7, 12, 18–22, 25, 33–34, 40–42, 45–46, 107, 107n.16, 109–10, 116, 130–31, 135, 140–41, 201–2, 209–10, 210n.34
    alternative, 21–22, 41–42
fake news, 38–39
fascism, 18, 103–4, 175–76
fear, 5–6, 10, 15n.40, 24, 36, 38, 42–43, 64, 71–72, 103, 112–13, 132, 139–40, 141–42, 186–87, 202–3, 205–8, 206n.26, 211–12, 218–19
feminist, 21–22, 21n.64, 57n.19, 191–92, 200–1, 219–21, 220n.63
fiction, 6–7, 20–22
    pandemic, 6–7
Firstenberg, Suzanne Brennan, 76f
Floyd, George, 23–24, 175–78
football, 2–3, 3n.6, 45
Forman, Werner, 174f
France, 3–5, 9, 16, 103–4, 175–76, 179–80, 182–83
Frankenstein, 153–54
fraternity (*fraternité*), 55–56

freedom, 1–2, 4–6, 11, 17, 23–24, 108–9, 137–38, 175–76, 199, 218–19
Freeland, Cynthia A., 23, 163n.57, 168n.63, 169n.65
Fürst, Paul, 126f

gender, 21–22, 53–55, 56n.16, 58–59, 61n.32, 62–63, 66–70, 71–73
global, 21–22, 31–32, 38–39, 57n.18, 66–69, 97, 131n.4, 141–42, 167–68, 176–77, 207–8, 219–21
    pandemic, 219–21
Gluck, Christoph Willibald, 40, 68–69, 189–90
God, 40, 42–44, 42n.48, 43n.50, 43n.52, 44n.55, 44n.57, 94–95, 135, 136–37, 148, 155, 157–58, 165, 166, 168
Grand, Joseph (character), 13, 40, 55, 119
Gray, Margaret E., 56n.16, 66–67, 66n.49, 67n.53
grief, 23, 103–4, 109–15, 109n.18, 111nn.24–26, 113n.30, 113n.31, 116–17, 122–24, 123n.54, 132, 136, 207–8
    anticipatory, 23, 112–13
    collective, 112–13

habitual experience, 81–82
happiness, 40, 95–96, 96n.84, 115, 115n.35, 122–23, 165, 201–2
Harris, Kamala, 12–13, 177–78, 178n.8
healers, 9–10, 12–13, 123, 137, 140–41, 200–1, 219–21, 220n.62
health care workers, 53–54, 69–70, 72–73, 137–38, 139–40, 206
heat, 147, 154, 155–56, 157, 159
Heidegger, Martin, 22–23, 78–79, 83–87, 84n.33, 84n.36, 84n.38, 84n.40, 85nn.41–42, 86n.44, 86nn.45–46, 88–89

228 INDEX

hermeneutic(s), 78–79, 85–86, 89–91, 92–93, 94–95, 100
hero, 14–15, 68–69, 119, 170–71, 212–13, 219
heroic, 12–13, 22, 23, 24, 54–55, 58–59, 66–67, 140–41, 148, 200–1, 212–13, 214–16, 218–21
solidarity, 212–13, 214–16, 218–21
Higgins, Kathleen, 23
Hitler, Adolf, 9, 11
Holbein, Hans the Younger, 198*f*
Holocaust, 165–67
l'homme absurde (the absurd person), 81
hopeless, 181–82, 193, 200–1
hopelessness, 71–72
horror, 23, 68–69, 147–48, 149, 150–52, 151n.8, 153–54, 158, 162–63, 163n.56, 163n.57, 168–69, 168n.63, 169n.65, 170, 218–19
Hudson, Craig, 76*f*
human condition, 5–6, 46–47, 81–82, 84, 116–17
humanity, 5–6, 24, 42–44, 48, 79–80, 116, 129–30
Husserl, Edmund, 83–84, 85–86
hydroxychloroquine, 38–39

"I Can't Breathe," 23–24, 175–78
illness narrative, 62–63
incredulity, 105, 109, 110, 111–12
India, 1–2, 7–8, 8n.18, 14–15, 61n.30
indifference, 10, 111, 121, 135, 136–37, 165–66, 169, 170, 185
indigenous, 2–3, 6–7, 8, 17–18
individual, 1–2, 17, 36, 84, 100, 116, 166, 170–71, 190–93, 203
injustice, 9–10, 12, 18, 20, 43–44, 45–46, 91–92, 99, 117n.38, 139, 164–65, 167–68, 176–78
innocent, 13, 42, 43–44, 94–95, 148, 159, 162–63, 165–66, 167
insurrectionists, 48

intentionality, 83
internalized representation, 115
isolation, 5–6, 23, 36, 85–87, 89–90, 103, 106–8, 106n.14, 109, 111, 112, 113–14, 122–24, 130–31, 134, 134n.16, 136–37, 139–40, 151n.8, 186–89, 191–92
isolationism, 192–93

January 6, 2021, 1–2, 48, 210
Jesuit, 13, 43–44, 89, 119
Jewish, 108, 152
Jews, 33–34, 106n.14, 155
Journal of the Plague Year, A, 16, 16n.43, 31, 32–33, 60–61

Kellman, Steven G., 2–3, 2n.5, 5n.10, 18n.53, 22, 104n.1, 104n.3, 106n.14, 108n.17, 115n.35, 121n.46, 121n.47, 122–23, 122nn.51–52, 123n.54
Kollwitz, Käthe, 102*f*
Kübler-Ross, Elisabeth, 109–10, 109n.18, 111n.24, 205–6, 206n.26

long Covid, 97–98
love, 2–3, 5–6, 14–15, 43–44, 56n.14, 67–68, 83, 94–95, 117, 118–19, 121–22, 141–42, 168–69, 186–87, 203
lungs, 160, 175–76, 180–82, 193

masks, 1–2, 14–15, 34–35, 37–38, 44–46, 48, 181–82, 190–92, 191–92nn.56–58, 208–9, 210
meaningless, 46–48, 77–78, 85–86, 93, 99, 204
meaninglessness, 83–84
medical care providers, 141–42
medicine, 57–63
memorial, -ized, -izing, 12–13, 122–24, 139, 164–65, 208–9

INDEX 229

memory, 105–6, 209
MERS (epidemic), 97
metaphor, 40, 46–47, 72–73, 92, 182
modern, 11, 24, 24n.65, 31, 32–33,
  53nn.2–3, 56n.17, 57–58,
  59–60, 69–70, 71–72, 89, 97,
  127–28, 130–31, 137, 139–40,
  165–66, 167, 199, 201–12, 213,
  218–21
Mortensen, Viggo, 9n.24
mother, Rieux's (character), 58–59,
  63–64, 149, 212–13
Mulvey, Laura, 57n.19
Munch, Edvard, 52*f*
Muslim, 46–47

natural evil, 23, 148, 162–71,
  168n.63, 169n.65
natural phenomena, 23, 148, 169
nature/Nature, 97, 98, 99, 147, 148,
  150, 153, 154, 161–62, 163, 164,
  165–66, 168, 169
nausea, 80, 80n.14
Nazi, 9, 18–19, 33–34, 78n.3, 103–4,
  169, 175–76
Nazism, 10, 18–19, 33–34, 166–67,
  168
Nobel Prize in Literature, 4–5,
  16n.42, 127–28
nonfiction, 6–7, 200
normal, 7–8, 115, 128–29,
  136–37
normalcy, 13–15, 112–13, 160
Nosferatu the Vampyre, 151
nursing, 57–63

oleandrin, 38–39
oppression, 6–7, 17, 18–19, 23–24,
  66n.49, 155, 156, 175–78
Oran, xviii*f*, 3–4, 5–6, 7–8, 11,
  13–14, 17, 18–19, 19n.56, 20–
  21, 22, 23, 24, 32–35, 36–37,
  38–39, 45–47, 53–55, 57–58,

63–64, 65–69, 78–80, 81–82,
  88, 88n.51, 89, 92–93, 94–98,
  96n.84, 99–100, 106–7, 108–9,
  111–12, 118, 123–24, 127–28,
  133, 147, 148–49, 150, 153–54,
  155, 164, 165, 179–80, 182–90,
  193, 199, 200, 201–4, 206,
  207–8, 212–19
Orpheus and Eurydice, 39–40, 68–69,
  88n.51, 189–90
Othon, Jacques (boy/son)
  (character), 42, 43–44, 159, 160,
  170–71, 213–14
Othon, Monsieur (character), 55–56,
  58–59, 114, 115, 212–13
Othon, Madame (character), 55–56,
  63–64

pandemic literature, 14–15
Paneloux, Father (character), 13,
  40, 42–44, 55–56, 58–59,
  64–65, 72–73, 79–80, 88–89,
  94–96, 97, 98–99, 119–20,
  121, 121n.46, 136nn.24–25,
  154–55, 156, 158–60, 165,
  170–71, 180–81, 213–14
Paris, 2–4, 13, 32–34, 38, 45–46,
  78n.3, 97, 118–19, 133
Paris-Soir, 3–4
patriarchal, 55n.12, 56–57, 61–62,
  68–70
peace, 12, 91–92, 139, 164–65, 170–71,
  213, 219–21
personal protective equipment
  (PPE), 139–40, 181–82
pestilence, 9–10, 12, 25, 31, 32,
  36–37, 48, 77–78, 87, 91–92,
  94–95, 100, 132, 137, 139, 153,
  161, 164–65, 219–21
phenomenology, 22–23, 78–79,
  82–87
philosophical suicide, 79–80, 81,
  82–83, 94–95

230 INDEX

physician, 9–10, 23, 40–42, 47–48, 58–59, 62–64, 66–67, 72–73, 104–5, 117–18, 123, 127–31, 132–33, 134, 135, 137, 139–41, 200–2, 204, 205–6nn.25–26, 212–13, 214
physician's hand, the, 61–62, 61n.33
pied-noir (black foot), 2–3, 45–46
plague bacillus, 5–6, 11, 46–47, 141, 148, 161–62, 167, 194, 199–200
pneumonic, 58–59, 64, 127–28, 180–81
politics, 18, 44–45, 54n.5, 57–58, 69–71, 208–9, 218–19
Prefect, The (character), 34–35, 45, 184–85
president, 1–2, 7–8, 12–13, 22, 34–35, 40–43, 44–45, 167–68, 177–78, 184–85, 190–91, 191n.53, 208–9, 210, 215–16, 219–21
price gouging, 37–38, 38n.26
protest, 107–8, 121–22, 162–63, 176–78, 177n.7
public health, 34, 40–41, 41n.43, 54–55, 69–70, 127–28, 191–92
purposelessness, 123–24

quarantine(s), 38–39, 45, 63–64, 105, 106–7, 106n.12, 108, 114, 121–23, 133, 182–83

race, 10, 17, 69–70, 175–76
racism, 18–19, 69–70, 175–76
Rambert, Raymond (character), 13, 32–33, 36–37, 38, 40–41, 45–47, 48, 55–56, 58–59, 72–73, 95–96, 99, 107–9, 118–19, 121–22, 121n.46, 135–36, 162–63, 179–80, 210, 212–13, 214
Raoul (character), 36–37
rats, 11, 23, 130–31, 141, 147, 148–52, 153–54, 160–63, 180–81, 192–93, 199

Resistance, French, 3–4, 166–67
Richard, (character), 34, 58–59, 194
Rieux, Bernard (character), 1–2, 5–6, 9–10, 11, 12, 13–15, 22, 23, 32–33, 34–35, 36–37, 38–39, 40–42, 44, 45–48, 55–57, 58–59, 59n.23, 62–67, 66n.49, 68–69, 72–73, 77, 87, 89, 91–96, 100, 104–5, 108, 112, 114, 118–20, 121, 121n.46, 122–24, 123nn.53–54, 127–28, 129, 131, 132–9, 134, 135–37, 136nn.24–25, 138, 139–41, 148–49, 154, 156–57, 158–61, 164, 165, 167, 170–71, 179–81, 182, 184–86, 187–89, 190, 191–92, 193–94, 199–202, 210–11, 212–14, 217–18, 219
Rieux, Madame (character), 58–59, 64–65, 68–69
Robertson, Pat, 42–43, 43n.51
routine, 47–48, 107n.16

Said, Edward, 17, 69–70
sanitizer, 37–38, 37n.25
SARS (epidemic), 97
Sartre, Jean-Paul, 3–5, 4n.7, 16n.41, 17, 80, 80n.14, 117n.38
Schultz, Jane E., 22
sermon, 43–44, 79–80, 94–95, 154, 155, 159–62
serum, 5–6, 13, 47–48, 65–66, 71–72, 97–98, 133, 161–62, 200–1, 213–14, 219
Sherman, David, 20n.61, 84, 84n.35, 84n.37, 116n.37
shortages, 7–8, 37–38, 199, 218–19
solidaire (solidarity), 122–23
solidarity
heroic, 24, 117–23, 200–1, 212–13, 214–16, 218–21
unheroic, 212–13, 215–16, 219–21

INDEX 231

solitaire (solitary), 122–23
Solomon, Robert, 17, 17n.48, 17n.50, 115n.35, 123n.53, 199, 199n.3, 201–2, 201n.9, 203–4, 219, 219n.60
Stoker, Bram, 149, 150, 150n.6
suffering, 156–58
suffocation, 23–24, 53–54, 175–76, 179–80, 182, 189–90
suicide, 79–80, 81, 82–83, 94–95, 120, 131, 185, 187–89, 202–3, 212–13, 215–16

Tarrou, Jean (character), 9–10, 12n.31, 13, 24, 36–37, 38–41, 42, 46–47, 55–56, 58–59, 62–64, 72–73, 81–82, 87–89, 91–96, 99, 106–7, 112, 117n.38, 118–19, 120, 121–23, 121n.46, 135, 140–41, 158–59, 160–61, 165, 166–67, 170–71, 180–81, 187–90, 193, 199, 210, 212–14, 217–18
temporality (*Zeitlichkeit*), 65–66, 81, 85, 88–89, 90–91, 92, 93–94, 96, 100, 109, 110
terror management theory, 207–8, 209, 216–17
theodicy, 42, 159
Thucydides, 16, 132, 132n.11, 152, 152n.11, 156–58, 157n.30, 206
timelessness, 21–22, 111
tragedy, 23–24, 70–71, 175–76, 175n.2
tribal, 214–15
Trump, Donald J., 1–2, 2n.3, 12–13, 22, 24, 34–35, 34n.13, 35n.18, 37, 41–42, 44–45, 45n.58, 98–99, 167–68, 176–78, 184–85, 185n.36, 190–91, 192–93, 208–9, 209n.31, 210–13, 211n.35, 214–16

Trumpism, 15–16
truth, 5–6, 25, 34, 41–42, 121, 159–60, 184–85, 209–10
tuberculosis, 2–4, 179–80, 187–89, 219

unbreathable, 53–54, 175–76, 177–78
United States, 1–2, 3–4, 7–8, 7n.15, 34–35, 37–38, 40–41, 42–43, 44–46, 53–54, 59–61, 76f, 103, 104–5, 108, 130–31, 139–40, 177–78, 182–85, 200, 205–6, 207–8, 218–21
United States Capitol, 1–2, 48, 210
unmeaning (*unsinniges*), 84, 86–87, 88–89, 90–91, 94–96, 97–98, 99–100

vaccination, 99, 187–89, 215–16, 218–21
vaccine, 1–2, 7–8, 8n.21, 12–14, 47–48, 70–71, 103, 127–28, 184–85, 194, 210, 211–12, 215–16, 218–21
variant, 7–8, 8n.17, 13–14, 64, 71–72, 180–81, 182–83, 187–89, 194, 206, 211–12, 218–19
   Delta, 13–14, 61n.31, 64, 206, 218–19
   Omicron, 8n.17, 13–14, 206, 211–12, 218–19
ventilator, 8, 23–24, 181–82, 206
vice-president, 12–13, 177–78
victim, 3–4, 8n.19, 9–10, 12–13, 21–22, 25, 36–37, 40, 68–69, 92–93, 99, 107–8, 119, 122–23, 150, 154, 158, 160, 167, 174f, 180–82, 193, 200–2, 204, 208–9, 210, 219–21
violent, 48, 153–54, 159–61
virtue ethics, 139

232 INDEX

vulnerable population, 6–7, 215–16, 217–18, 221

weather, 153–56, 159, 160–62, 163–64, 169–70
Weiser, Edward B., 23
Weiser, Peg Brand, 24
Western, 45, 58–59, 68–70, 70n.63, 71–72, 98–99, 130, 152, 152n.12
White House, 182–83, 190–92, 208–9, 211, 214–15

WHO (World Health Organization), 2n.3, 7–8, 131n.4
wind, 23, 147, 153–56, 159–61, 162–63, 180–81
women, 63–66
World War I, 2–3, 204
World War II, 3–4, 9, 45, 53–54, 59–60, 168–69, 175–76, 179–80
Wuhan, China, 7–8, 32, 152, 167–68, 184–85

zoonotic villains, 23, 151

Printed in the USA/Agawam, MA
December 5, 2022

802381.011